BT
57
54
1998

REMEMBER THE POOR

REMEMBER THE POOR

The Challenge to Theology
in the Twenty-First Century

JOERG RIEGER

TRINITY PRESS INTERNATIONAL
Harrisburg, Pennsylvania

Trinity Press International, P.O. Box 1321, Harrisburg, PA 17105
Trinity Press International is a division of the Morehouse Group.

Library of Congress Cataloging-in-Publication Data

Rieger, Joerg.
    Remember the poor : the challenge to theology in the twenty-first century / Joerg Rieger.
      p.   cm.
    Includes bibliographical references and index.
    ISBN 1-56338-256-3 (paper : alk. paper)
    1. Liberation theology.   I. Title.
BT83.57.R54   1998
230'.0464–dc21
                                                98-42316

Printed in the United States of America

98   99   00   01   02   10 9 8 7 6 5 4 3 2 1

To Helen and Annika and all the other three-year-olds
who in their own ways keep us honest
in the midst of the death of 35,000 children every day

They asked only one thing, that we remember the poor,
which was actually what I was eager to do.
— Galatians 2:10

The poor do not exist.
— Paraphrasing JACQUES LACAN

Religion must not go from the greatest to the least,
or the power would appear to be of men.
— JOHN WESLEY, *Works* III, 178

Contents

Preface

THIS BOOK is about the future of theology at a time when suffering and death are on the rise, despite the greater generation of wealth and prosperity all around the globe. At the beginning of a new millennium, "remembering the poor" and other people at the margins poses a major challenge for everybody, including those of us who profit from an increasingly global economy and other structures of privilege along the lines of gender, race, and class.

Yet this challenge is often diverted by the hope that the benefits of economic, political, and intellectual developments may finally start to "trickle down," a hope that seems to be mirrored in the various camps of mainline theology. There are still some expectations that our own theological achievements and good intentions might find their way to those "less fortunate" after all. But what if the gains of power and authority in the hands of a few were never designed to trickle down in the first place?

Encounters with the realities of marginalization, poverty, and oppression tend to shatter idealistic dreams and have the potential to wake us from our dogmatic (or systematic) slumbers. Herein lies the challenge of this book. Its main objective is to think through the impasse in mainline theological options in the Americas in light of those who are excluded, and to identify and further establish those theological trails that are already being blazed into a different future.

My motivation for writing this book is inextricably related to encounters with women, men, and children in both Americas and on both sides of the Atlantic who are witnesses to God's liberation breaking through into the present. My acknowledgments must begin with people in Germany, Peru, North Carolina, Texas, and new friends at the margins of the city of Dallas, in West Dallas, East Dallas, and South Dallas, who have, probably without knowing it, contributed much to keeping my theological thinking alive. Meeting God at the margins can change your life, an experience that others have shared with me, including my wife, Rosemarie Henkel-Rieger, and our three-year-old twins, Helen and Annika.

My friendship with Gustavo Gutiérrez, encounters with people connected with the Instituto Bartolomé de Las Casas in Lima, and close relations with members and leaders of the Methodist Church in Peru have deepened my appreciation for, and awareness of, those who are involved in similar struggles in different situations and under even greater pressure. As one of the few white male liberation theologians, the late Frederick Herzog of Duke University, teacher and friend, opened the way for new questions about the challenge of the underside of history to the future of theology as a whole. Fredric Jameson, well-known literary critic at Duke University, always encouraged my interdisciplinary ventures and initially sparked my interest in new readings of the psychoanalyst Jacques Lacan. Mary Fulkerson, also at Duke, kept me honest about specific modes of oppression that include women. John Havea, Ph.D. student from Tonga and my research assistant, reminded me of additional layers of meaning in the title "Remember the Poor." My colleague at Perkins School of Theology, Charles Wood, read the manuscript with the precision of a systematic theologian. Teresa Berger, M. Gail Hamner, Thomas A. Langford, Robert T. Osborn, and Kenneth Surin have made helpful suggestions in earlier stages of this project. And Harold W. Rast, publisher of Trinity Press International, caught on to the vision and saw the project to publication.

The works of two major theologians, Gustavo Gutiérrez and Frederick Herzog, and the work of Jacques Lacan provide the backbone of this book. Where available I have quoted the English translations of their writings. All other translations from the Spanish, the German, and the French are my own. I have also included some interviews with Herzog, Gutiérrez, and others that I have conducted over the years. A Tinker Field Research Grant supported some of my early research in Peru.

For contemporary readers the lack of inclusive language in the early works of all three thinkers is quite obvious. I have kept these idiosyncrasies, in order to leave in place some of those inconsistencies, frictions, and repressions that are always a part of our discourses and bear in themselves the necessity of transformation.

Dallas, Pentecost 1998

Abbreviations

GL Gustavo Gutiérrez, *The God of Life*, trans. Matthew J. O'Connell (Maryknoll, N.Y.: Orbis, 1991)

GW Frederick Herzog, *God-Walk: Liberation Shaping Dogmatics* (Maryknoll, N.Y.: Orbis, 1988)

IS Gustavo Gutiérrez, *Las Casas: In Search of the Poor of Jesus Christ*, trans. Robert R. Barr (Maryknoll, N.Y.: Orbis, 1993)

JC Frederick Herzog, *Justice Church: The New Function of the Church in North American Christianity* (Maryknoll, N.Y.: Orbis, 1980)

Job Gustavo Gutiérrez, *On Job: God-Talk and the Suffering of the Innocent*, trans. Matthew J. O'Connell (Maryknoll, N.Y.: Orbis, 1987)

LC Gustavo Gutiérrez and Richard Shaull, *Liberation and Change* (Atlanta: John Knox Press, 1977)

LT Frederick Herzog, *Liberation Theology: Liberation in the Light of the Fourth Gospel* (New York: Seabury, 1972)

PP Gustavo Gutiérrez, *The Power of the Poor in History*, trans. Robert R. Barr (Maryknoll, N.Y.: Orbis, 1983)

TF Gustavo Gutiérrez, *The Truth Shall Make You Free: Confrontations*, trans. Matthew J. O'Connell (Maryknoll, N.Y.: Orbis, 1986)

TL Gustavo Gutiérrez, *A Theology of Liberation: History, Politics, and Salvation*, Revised 15th Anniversary Edition, trans. Sister Caridad Inda and John Eagleson (Maryknoll, N.Y.: Orbis, 1988)

UG Frederick Herzog, *Understanding God: The Key Issue in Present-Day Protestant Thought* (New York: Charles Scribner's Sons, 1966)

WD Gustavo Gutiérrez, *We Drink from Our Own Wells: The Spiritual Journey of a People*, foreword by Henri Nouwen, trans. Matthew J. O'Connell (Maryknoll, N.Y.: Orbis, and Melbourne: Dove, 1984)

Introduction

A NEW THEOLOGICAL VISION for the twenty-first century is imperative for various reasons. Most theologians today are sensitive to
broad shifts on the level of ideas and worldviews that send us back
to our drawing boards. Ever since the Enlightenment, theology has
tried to keep up with this flow. Lately, the transition from modernity
to postmodernity has taken up much of our theological energies.

Underlying these shifts, however, is an even bigger crisis that often
does not reach the theological consciousness. Despite the much celebrated "victory of capitalism" in the 1990s, the situation of those who
do not share in this victory, people pushed to the underside of history,
has worsened, even in "first world" countries.[1] Statistics show that poverty levels have risen not only in faraway places but at home as well.
If nothing else, the increasing poverty of children even in the United
States and the death of 35,000 children every day throughout the world
from preventable causes must serve as a wake-up call.[2] As people of my
generation in Germany have asked our parents and grandparents about
their relation to the deaths of six million Jewish people, future generations will ask us about the deaths of nearly twelve million children each
year, and even well-meaning theologians will not be spared. This time,
however, it will be virtually impossible to respond that we did not know.
At this point we have not even touched the pain and suffering inflicted

---

1. I will use the designations "first world" and "third world" in quotation marks
to indicate that they are not unproblematic. I will keep the terms, however, because
they remind us of actual relationships of political and economic power. The use of other
terms such as "one-third" and "two-thirds" world has the disadvantage of covering up the
structures that have produced, and still keep in place, center and periphery.

2. See the United Nations' *Human Development Report 1996* (New York: Oxford
University Press, 1996). In an initiative on children and poverty the United Methodist
bishops point out that in the United States between 1979 and 1989, child poverty in-
creased by 21 percent while the gross national product grew by 25 percent. More than
fifteen million children in the U.S. live in poverty, and nine million lack basic health
care. Preschool vaccinations lag behind those in some "third world" nations. The Council
of Bishops of the United Methodist Church, *Children and Poverty: An Episcopal Initiative*
(Nashville: United Methodist Publishing House, 1996), 2.

along the fault lines of gender and race, and other manifestations of the underside of history that are relevant for the topic of this book. How does theology deal with this situation? At present there is a growing awareness that theology that responds to God's embrace of all of creation will have to learn to pay attention no longer just to the flow of ideas but to other aspects of reality as well, all the way to a new understanding of the forces of the economy.[3] Theology dealing with all aspects of life will need to investigate, furthermore, how all these things come together. Yet while broadening the theological perspective in these ways, we also need to explore how those whose pain interrupts our well-ordered reflections are becoming part of the theological enterprise as a whole. That is the overarching challenge that I will address in this book.

The Underside of History

In order to understand the potential contribution of people on the underside to theological reflection, we need to see what role they have played so far. While modern theology has generated a new concern for the "signs of the times," to use the famous expression that permeated the Second Vatican Council, few have had the courage to deal with the underside of those signs.

Even though everybody knows that there are now a growing number of theologies that have to do with poor, oppressed, and marginalized people, the extent of the challenge of these groups to theology as a whole is still little understood. This paradox points to a major blind spot in contemporary theology and requires a closer look at where we are. How well are the standard paradigms of contemporary theology equipped to deal with this challenge? The camps of mainline theology today seem to be reflected in two general interpretive frameworks whose force fields even extend to some theologies at the margins. In response to the challenge posed by people on the underside, one version tries to

---

3. The members of a panel in memory of Frederick Herzog at the American Academy of Religion in 1996 were amazed that their presentations converged by and large in the theological concern for economic structures. Those contributions have been expanded and included in *Liberating the Future: God, Mammon, and Theology*, ed. Joerg Rieger (Minneapolis: Fortress, 1998). Contributors are John B. Cobb Jr., Gustavo Gutiérrez, M. Douglas Meeks, Jürgen Moltmann, Susan Thistlethwaite, Gayraud Wilmore, and myself. A broadening of the theological perspective is also taking place in dialogue with the emerging field of cultural studies. See, for instance, *Changing Conversations: Religious Reflection and Cultural Analysis*, ed. Dwight N. Hopkins and Sheila Greeve Davaney (New York: Routledge, 1996).

elevate them to a prominent place of authority and control, not unlike the place occupied by the modern self in much of modern theology. The other version makes them into recipients of charity and well-meaning support from those who are better off. In both cases, however, people at the margins are merely integrated into existing theological frameworks. Both camps of mainline theology in their various manifestations have not yet understood that precisely at this point their binary logic has reached an impasse. Theological encounters with the underside call for a paradigm shift and new theological categories.

More aware of this problem than anyone else, many liberation theologians have explored new ways of listening to people at the margins that neither patronize them nor romanticize them by putting them in the place of ultimate authority. Nevertheless, the new vision unfolds only gradually and remains a continuing challenge for the future. In the world of late capitalism and its widening gaps through which more and more people are falling, this question becomes the ultimate challenge for any theology.

To be sure, none of us is in a position to settle this matter once and for all. Rosemary Radford Ruether's critique, which charges one of the fathers of liberation theology, Gustavo Gutiérrez, with patronizing women and even indigenous people and the poor, has received some attention recently.[4] But, apart from the fact that Ruether's case is debatable (especially when it comes to Gutiérrez's relations to poor and indigenous people) and that even some of her sources of information have objected to her argument,[5] this only shows the importance of the ongoing need to deal with the question of the role of the marginalized beyond patronizing them, on the one hand, and idolizing them, on the other.

Working through the fundamental challenge posed by people on the underside to contemporary theology as a whole, I will trace two different examples of an increasing awareness of the "other" in the work of two of the pioneers of liberation theology in the Americas, one North American, Frederick Herzog, and the other Latin American, Gustavo Gutiérrez. Yet in order to appropriate and develop their contributions, we need new theological modes of perception. Since the marginalized and the poor often make their presence felt by interrupting the

---

4. Rosemary Radford Ruether, "Rift between Gutiérrez and Peru Women," *National Catholic Reporter* 32:44 (October 18, 1996), 28.

5. See especially the response in defense of Gutiérrez by "Talitha Cumi," a group of Peruvian feminist Christians to which Ruether referred in her article, in the *National Catholic Reporter* 33:12 (January 29, 1997), 32.

dominant flow of ideas, for instance, the theological challenge of the underside of history can never be quite grasped in terms of a conventional history of ideas approach.[6] In this context, theological changes in emphasis do not necessarily signify inconsistencies or breaks, but can also mark readjustments in an ongoing relationship. Here the contribution of the underside of history is most visible and most productive in the formation of theological thought. The trail into the future of theology will be blazed, therefore, through understanding the shifts and adjustments of theology in relation to the marginalized, poor, and oppressed. In Herzog's words: "Liberation theology begins as the poor begin to listen to each other before God. Liberation theology continues as we listen to the poor before God."[7]

One caveat: While in this book I variously refer to the marginalized, the oppressed, people on the underside of history, the poor, and the other, this makes sense only if they have actual names and stories.[8] "The poor" to which the title of this book refers, like "the oppressed" or "the marginalized," do not exist as universals. Any generalizing reference to "the poor" or "the marginalized," if it is produced by those in power rather than by those in touch with the underside, must fail due to the asymmetry between oppressors and oppressed.[9] At the same time, however, this does not mean that the reality of people on the underside would wither away into postmodern pluralism. Where the false universals of those in power are exposed, new forms of solidarity develop. For this reason, I continue to use the general expressions, emphasizing that I refer not only to individual poor or marginalized persons but also to whole groups or classes, produced and drawn together by mechanisms of oppression and repression. In other words, when I am talking about encounters with the poor, the marginalized,

---

6. These approaches usually circle around one thing, namely, as José Míguez Bonino has pointed out in relation to the work of Gutiérrez, that, positively or negatively, "you must somehow find a way of saying that there is a first and a second Gustavo Gutiérrez." Bonino, "Statement of José Míguez Bonino," in *Theology in the Americas,* ed. Sergio Torres and John Eagleson (Maryknoll, N.Y.: Orbis, 1976), 275.

7. Frederick Herzog, *God-Walk: Liberation Shaping Dogmatics* (Maryknoll, N.Y.: Orbis, 1988), xxii.

8. Even the apostle Paul, whose concern for remembering the poor in Gal. 2:10 provided the title of this book, did not simply talk about the poor in general. In this passage he had in mind a specific group of poor people connected to the church in Jerusalem.

9. In regard to the relation of black and white in North America, James H. Cone, *A Black Theology of Liberation,* 2d ed. (Maryknoll, N.Y.: Orbis, 1986), 108, has formulated the basic challenge of this asymmetry that will need to be addressed in the course of this book: "Oppressors are not only rendered incapable of knowing their own condition, they cannot speak about or for the oppressed."

and the oppressed, this includes both interpersonal and transpersonal aspects.[10]

Theologians like Herzog and Gutiérrez have led the way. The genesis of their theological reflections begins not with general reflections on the nature of oppression and its role in theology, but with actual encounters with those who suffer.[11] Even in these encounters, however, we need to be extremely careful not to end up exploiting oppressed and marginalized people once more, this time theologically.[12]

Alternative Theology

The new vision does not quite fit any of the major paradigms of contemporary theology. Many of the "first world" labels that have been used to describe theologies from the underside such as "situational theology," "contextual theology," "social gospel," "orthopraxis," "political theology," and even "theology from below" fail to convey the difference introduced by the perspective of the underside of history since they work with existing theological frameworks, typically of liberal provenience.[13] As initial encounters with the underside in theology have indicated, taking seriously the role of the marginalized leads to new ways of dealing with the two fulcrums that have alternatively served as the Archimedean points of much of modern theological thought: the modern self and the texts of the tradition (including the Bible).

Although listening to marginalized people leads back to interactions with both the modern self and the traditional texts, the new theological vision that emerges at this point cannot be understood exclusively in terms of one or the other. How strong the theological pull of those

---

10. Similarly, when I talk about the "modern self," I refer not only to certain individuals in power in modern times but also to larger groups of people such as the middle class.

11. Writing from a Latin American perspective, Gutiérrez mainly talks about the world of the poor and oppressed. The early beginnings of Herzog's reflections, on the other hand, are closely related to the marginalization of African Americans, a perspective that is broadened later in the encounter with the oppression of the poor, Native Americans, and women. In one of my last conversations with Herzog shortly before his death in 1995, he expressed concern that notions like the "underside of history" may not be understood by people who do not live there, thus becoming free-floating theological catchwords without bite. This book is an attempt to counteract that tendency.

12. In Herzog's *God-Walk*, the rejection of the theological exploitation of the poor is a major theme.

13. For a critique of the application of the labels of "contextual theology" or "special interest theology" to theologies from the underside see Joerg Rieger, "Developing a Common Interest Theology from the Underside," in *Liberating the Future: God, Mammon, and Theology*, ed. Rieger.

two alternatives still is can be seen in the fact that most interpreters of current theologies from the underside have tried to understand the phenomenon either in terms of one central doctrine (text) or in terms of a new theological agent (self) assuming control. Yet neither a reading on the level of the authority of texts of the church alone (dogmatics) nor a reading on the level of the authority of the human self (systematics) can fully grasp the contribution of the underside to theological reflection. In the encounter with the marginalized other before God, both the concern for the texts of the church and the concern for the human self are transformed.

The irruption of the underside of history into theology reminds theologians that even our best intentions can fail. Encountering the reality of marginalization, poverty, and oppression, the way into the theological future can no longer afford to start with lofty ideals and dreams. Theologians in touch with the underside have set the course when they remind us that we need to shift from "theologizing about an ideal church" to "analyzing the actual church."[14] The new theological vision cannot grow out of well-meaning charities, utopian dreams, stout political activism, or moralistic guilt trips. A self-critical look at theology and the church in actual solidarity with the victims will help to clear the view.

Such analysis will broaden the field of theological reflection. For example, theology done together with people on the underside cannot help but notice the intersections of theological authority and power. Where theological authority is reconsidered in the encounter with the underside, we can begin to map the connections between the production of theological authority and the prevailing structures of power in actual historical settings, and develop new blueprints for the future.

In one of his last notes Herzog reminds us that "only if we change ourselves in view of these 'invisible' people, will we become aware of the 'invisible God.' Here anchors our theological future."[15] Let me add that without new encounters with the other at the margins, claims of

---

14. Frederick Herzog, *Justice Church: The New Function of the Church in North American Christianity* (Maryknoll, N.Y.: Orbis, 1980), 11. Gutiérrez reminds us that the theological task is to "formulate a theology, not of what the church ought to be but of what the church is in the concrete." Gustavo Gutiérrez, "The Irruption of the Poor in Latin America and the Christian Communities of the Common People," in *The Challenge of Basic Christian Communities,* ed. Sergio Torres and John Eagleson (Maryknoll, N.Y.: Orbis, 1981), 119.

15. Frederick Herzog, "New Birth of Conscience," *Theology Today* 53:4 (January 1997), 483, also included in *Liberating the Future: God, Mammon, and Theology,* ed. Rieger.

encounters with the Otherness of God can be dangerous illusions, an insight that can be traced all the way back to the biblical texts.[16]

North and South

Finally, theology listening to the underside implies a new global vision. While the reality of suffering and oppression transcends national or geographic boundaries and points us toward global structures, the fact that those on the underside have different names and stories in different parts of the country and the world reminds us that we must not neglect differences.

A new global outlook on theology can, therefore, no longer be achieved in terms of a theological import-export business at the level of ideas. In order to mine the insights of new theological encounters with the marginalized we need to draw together both global implications and local differences. In the past, many "first world" interpretations of "third world" theology have failed, for instance, to understand the significance of different social locations. Insights developed elsewhere were often imported, not unlike other cultural artifacts and styles. The imported elements were then attached to existing theological models. For example, the Latin American concern for orthopraxis has been interpreted in terms of a "first world" concern for social activism. In this case the fundamental difference between activism propelled by modern autonomous selves and the praxis of people on the underside of history was overlooked. Failure to take into account the differences of theological thought in other parts of the world inhibits a constructive and self-critical encounter with one's own theological heritage. Encountering the poor in our own backyards, we need to start again where differences have often been overlooked. This might, in turn, lead to a reordering of some of our own priorities in the "first world."[17]

---

16. See 1 John 4:20: "Those who say, 'I love God,' and hate their brothers or sisters, are liars; for those who do not love a brother or sister whom they have seen, cannot love God whom they have not seen." This well-known passage looks fairly harmless at first sight since most of us assume that we love others. But what if those who do not respect the difference of the other (an often forgotten aspect of "love") are indeed unable to respect the difference of God?

17. Fredric Jameson has formulated the dilemma on the level of the textual material. The difficulty in taking a "third world" text seriously, he argues, is that "we would have to give up a great deal that is individually precious to us and acknowledge an existence and a situation unfamiliar and therefore frightening — one that we do not know and prefer *not* to know." Fredric Jameson, "Third-World Literature in the Era of Multinational Capitalism," *Social Text* 15 (Fall 1986), 66.

In dealing with those who are different, other, there is always the danger of assimilating them to serve one's own purposes. This danger is particularly prominent in the universalizing vision of modernity and its attempt to integrate that which is different into a firmly established worldview. Theology encountering the poor needs to deal with radical differences between rich and poor, oppressor and oppressed, and North and South. Unfortunately, this task does not seem to become much easier in postmodern times. Rather than being challenged, the contemporary postmodern mind is often entertained by differences in taste and style, reaching all the way into the theological arena, where notions of otherness and difference are now becoming more and more fashionable. Only where differences are taken seriously, however, can we think about unity. Only by keeping in mind the fundamental asymmetries will we be able to realize what we have in common, rich and poor, and North and South. The poor remind us that a "common tradition" cannot be built from the top down but needs to grow out of the underside of history.[18] Herzog recalls the ultimate challenge of such an attempt: "I have often heard it said in debates about liberation theology that first of all we must define oppression and who the oppressed are. I believe it's the other way around: the oppressed define us."[19]

A Conceptual Framework

In the search for a theoretical framework that would help to understand the role of the underside of history in theology and transcend the confinement of much of contemporary theology to either the authority of the modern self or some ecclesial text, the work of the French philosopher and psychoanalyst Jacques Lacan bears promise.

Working out of postmodern France, Lacan has dealt extensively with the most influential modern and postmodern theories and has also shown interest in the situation in the United States. His notion of the "real" is an attempt to recover those moments of oppression and repression that have been left out by both modern thinkers and their critics alike. The encounter with the "real" reshapes both the modern turn to the self and the postmodern turns to language and the text. Lacan's

18. Herzog talks about a *tradición común* that ties together both Americas. Frederick Herzog, "Tradición Común Shaping Christian Theology: Mutualization in Theological Education," Working Paper Series 12, Duke-UNC Program in Latin American Studies (April 1994); also included in *Theology from the Belly of the Whale: A Frederick Herzog Reader*, ed. Joerg Rieger, forthcoming from Trinity Press International.

19. Frederick Herzog, "From Good Friday to Labor Day," *Journal of Religious Thought* 34:2 (Fall–Winter 1977–78), 22.

reflections open up a new way of accounting for the specific difference that the encounter with the underside makes. The notion of the real creates a conceptual opening for the underside of history.

In this book the Lacanian perspective does not function as a rigid system, however, to be superimposed on the theological vision. I do not consider Lacan's thought as normative for theological decisions. He simply provides an analytic perspective, a mirror, in which we can observe structures of authority and power at play. Lacanian thought can help us map and specify the (mostly unconscious) basic identifications and alienations that shape societal, intellectual, and even theological production. In determining these, we can then proceed to search for alternatives and raise questions as to how established situations might be changed.[20]

The Lacanian perspective reminds us that understanding the actual location of authority is necessary in order to allow for transformation. Such analysis works in solidarity with the oppressed rather than in place of, or for, the oppressed. Yet while Lacan provides tools for a better understanding of the challenge of the underside, Lacanian thought itself will benefit a great deal from a closer encounter with actual situations of oppression along the lines of class, race, and gender.[21] The perspective of the poor, the marginalized, and the oppressed prevents its reduction to a mere psychocritique.[22] Readers interested in the theoretical paradigm will find new ways of dealing with Lacan in these pages.

The Question

Gustavo Gutiérrez has reminded us that "those who change the course of history are usually those who pose a new set of questions rather than those who offer solutions."[23] This book deals with the following ques-

---

20. Mark Bracher, *Lacan, Discourse, and Social Change: A Psychoanalytic Cultural Criticism* (Ithaca: Cornell University Press, 1993), 73, makes the useful comment that the fundamental dynamic of change must involve not only changes in laws and political processes but also, and more important, changes in those repressions of the unconscious where basic identifications and desires are located.

21. A number of feminist thinkers, while making use of Lacan's critiques, have emphasized his limitations as well. Cf., e.g., Elizabeth Grosz, *Jacques Lacan: A Feminist Introduction* (London: Routledge, 1990). In any case, Lacanian analysis is useful only where it is understood that Lacan does not describe the way things are and always will be, but rather the way power and authority are structured in specific social contexts, laying the ground for transformation and change.

22. This reduction is not necessarily the problem of Lacan's own work, but of some of the later "Lacanians."

23. Gustavo Gutiérrez, "Introduction," in *Between Honesty and Hope*, ed. Peruvian Bishops' Commission for Social Action (Maryknoll, N.Y.: Orbis, 1970), xxiii.

tions: In light of the growth of marginalization and suffering that we encounter today, how can those at the margins help theology to become more aware of, and accountable to, what God is doing? How can we create more space for God's work, which seems to be under constant tutelage in much of contemporary theology as it identifies ultimate theological authority alternatively either with the modern self or the traditional texts of the church rather than with Godself?

Despite necessary differences, theology as a whole will benefit from the ongoing attempt to rethink the movement of God's praxis in relation to Christian praxis and the underside of history. The theological task is to draw together, in light of the Gospel and the traditions of the church, the implications of the eruption of people on the underside and God's irruption.

This book is structured in three main parts. Part I, rereading the spectrum of mainline theology from a position that includes the poor and oppressed, has two chapters. In the first chapter, I will look at liberal Protestant theologies in North America, and major alternatives offered by their critics, from a perspective that includes the underside of history. A discussion of Jacques Lacan's notion of the imaginary and symbolic orders provides the analytic framework. The second chapter goes on to examine Roman Catholic Christendom and variations of modern theology in Latin America from the same perspective.

Part II introduces the Lacanian notion of the real in chapter 3, exploring ways in which the marginalized are pushing for a new theological future. Chapters 4 and 5 trace the progressive integration of the voice of people at the margins in the theological works of Herzog and Gutiérrez, thereby developing clues for alternative theological paradigms.

In part III, I will draw together the most important elements of a new theological paradigm that grows out of an encounter with the underside of history. This part includes a theological reflection on history from the underside (chapter 6), a chapter on power and authority in the Protestant North and the Roman Catholic South and new ways of developing theological understanding and solidarity (chapter 7), and a chapter on the way in which the eruption of the marginalized relates to the irruption of God (chapter 8). Chapter 9 develops the implications of encounters with the underside for a new theology and new theologians.

Part I

DEALING WITH THE IMPASSE IN CONTEMPORARY THEOLOGY

THE ADVENT of the poor and oppressed on the theological map poses a new challenge. In this part, I will reread the spectrum of mainline theology in the Americas from a position that deals with this challenge. Since the theological spectrum differs considerably in North and South, I offer one chapter on each setting. In the process I make use of a number of clues scattered throughout the work of Herzog and Gutiérrez. The parallels that emerge are highly instructive. The overall problem seems to be a certain myopic restriction in perspective that prevents theology, no matter how hard it may try, from dealing with those who are other and from discerning God's work in the world. The thought of Jacques Lacan will help in analyzing some of the remarkable similarities of the mechanisms that blind theology and theologians in different parts of the world.

Beginning with the location of theological authority, I clarify the basic liabilities and starting points of the paradigms of the theological mainline. In a next step this reflection leads to the question of how theological authority structures are related to more general ways of distributing power, a process that often takes place unconsciously. This insight into the interrelation of authority and power that I address at various points throughout this book is not based on a universal conceptual account of how both notions might be related in general. It is one of the products of an encounter with the underside of history. The view from the underside reminds us that authority and power are tied together historically, in real-life settings, a fact often overlooked by those in power. One of the basic insights of the theologies of liberation in dialogue with oppressed people has been the increasing awareness that power and authority can no longer be treated as completely separate issues in theological discourse. My own reflections on the relationship of authority and power develop those concerns further.

These reflections result in a more comprehensive understanding of authority and power in theological discourse. Even though neither term can be defined exhaustively in abstract, a priori fashion, there are some basic characteristics that help guide the search: Authority is understood here as that which produces identity and consciousness. Authority includes the ideological as well, what Karl Marx has called "false consciousness."[1] Power, on the other hand, relates more broadly to those larger structures of societal control that produce obedience.[2] In this context, the thought of Jacques Lacan helps us understand better the various ways in which identity is produced, and how the mechanisms of identity both produce and confirm power structures.

This approach finally leads to the insight that the analysis of power and authority cuts both ways in that the analysis of theological authority leads to new insights into its impact on issues of power, and the analysis of actual power struggles contributes to a double check of notions of theological authority. I will take up these issues in part II and show that, in listening to the underside of history, new understandings of authority develop that feed back into new understandings of power. In this interrelation of authority and power the new theological vision takes shape.

---

1. In this definition the causative aspect of authority is of special importance, assuming that the normative aspect, which I will not address as a separate issue, has always a part in it.

2. According to this initial understanding, authority and power can be related in two ways. Where one person controls another, a relationship of power is established. A relationship of authority is established if one person determines the identity of the other and shapes its interests. Cf. David Chidester's three-dimensional model of political power in his book *Patterns of Power: Religion and Politics in American Culture* (Englewood Cliffs, N.J.: Prentice-Hall, 1988), 7: "A three-dimensional model of political power might recognize those situations in which x not only controls y, and not only controls the situations within which y might struggle for power, but even creates y's own interests."

Chapter 1

Authority and Power in Mainline Protestant North American Theology

WHEN THEOLOGY started to become aware of the underside of history in the United States in the late sixties, the opposition of liberal and neoorthodox theologies was still in full swing. In this context, the new theological impulse was often identified with the liberal camp. It was assumed that people on the underside of history were to take the place of the modern self in theology. Only recently has the concern for the underside also been set in relation to those theologies critical of the liberal approach.[1] In both cases, however, the concern for people on the underside has not yet been seen for what it really is: a new theological impulse that opens up new vistas and provides a way out of the theological two-party system.

It is surprising at first sight that even at a time when we seem to be more and more lost in the limbo of theological pluralism, the undercurrents of the two-party system can still be felt. The respected sociologist of religion Robert Wuthnow, for instance, has pointed out that today we have not one but two civil religions, one "conservative" and the other "liberal."[2] Some leading theologians share similar views. A couple of years earlier, James Cone had realized that white theology was unable to search for a new theological basis together with blacks because of its restriction to "outmoded neoorthodox and liberal theological ideas."[3] David Tracy, whose analysis of theological paradigms is widely recognized, has come to a similar conclusion: "It would seem that the

---

1. See, e.g., Terrence Tilley, *Postmodern Theologies: The Challenge of Religious Diversity* (Maryknoll, N.Y.: Orbis, 1995), 128. Tilley argues that the work of Gustavo Gutiérrez addresses the problems of modernity and concludes that "liberation theology is a postmodern theology of communal praxis which sees that knowing the truth is possible only for those who first make the vision of the kingdom come true."

2. Robert Wuthnow, *The Restructuring of American Religion: Society and Faith since World War II* (Princeton: Princeton University Press, 1988).

3. James H. Cone, *For My People: Black Theology and the Black Church* (Maryknoll, N.Y.: Orbis, 1984), 15.

liberal vs. neoorthodox clash continues to dominate much of contemporary Christian theology."[4] Recently, Tracy has repeated this judgment in slightly different form. Theology is divided, he points out, between those who continue to follow modern models of reason and those who reject these models.[5] Frederick Herzog, throughout his work, has also noted the limiting aspects of the two fronts.[6] I strongly suspect that this tug-of-war still prevents much of mainline theology from understanding the challenge posed by those on the underside of history. In this chapter, I will discuss the two major alternatives in contemporary North American theology.

Liberal Theology: The Turn to the Self

Liberal Theology, Authority, and the Underside of History

Liberal theology, in all its different manifestations, is part of the wider concentration on the human self as the focal point of modern thought. With the Enlightenment, the concern for human subjectivity starts to compete with the traditional emphasis on objective truths. In some cases, the concern for the objective component all but disappears. As a result, the human self moves into the center of the modern world. Already in the seventeenth century, the French philosopher René Descartes argues that the self remains the only secure foundation in a world where everything else has become subject to radical doubt.[7]

Responding to similar moves in modern thought and culture later on, the father of theological liberalism, Friedrich Schleiermacher, starts

---

4. David Tracy, *Blessed Rage for Order: The New Pluralism in Theology* (New York: Seabury, 1975), 30. In this book Tracy elaborates five different models. Using his typology, it would not be difficult to support the existence of two major theological camps, for Tracy realizes a certain closeness of his first and third models, orthodoxy and neoorthodoxy, particularly in the work of Karl Barth; 37 n. 30. Models four and five, radical and revisionist theology, share the specific mark of liberal theology, the attention to the self.

5. See David Tracy, foreword to Jean-Luc Marion, *God without Being: Hors-Texte* (Chicago: University of Chicago Press, 1991), ix.

6. Already in his early writings Herzog deals with those conflicting theological approaches typical of white North American Protestant theology that he describes in his last book, *God-Walk*, as "liberal" and "orthodox" (or "neoorthodox"). Frederick Herzog, *God-Walk: Liberation Shaping Dogmatics* (Maryknoll, N.Y.: Orbis, 1988); see especially the diagram on 3 (abbreviated: GW). In his earlier work, Herzog finds the orthodox perspective represented by southern culture religion and the liberal perspective by the northern centers of theology.

7. Descartes's motto "I think, therefore I am" is well known. See René Descartes, *Discourse on Method*, trans. John Veitch, Religion of Science Library no. 38 (La Salle, Ill.: Open Court, 1952), 35.

theology with the insight that "any proclamation of God which is to be operative upon and within us can only express God in His relation to us."[8] We can no longer claim to know God in Godself. God can only be understood in relation to the self of the theologian. Although Schleiermacher, as this argument shows, tries to keep together subjective and objective elements, he insists that the (objective) traditions of the church must be interpreted in light of the (subjective) modern self. Schleiermacher, thus tilting the theological balance toward the subjective element, concludes that "Christian doctrines are accounts of the Christian religious affections set forth in speech."[9] Objective tradition is rooted in subjective sensitivities.

Even though Schleiermacher and many of his liberal successors seek to maintain a certain balance, the location of theological authority shifts in tendency from objective to subjective realities, from Scripture and tradition, for instance, to experience and reason. Theology in search of basic points of identity between humanity and God now listens more closely to human concerns and questions in order to understand God. A first theological opening is created at this point. Theology, broadening its horizon, learns to pay closer attention to the concerns of humanity. Yet we must not forget that this horizon is still fairly limited: Liberal theology listens to the voice of the modern self at the center of history, rather than to the other on the underside.[10]

While the theological movement toward the self shows similarities in Germany and North America, North Americans seem to surpass their German teachers at a certain point. According to Langdon Gilkey, for instance, the theologian has to start with him- or herself, on the level of his or her personal experiences.[11] The modern self is becoming more

---

8. Friedrich Schleiermacher, *The Christian Faith*, ed. H. R. Mackintosh and J. S. Stewart (Edinburgh: T. & T. Clark, 1986), 52.

9. Ibid., 76.

10. Obviously Schleiermacher's concern for relationship includes a relationship to the human other, but this concern has often been idealized. Manfred Frank, *Das Sagbare und das Unsagbare: Studien zur neuesten französischen Hermeneutik und Texttheorie* (Frankfurt: Suhrkamp, 1980), 133, for instance, goes too far when he talks about Schleiermacher's awareness of the radical *"Nicht-Einvernehmbarkeit"* of the other. Even in its relation to others, the self never needs to give up control since access to truth lies within the reach of its own intuition.

11. See Langdon Gilkey, *Naming the Whirlwind: The Renewal of God-Language* (Indianapolis: Bobbs-Merrill, 1969), 11. See also Herzog's discussion of this issue in "Ein neuer Kirchenkonflikt in den USA?" *Evangelische Theologie* 32:2 (March/April 1972), 174, and Frederick Herzog, "Dogmatik IV," in *Theologische Realenzyklopädie*, vol. 9, ed. Gerhard Krause and Gerhard Müller (Berlin: Walter de Gruyter, 1982), 106ff.; a translation is included in *Theology from the Belly of the Whale: A Frederick Herzog Reader*, ed. Joerg Rieger, forthcoming from Trinity Press International. Herzog's examples of early North Ameri-

and more the central point of reference in the development of North American theology. Not even the Social Gospel movement is different in this regard since the added concern for transforming the social order does not challenge the position of the modern self at the heart of theology. The self remains firmly in control.[12] A theological position that starts listening to the marginalized and disempowered other rather than to the self can therefore not easily follow in the footsteps of modern theology.

While the shock waves of the twentieth century dampened the liberal trust in the integrity of the modern self on a global scale, liberal theology remained strongest in the United States. Whereas German theology could not easily forget liberal theology's complicity in two world wars and the Holocaust, English-speaking theology preserved more of the liberal optimism. In North America the parameters of liberal theology remained in place, and the alternatives offered, for instance, by Karl Barth and the so-called neoorthodox theology were seen more as an option than as radical challenge. In the 1970s, John Macquarrie announced that mainline theology had returned once more to Schleiermacher.[13]

While in North America the liberal theological turn to the modern self has lately been critiqued by postmodern voices, it seems that much of theology continues to rely on the experience of the self as primary source of authority in one way or another. No doubt, in the postmodern situation the notion of experience is no longer as monolithic as in the classic liberal approaches. Theology is no longer guided by the experience of the educated middle class alone. Movements as different as New Age spirituality and Pentecostalism have broadened the range of experiences in control. Yet while the notion of experience has become more pluralistic, the theological reliance on experience as such often has not been called into question.

In this regard, encounters with the experience of the other will introduce a major challenge. Born in suffering, the experience of the oppressed can no longer be experience in control. While liberal the-

---

can theology include Nathaniel William Taylor and Horace Bushnell, the latter under the direct influence of Schleiermacher.

12. Cf. Herzog, "Dogmatik IV," 111, and Frederick Herzog, "Die Gottesfrage in der heutigen amerikanischen Theologie," *Evangelische Theologie* 23:2.3 (February–March 1968), especially his critiques of John B. Cobb Jr., 136, Schubert M. Ogden, 140ff., and John Macquarrie, 143ff.

13. John Macquarrie, quoted in Frederick Herzog, *Justice Church: The New Function of the Church in North American Christianity* (Maryknoll, N.Y.: Orbis, 1980), 56 (abbreviated: JC).

ology rests on the assumption of some basic analogy between humanity and God — herein lies the foundation of the theological authority of the self; theology in dialogue with people on the underside of history must take into account more specifically the experience of brokenness and of separation from God as well. In the liberal paradigm, the essential relation of humanity and God, based on the analogy of the human spirit and the divine Spirit,[14] always implies some relation between ultimate reality and the reality of the human being. This connection, as history has shown, can easily lead to an implicit sanctification of the way things are. If our human reality is somehow grounded in ultimate reality, things must not be so bad after all. Where the religious sensitivities of the modern self guide the search, ultimate reality can never become a fundamental challenge of the reality of this self. In other words, although God may be at work in evolutionary processes and gradual improvements of what is, God can never be a revolutionary.[15] The encounter with the marginalized, on the other hand, might help turn things around. If things are not the way they are supposed to be, theology needs to develop a new understanding of the difference God makes.

The relation of human reality and ultimate reality in liberal theology, of the human spirit and God's Spirit, has far-reaching implications for the question of theological authority. Paul Tillich's well-known method of correlation may serve as an example, connecting the existential questions of humanity and the corresponding theological answers. This method starts with the presupposition that the human self is able to ask the right questions. Humanity may not have all the answers, but its concerns set the stage for the theological enterprise. In fact, Tillich does not indicate a possible transformation of the existential questions by the theological answers except perhaps on the formal level, thus giving the existential questions a certain autonomy and the ability to determine the theological answers.[16] In this approach, a certain amount of theological authority is attributed to the modern self that formulates the

---

14. Cf., e.g., Friedrich Schleiermacher, *Christian Faith*, 65.

15. Paul Tillich's discussion of miracles provides the ontological underpinnings for this type of argument. Miracles do not "destroy the structure of being in which [they] become manifest"; it is inconceivable that "the manifestation of the ground of being would destroy the structure of being." Paul Tillich, *Systematic Theology*, vol. 1 (Chicago: University of Chicago Press, 1951), 115, 116.

16. This position is developed more strongly in the second volume of *Systematic Theology*. See Paul Tillich, *Systematic Theology*, vol. 2 (Chicago: University of Chicago Press, 1957), 16: The theologian must approach the existential questions "as though he had never received the revelatory answer."

questions. In agreement with Schleiermacher, Tillich searches for what he calls a "principle of identity," based on the premise that the self is essentially related to the divine by way of an underlying reality, a common ground. Tillich is more aware than Schleiermacher of the psychological limits of the self (Sigmund Freud's thought has made a difference), but he preserves its authority and puts it on an even stronger basis that is now defined ontologically.[17] Even though Tillich's work today belongs to the history of theology, his influence must not be underestimated in setting the hermeneutical course for contemporary North American theology.

Herzog broadens our analytic framework when he reminds us that similar mechanisms of correlation have been at work in legitimizing the doctrine of Manifest Destiny in the United States.[18] By creating close links to God's will, the actions of the modern self are not only left unquestioned but are sanctioned. In this context Herzog concludes that liberal theologians like Tillich "did not offer us a revolutionary principle that would have radically questioned the bourgeois system in a theological way."[19] The syntheses of theology and culture of nineteenth-century European Protestant theology are perpetuated on North American soil in their own ways.

In liberal theology starting with the Enlightenment, the modern self, assured of its autonomy not only by the philosophical trends but also by political and economic success, takes on a prominent position of authority in the construction of theological discourse. In the process, the subjective element is placed more or less in competition with the objective traditions of the church. While the theological concern for the oppressed has often been interpreted in this context, there are significant differences. Their position does not necessarily imply, for instance, the aspect of control tied to the role of the self. As I will show in part II, the struggle of oppressed people for liberation cannot easily be identified with the modern self's struggle for autonomy.

---

17. Tillich talks about the "principle of identity" in *Perspectives on 19th and 20th Century Protestant Theology*, ed. Carl E. Braaten (New York: Harper & Row, 1967), 94. He distances himself from Schleiermacher mainly at the points where the latter is not going far enough in establishing the theological place of the self. Ultimately, however, Tillich points out that Schleiermacher's notion of "[feeling of] unconditional dependence is only a slightly narrower way of saying 'unconditional concern....' It has the same basic motives and is an expression of a total experience, the experience of the holy." Ibid., 105. He makes the same point in his *Systematic Theology*, vol. 1, p. 42.

18. Herzog, "Introduction: On Liberating Liberation Theology," in Hugo Assmann, *Theology for a Nomad Church* (Maryknoll, N.Y.: Orbis, 1976), 7, also included in *Theology from the Belly of the Whale: A Frederick Herzog Reader*, ed. Rieger.

19. Ibid., 9.

Liberal Theology and Power

Looking at the liberal paradigm from the underside of history, it becomes clear that theological authority in liberal theology is not in the hands of humanity in general but in the hands of a certain segment of society, the class that is rising to power in modernity, the middle class. It was no accident that Schleiermacher addressed theology to the cultured among the despisers of religion. Tillich, too, wrote his *Systematic Theology* for the educated. While the location of authority in liberal theology is widely recognized, the relation of authority and power is often neglected. The view from the underside of history puts the theological question of authority in a broader perspective. The insight that authority in liberal theology is not in the hands of humanity in general is only a first step. How are power and authority related? From a Latin American perspective, for example, Enrique Dussel has pointed out that the modern paradigm shift did not start with Descartes's turn to the self but with the reaffirmation of the European self in the conquest of the Americas one hundred years earlier.[20]

A closer look at Schleiermacher's theology and the problem of power might give us another clue. As we have seen, the modern self assumes an important position in modern theological thought. The self is in touch with God through what Schleiermacher calls the "feeling of absolute dependence." God is experienced as the absolute cause of one's being and of all that is. Even where this relationship of God and humanity is toned down in the work of other liberal theologians, the self is still somehow in touch with the way things are and thus a reliable theological guide.[21] Schleiermacher's reflections on the doctrine of God may serve as an example for the role of the self. Where traditional statements about God conflict with the experience of the modern self, theology follows the lead of the self. "Conceptions of divine modes of action" are permissible only, according to Schleiermacher, if they can be developed out of propositions in tune with the "realm of inner experience," the only place where "nothing alien can creep into the system of Christian doctrine."[22] Prevailing on the level of authority, the power of

---

20. The "I conquer" precedes the Cartesian "I think, therefore I am" by almost one hundred years. See Enrique Dussel, *Von der Erfindung Amerikas zur Entdeckung des Anderen: Ein Projekt der Transmoderne*, Theologie Interkulturell 6 (Düsseldorf: Patmos 1993), 10.

21. Even though Tillich, *Systematic Theology*, vol. 1, 9, suspects that Schleiermacher is too closely identifying the "experiencing subject and the ultimate," the projects are similar. Both attempt what Tillich has called a "synthesis" between "the Christian message" and "the modern mind." Ibid., 7.

22. Schleiermacher, *Christian Faith*, 126.

the modern self is reaffirmed as well. God's power supports the powers of modern society, since God is not primarily the God of Abraham and Isaac, a potentially disruptive figure, but, according to the experience of the modern self, the absolute cause of all that is. God's power and the power of modern society go hand in hand. Schleiermacher concludes that, in view of the great power of the Christian nations of modernity, we do not even need a demonstration of God's power in miracles anymore.[23]

Schleiermacher's God affirms the social context of the modern person. Without neglecting the obvious differences between Schleiermacher's approach and other liberal theologies such as Paul Tillich's, there is a parallel in the fundamental lack of a critique of the modern self and its context. The oppressed other never appears on the theological scene. In this way the modern self, authorizing the theological enterprise, ends up sanctioning the power structures of modern society and contributes to their fixation.

At the same time we must keep in mind that this relation of authority and power takes place on an unconscious level. In fact, the modern self is quite unaware that it is part of a struggle for power at all. Having created a theological vision of harmony and peace in the relation of God and humanity,[24] Schleiermacher applies this vision to society at large. Liberal theology thus tunes out the contradictions and conflicts of real life, thereby reinforcing theologically the blindness of the self for its own role in the power struggle of the modern world.[25] Gregory Baum's portrait of North American middle-class religion provides a contemporary description of this phenomenon: "Middle class religion easily speaks of unity and reconciliation. It disguises the real conflicts in the community and the inequality of power and pretends that love can unite all people in a common humanity. Middle class religion entertains the hope that the great injustices in the world, including the gap between rich nations and poor nations, can be overcome through greater love."[26]

It is absolutely crucial to understand that what is at stake here is not primarily a matter of "social concern." Schleiermacher's or liberal

23. Ibid., 450: "In view of the great advantage in power and civilization which the Christian peoples possess over the non-Christian, almost without exception, the preachers of to-day do not need such signs." Quoted also in Herzog, JC, 57. Herzog is one of the few in the English-speaking world to address the relation of power and authority in Schleiermacher.

24. The notion of peace is also a central theme of Schleiermacher's later sermons.

25. Cf. Herzog, JC, 65.

26. Gregory Baum, "Middle Class Religion in America," *Concilium* 125 (1979), 21.

theology's sense of social responsibility is not in question. Neither is the charge that Schleiermacher was politically passive or unproductive.[27] The point is that Schleiermacher and much of liberal theology fail to self-critically analyze actual social practices and political identities with regard to their underlying identifications in terms of authority and power. Herzog identifies two diametrically opposed options: *"There is the solidarity of the powerful in-group that controls civilization. And there is a solidarity that includes the powerless, the voiceless poor."*[28] Here is the crucial issue: The powers that be fail to understand that the suffering other is in fact part of the modern self. Herzog suspects rightly that "underlying the power corruption is the exclusion of the other from one's selfhood."[29]

At this point, a shift in relations of power might lead to a new vision of authority as well. No doubt, the theological authority of the modern self closely resembles its power to make things happen in the modern world. From the perspective of modern self, authority is related to the ability to control. From the perspective of those on the underside, on the other hand, control has never been a way of life. For this reason alone the notion of authority may take on different forms when reconsidered from the underside. Unfortunately, since we do not yet have a theological paradigm for the interrelation of authority and power, mainline theology still has a hard time following this train of thought. An observation made by Herzog more than twenty years ago still rings true: We need to realize first of all that "there *is* a history of power in Protestant systematic theology."[30] There is still the danger that, unaware of its theological ties to those who are in power, mainline theology ends up on the side of the powers that be. We need to learn how to examine theological statements in terms of what "authorizes" them as well as what "empowers" them.

Without necessarily putting as much faith in the religious abilities of the modern self as Schleiermacher, liberal theology still considers the

---

27. This is the misunderstanding of Richard Crouter in his article "Schleiermacher and the Theology of Bourgeois Society: A Critique of the Critics," *Journal of Religion* 66 (July 1986), cf., e.g., 303. Crouter's claim on 309 that Herzog "leaves us with a Schleiermacher whose views are passivist and culturally unproductive" misses the point.

28. Herzog, JC, 58. Emphasis in original.

29. Frederick Herzog, "Jesus and Power," in *Philosophy of Religion and Theology: 1975 Proceedings*, American Academy of Religion Section Papers, ed. James Wm. McClendon Jr. (Missoula, Mont.: Scholars Press, 1975), 207. A later version of this article can also be found in Herzog, JC, chapter 2.

30. Frederick Herzog, "Whatever Happened to Theology?" *Christianity and Crisis* 35:8 (May 12, 1975), 116–17.

modern middle-class self's experiences as a reliable guide in theological matters. How much this self, tying together authority and power, is still at the center of both North American society and the churches is illustrated by that famous best-seller of Norman Vincent Peale's, originally written in the fifties: *The Power of Positive Thinking.* The thirty-fifth anniversary edition in 1987 starts out with this imperative: "Believe in yourself! Have faith in your abilities! Without a humble but reasonable confidence in your own powers you cannot be successful or happy." All this is grounded theologically. Peale gives one of his patients this formula, to be repeated every day: "I can do all things through Christ which strengtheneth me" (Phil. 4:13), with the following comment: "Now, follow that prescription, and I am sure things will come out all right."[31] But what may in fact work for the average middle-class reader, white and male, may not work for most others.

The Modern Self and the Struggle for Power and Authority

In order to understand better the nature of the problem, we need to clarify some of the mechanisms that are at work in the identifications of the modern self in terms of authority and power. In the process I will show how the concern for the underside of history cannot be an extension of liberal theology but becomes its crisis.

The reflections of Jacques Lacan are helpful because they address the tensions of the modern world — Lacan calls it the "era of the 'ego.'"[32] Lacan describes therefore not so much the human being in general but its specific alienations and fragmentations in modern society with a special interest in North American phenomena.[33] Furthermore, by not separating individual and collective realities, Lacan does not fall into the individualizing mode of much of psychoanalysis.[34] In this respect, a Lacanian interpretation is particularly fruitful in relation to

31. Norman Vincent Peale, *The Power of Positive Thinking* (New York: Prentice-Hall, 1987).

32. Jacques Lacan, "The Function and Field of Speech and Language in Psychoanalysis," in Jacques Lacan, *Écrits: A Selection*, trans. Alan Sheridan (New York: W. W. Norton, 1977), 71.

33. Cf. Fredric Jameson's observation in "On *Habits of the Heart*," *South Atlantic Quarterly* 86 (Fall 1987), 549–50, that "many of those European theories are in reality secretly North American in their content, if not their form. The hidden reference point of much postcontemporary speculative description of the decentered self or ego, the schizophrenic consciousness, is not European psychology, but North American psychology and behavior as that fascinates the European intellectual." The close relation of Lacan's work to the problems of contemporary society is also stressed by Shoshana Felman, *Jacques Lacan and the Adventure of Insight* (Cambridge, Mass.: Harvard University Press, 1987).

34. Cf. Lacan, "The Function and Field of Speech and Language," 80.

"third world" texts since here the Western split between the private and the public is not presupposed to begin with.[35] I will read Lacan's observations in the context of the complex interrelationship of "super-structure" and "infrastructure," of authority and power, often repressed by Western consciousness.[36] Using Lacanian thought in this way, at the intersection of authority and power, will throw new light on Lacan's own work as well.

The Lacanian notion of the ego's era circles around the modern self as its center, caught up in a narcissistic structure. This interpretation of modernity is in line with a good number of other highly influential critiques of modernity. Yet unlike most other critics, Lacan provides tools that permit a broader understanding of the modern predicament. Charles Taylor's brilliant study of the modern self's emancipation from objective reality, for instance, fails to reflect on the relationship of self and other in modernity. Taylor's focus on authority (in terms of moral authority) leaves out a reflection of the ways in which the modern self assumes a position of power in relation to the other.[37] Lacan will help us keep these elements together. Christopher Lasch's well-known book *The Culture of Narcissism*[38] also reflects on the self-centered and neurotic culture of modernity. Lasch and others, however, treat the problem in a moralistic way, implying that we could be different if we only tried, obviously another version of the modern self's dreams of control. Lacan, on the other hand, points us to the need for analysis, for without a deeper understanding of what really motivates and drives the modern self change will not be possible. In this context, the history of the modern self and its conquests, to be discussed further in chapter 2, cannot be neglected. Once more, authority and power need to be seen together.

Lacan relates the ego's era to what he calls the "imaginary order." This constellation emerges out of the so-called mirror stage, which can be compared to the way small children identify with a mirror image. A mirror image (any image outside the self) allows the child to create,

35. See Fredric Jameson, "Third-World Literature in the Era of Multinational Capitalism," *Social Text* 15 (Fall 1986), 69.

36. An observation by Jameson is particularly helpful in my attempt to keep several dimensions together: "When a psychic structure is objectively determined by economic and political relationships, it cannot be dealt with by means of purely psychological therapies; yet it equally cannot be dealt with by means of purely objective transformations of the economic and political situation itself, since the habits remain and exercise a baleful and crippling residual effect." Jameson, ibid., 76.

37. See Charles Taylor, *Sources of the Self: The Making of the Modern Identity* (Cambridge, Mass.: Harvard University Press, 1989).

38. Christopher Lasch, *The Culture of Narcissism: American Life in an Age of Diminishing Expectations* (New York: W. W. Norton, 1978).

for the first time, an (illusory) identity that did not exist before.[39] This image, which can be produced in an encounter with the caregiver or another person, appears to the child as unified and whole. In relating to this unified image and appropriating it, the child, which up to this point had no particular sense of being a self, creates the illusion of its own self as a perfect self. Here a first relation between self and other, between inside and outside, is instituted. This self is born, therefore, not in isolation but in the identification with a mirror image, an other.[40] By the same token, the history of the modern self as a self "come of age" needs to be understood in relationship with its others, starting as early as the conquest and continuing through colonialization, industrialization, and into late capitalism.[41] In this context it becomes clear that "the self" is not just the individual subject but refers to the class in power in modernity.

The problem, according to Lacan, is that in this way of relating self and other the difference between the mirror image and the self is not recognized. The imaginary-order self is not aware of the actual gap between the self and the other. Lacan talks about a "misrecognition." This leaves the newborn self in a narcissistic trap. While the self is born in relation to the other, the other is turned into an object, made to serve as prop for the self.

This narcissistic tendency is paralleled by aggressivity. Lacan notices an "aggressive competitiveness,"[42] linked to a "passionate desire peculiar to man to impress his image in reality."[43] The modern self asserts its own value by conquering the other. This struggle is facilitated by that narcissistic transitivism in which the other and the self can no longer be

---

39. See Jacques Lacan, "The Mirror Stage as Formative of the Function of the I as Revealed in Psychoanalytic Experience," in *Écrits: A Selection*, 2.

40. Ibid., 4.

41. Albert Memmi, *The Colonizer and the Colonized*, trans. Howard Greenfeld (New York: Orion, 1965), 66, for instance, has shown how the existence of the colonized is indispensable to the existence of the colonialist, despite the latter's belief that "everything would be perfect...if it weren't for the natives."

42. Jacques Lacan, "Aggressivity in Psychoanalysis," in *Écrits: A Selection*, 19. Lacan, ibid., 20, sees this insight already foreshadowed in Augustine's statement that "I have seen with my own eyes and known very well an infant in the grip of jealousy: he could not yet speak, and already he observed his foster-brother, pale and with an envenomed stare." Memmi, ibid., 55, notes that even though the colonialist can be "a warm friend and affectionate father," in the relation to the colonized he "cannot help but approve discrimination and the codification of injustice."

43. Lacan, ibid., 22. Memmi, *The Colonizer and the Colonized*, 83, shows how, "far from wanting to understand him as he really is," the colonizer tries to mold the colonized to serve to his advantage.

clearly distinguished, a situation where the "slave [is] identified with the despot, the actor with the spectator, the seduced with the seducer."[44]

Liberal theologies in their own ways share in the modern self's "misrecognition" of the other. Even the Social Gospel movement, strongly determined to help the disadvantaged, did not yet fully understand that the other co-constitutes the self and therefore might call the self to account. Closer encounters with people on the underside of history have helped to realize the problem. Exploring the relationship of black and white in the southern United States, Herzog realizes that the relationship between self and other "can be seen as much more determinative of self-consciousness than appears on the surface." Even though whites are not aware of it, "the white does not have his self-consciousness apart from the black's dependence on him."[45] In this way theology hits on the paradox that the making of the modern self, despite all its connotations of individualism and autonomy, is entirely social. The modern self comes into being in a power struggle in which the other is subdued and turned into an object.[46]

The idiosyncrasies of the modern self can be explored further by taking a look at the distortions of the imaginary order. In what psychoanalysts call neurosis, the imaginary self takes over completely, closing off all other aspects of reality. This confines neurotics to their own prefabricated world, making them believe their self-centered myths over truth.[47]

Here is an important parallel to the issue of theological authority. In liberal theology, theology is often constructed around the immediate experiences of the modern middle-class self. The other is neglected by default. We are able to understand now why this way of going about the business of theology is always in danger of constructing closed intellectual systems. In asking and answering the questions of an imaginary-order self that, even where it is concerned about social issues, is not able to adequately take into account the difference between self

44. Lacan, ibid., 19.

45. Frederick Herzog, "Reorientation in Theology: Listening to Black Theology," in *The Context of Contemporary Theology*, ed. Alexander J. McKelway and E. David Willis (Atlanta: John Knox Press, 1974), 227–28.

46. Already Hegel began to realize that both individual self-interest and the mutual dependence that grows out of this are elements of bourgeois society. See Georg Wilhelm Friedrich Hegel, *Grundlinien der Philosophie des Rechts*, 3d ed. (Berlin: Duncker and Humbolt, 1854), pt. 3, sec. 2, par. 182ff., "Die bürgerliche Gesellschaft."

47. Lacan, "The Function and Field of Speech and Language," 69. Cf. also Ellie Ragland-Sullivan, *Jacques Lacan and the Philosophy of Psychoanalysis* (Urbana: University of Illinois Press, 1986), 264 and 266.

and other, theology will end up going in circles. The totalizing and universalizing tendencies of liberal theology that have come under attack lately from various sides grow directly out of this phenomenon.

The Power of the Modern Self

Connecting authority and power, Lacan gives us some clues as to the manifestations of imaginary narcissism and aggressivity and their role in "modern neurosis and in the 'discontents' of civilization."[48] Modernity must be understood not only in terms of the identity of the modern self but also in terms of the self's production of actual structures of power. The theories of Charles Darwin, for instance, which establish the modern self at the peaks of evolution are, as Lacan points out, closely related to the "predations of Victorian society and the economic euphoria that sanctioned for that society the social devastation that it initiated on a planetary scale."[49]

The "Darwinian century" as a whole is shaped by an increasing power struggle in which the middle class takes over on a broad scale that includes economy and politics. Nevertheless, this struggle never quite reaches consciousness. Only from the perspective of the unconscious, that which is repressed to the underside of history, can the devastating power of those subterranean conflicts, carefully covered up by the modern self, be assessed. The self assumes absolute power in the historical development of the neuroses of modern bourgeois society and the "psychasthenic forms of its derealizations of others and of the world."[50] This process is perhaps most clearly visible in the relationship to the "third world," a term that in itself is a derealization. The encounter with the underside of history makes it clear that the emerging authority of the self in modern theology cannot be separated from its gain in power.

In the ego's era the interrelation of authority and power is rooted in the modern self's conquest of the other. The usurpation of the other is not only the process by which the self acquires its own identity and authority. Here is also the basis for the self's power, which grows more and more absolute as time goes on and guarantees even the power of those who, while perhaps not completely in the position of the modern self, benefit from it.[51] This insight corresponds to one of the basic

---

48. Lacan, "Aggressivity in Psychoanalysis," 25ff.
49. Ibid., 26. Lacan also mentions the social location of Hegel's "Master and Slave" and the battle between the sexes.
50. Ibid., 28.
51. Memmi, *The Colonizer and the Colonized*, 11, describes the situation of the less

theological lessons to be learned in the encounter with the underside of history: Both power and authority are corrupted at the point where the other is objectified.[52]

Lacan suspects that the modern self's rigidities worsen over time. In the words of one of his interpreters: "On a social scale, they are worse now than they were a few centuries ago. And the place where they are absolutely worst of all is America."[53] In this perspective it is hardly a coincidence that in the early stages of the North American encounters with the underside, Herzog concentrates on the phenomenon of the modern self and its narcissism, related to the inability to understand the pain of the other. As we have seen, this rigidity of the self corresponds with the tendency to make the world into one's own image. Anxious to preserve this constellation, the modern self is controlled by dreams of fixation and objectification as well as control and power. And since today this self is increasingly able to make the world over in its own image, as a result of technological advances and the international expansion of capitalism, we need an even broader critique of the ego's era, including its economic and political structures. The continuing drive to appropriate new worlds, itself symptomatic of the rise of modernity and the ego's era, has exported the power structures of modernity to other places. The powers of modern self are not confined to Europe and North America. In the next chapter, I will show how even the history of Latin America is tied up with the powers of the ego's era.

Having analyzed the structure of the imaginary self, Lacan develops an antidote. The most basic critique that dismantles the aura of the modern self is the insight that "I is an other."[54] The modern self needs to realize its basic connectedness to the other. In this sense, the encounter with that which is repressed, the other, the marginalized, the oppressed, the poor, amounts to nothing less than another Copernican

---

privileged colonizers thus: "If the small colonizer defends the colonial system so vigorously, it is because he benefits from it to some extent. His gullibility lies in the fact that to protect his very limited interests, he protects other infinitely more important ones, of which he is, incidentally, the victim. But, though dupe and victim, he also gets his share."

52. In Herzog's words, power is corrupted "where the weak, the poor and the maimed are viewed as non-persons." And, he continues, "absolute power corrupts absolutely where everyone beside oneself is viewed as non-existent except as prop for one's self-aggrandizement." Herzog, "Jesus and Power," 205, 206. Memmi, ibid., 86, talks about the "extraordinary efficiency" of this process in the colonial situation where the colonialized "should exist only as a function of the needs of the colonizer."

53. Teresa Brennan, "History after Lacan," *Economy and Society* 19 (August 1990), 282.

54. Referring to Arthur Rimbaud's well-known dictum.

revolution that questions "the place man assigns to himself at the cen-
tre of the universe."[55] The new focus that the encounter with people on
the underside of history brings to theological reflection is, therefore, in
the most literal sense, a "self-"critical one. Herzog envisions the theological direction of the future: "The commandment to love the other
as oneself is . . . an invitation . . . to discover the other as co-constitutive
of one's self."[56]

Alternatives to Liberal Theology: The Turn to the Text

While theological liberalism affirms the modern self in various ways,
its critics do not trust it, especially in matters of theological authority. Here is an interesting parallel to the general critique of the self
in "postmodern" times, displayed, for instance, in the critique of the
idea of authorship (Michel Foucault) and the emphasis on the power
of the text (Jacques Derrida).[57] The encounter with the underside of
history challenges us to find out whether those critiques might help to
effectively overcome the power structures of modern society and the
authority of the modern self.

Authority, Theology after Liberalism,
and the Underside of History

Most critics of liberal theology agree at least on one issue: The modern self is no longer a reliable theological guide. Theological authority,
therefore, can no longer be rooted in experience or reason. Usually,
some form of a "turn to the text," or a "turn to language,"[58] to Scripture
and tradition, is suggested as alternative.

In the North American context, some of the early mainline critics of
liberal theology were neoorthodox thinkers. Neoorthodox thought, dating back as far as the 1930s, opposes modern liberal theology on several
counts. Reacting against the modern trust in the power of the self, one
of the common denominators of neoorthodoxy is the rediscovery of the

---

55. Jacques Lacan, "The Agency of the Letter in the Unconscious or Reason since
Freud," in *Écrits: A Selection*, 165.

56. Herzog, "Jesus and Power," 207.

57. See, for instance, Michel Foucault, "What Is an Author?" in *Language, Counter-
Memory, Practice*, trans. Donald F. Bouchard and Sherry Simon, ed. Donald F. Bouchard
(Ithaca: Cornell University Press, 1977), and Jacques Derrida, *Of Grammatology*, trans.
Gayatri Chakravorty Spivak (Baltimore: Johns Hopkins University Press, 1976).

58. David Tracy, "Theology and the Many Faces of Postmodernity," *Theology Today*
51:1 (April 1994), compares what he sees as two postmodern phenomena: a "turn to
language" and a "turn to the other."

notion of sin and a corresponding sense of the limits of human autonomy. In this context, neoorthodox theology argues for a relocation of
theological authority. Reaffirming the sovereignty of God, it develops a
renewed interest in the Bible as revelation.[59] In North America, neoorthodox theology has served as a call for mainline theology to return
to a closer encounter with the texts of the church.

Neoorthodox theologians often saw the work of the Swiss theologian
Karl Barth as a model for the new paradigm. Although Barth does not
fit the neoorthodox mold in some ways, his influence should not be
underestimated. Even at present Barth's work is still influential for many
of the alternatives to liberal theology, postliberal theology being only
one example.

Many of the critics of liberal theology followed Barth in relocating
theological authority from the modern self to the word of God. While
Barth himself talks about the word of God in three forms, as Jesus
Christ, the biblical text, and the sermon, his concern for the biblical
text has found the strongest resonance. His discovery of the "new world
of the Bible" helped to displace liberal theology's confidence in the self
as theological guide.[60] At a time when the modern self had discred-
ited itself by its actions in two world wars and the Holocaust, theology
could no longer start with the identity between God's Spirit and the
human spirit, one of the basic foundations of liberal theology. Theology
now started with God's self-revelation put forth in Scripture. Here is an
often overlooked parallel to the early encounters with the oppressed in
liberation theology. Many communities on the underside in both North
and Latin America also supported a new concern for the Bible that
would help to break the spell of the liberal status quo.[61]

Many of the critics of liberal theology who followed Barth and neoorthodoxy seemed to overlook, however, that Barth was fighting on a
dual front. While he rejected the liberal idea that theology is based on
the experience of the modern self, he also rejected the idea that the-

---

59. Cf., e.g., Dennis Voskuil, "Neoorthodoxy," in *Reformed Theology in America: A
History of Its Modern Development*, ed. David F. Wells (Grand Rapids: Wm. B. Eerdmans,
1985), 255.

60. Karl Barth, *The Epistle to the Romans* (1922), trans. from the sixth edition by Ed-
wyn C. Hoskyns (London: Oxford University Press, 1968), 12: "It has been my 'Biblicism'
which has compelled me to wrestle with these 'scandals to modern thought.'"

61. Frederick Herzog found a new emphasis on the Bible among African Americans
in North Carolina that was at least as strong as that of his teacher, Karl Barth. (Herzog
studied theology in Bonn, Germany, and Basel, Switzerland. Having met Karl Barth in
Bonn, he served as his graduate assistant in Basel for three years. He completed his Th.D.
at Princeton under Paul Lehmann.) The concern for the Bible of the Latin American
base communities is well known.

ology was more or less a collection of (and commentary on) the truths contained in the texts of the church.[62] According to Barth, authority could be located neither immediately in the self, as liberal theology argued, nor in the reality of the church and its tradition and texts, a claim that he found in Roman Catholicism and Protestant Orthodoxy.[63] In both cases, theology has a tendency to proceed as if it had its subject matter at its disposal.

Whereas Barth tries to keep open the ultimate position of authority, convinced that the texts and traditions of the church need to be reconstructed in relation to Jesus Christ as the highest form of the word of God, most of his neoorthodox and postliberal followers in North America and elsewhere are not as concerned about this issue. No wonder that in this context the concern for the underside of history had to be understood, once more in terms of the two-party system, either as condoning the authority of the oppressed as autonomous selves or the authority of the ecclesial texts. It has hardly been noticed, however, that the approach to authority from the underside is much closer to Barth's initial vision. Oppressed people, excluded from the structures of power, are not necessarily in the control mode, and therefore not necessarily ready to attribute ultimate authority either to themselves or the texts of the church. In the next part I will show what the oppressed might be able to teach theology about how to keep the place of authority open for God.

In this sense, a fresh encounter with the underside of history might help pull theology out of its current impasse. Perhaps Barth himself unconsciously contributed to the impasse. Once the modern self is displaced from the position of authority, what is put in its place? Herzog notes the obvious, that to follow Barth's approach "for a lot of people . . . ended up in neoorthodoxy."[64] Here, the modern control mode continues in different forms. The authority of the self is replaced by the authority of the text. Barth himself, focusing most of his attention on the critique of liberalism, seems to have trouble keeping the place of ultimate authority open. In developing his theology, he finally ends up building theology around the textual reality of the Bible and the creeds or dogmas of the church as the factual authority.[65] As Herzog points

62. See Karl Barth, *Church Dogmatics*, vol. I, 1, ed. G. W. Bromiley and T. F. Torrance (Edinburgh: T. & T. Clark, 1975), 265: Dogmatics "cannot be 'dogmatics' in the sense of the Roman Catholic Church, i.e., the development of the truths of revelation immanent in the Church, nor the 'doctrine of faith' in the sense of Protestant Modernism, i.e., the exposition of the faith of the men united in the Church."

63. See ibid., 14.

64. Herzog, JC, 122.

65. His *Dogmatics in Outline*, trans. G. T. Thomson (New York: Harper & Row, 1959),

out, this move "often led him to preference of the concept as the crucial language vessel of Christian truth." In Barth's focus on the texts of
the church, on the conceptual language of doctrine, the suffering en-
dured by people at the margins makes little difference: "In the realm of
concept everything ultimately has its place and is realized."[66]

While in liberal theology it is difficult to envision the hidden fact
of a basic historical *struggle* since the self is unaware of its ongoing
competition with the other, the critics of liberalism often have trouble
understanding that there is an *ongoing* struggle *in history,* since both self
and other are displaced by canonized texts. Barth's battle with heresy
also takes place on the level of the text. The importance of this battle
can be seen, for instance, in documents like the Barmen Declaration,
which opposed Germany's Third Reich and called for resistance, but
later Jewish responses have made it painfully clear that the Jewish other,
for example, who suffered most under Hitler's reign is not part of the
picture.

At first sight, the urge to eliminate the authority of the self by focusing on the biblical and creedal texts seems logical. It was, after all, the
middle-class self of modernity, creating and domineering its world, that
caused most of the trouble associated with modernity. But by merely
dropping the issue and eliminating the self, the chance of reconstruction
is lost. Worse yet, if the self is merely eliminated or repressed, it might
return through the back door, unconsciously.[67] The power struggle at
the level of self and other to which the encounter with the underside
of history has opened our eyes, so carefully blended out in liberal theology, does not seem to be acknowledged in the theologies of the critics of
liberalism either. The main struggle of which Barth's theology is aware
takes place on a vertical level, between God (the wholly Other) and
human being. The struggle at the horizontal level between the positions
of oppressed others and the self is not reflected theologically.

In this situation, listening to the other introduces a radical transformation. As we have already seen, the modern self, the driving force not
only of liberal theology but of the political and economic transactions

---

for instance, uses the Apostles' Creed as a backbone, never quite overcoming one of its
basic weaknesses, the neglect of the life and ministry of Jesus.

66. Frederick Herzog, "Liberation and Imagination," *Interpretation* 32:3 (July 1978),
240.

67. Herzog indirectly hits on a similar problem in the discussion of Jesus' own self:
"Barth does not raise the issue of Jesus' personhood within Israel....So here too [as in
liberalism] the power conflict between the rabble and the powerful is overlooked *as a
significant factor of theological construction.*" Herzog, "Jesus and Power," 202. Emphasis in
original. Also in Herzog, JC, 36.

of the modern world, cannot be liberated from its dogmatic slumbers without an encounter with its other. A mere displacement of this self by the world of the text may not be sufficient. Furthermore, if the modern control mode is simply reproduced where the texts replace the self, the place of ultimate authority cannot remain open for God.

Only in listening to the underside do all three elements — selves, others, and sacred texts — finally meet. The modern control mode is only overcome where the self finally dares to face its other. In this process the text can be of help.

Power and the Alternatives to Liberal Theology

The critics of liberal theology expose the control of the modern self in matters of theology. This is part of the importance and promise of the critiques of liberalism and modernity, all the way from neoorthodoxy to contemporary postliberal theology. At first sight, the critics of liberal theology seem to be more on target in a postmodern world than their liberal colleagues. Rejecting the self-centeredness of the "ego's era," at least they do not immediately give in to the lurings of the modern self. Theology can no longer be driven by the modern self enchanted with its own mirror image.

But how are authority and power related in those alternative approaches? Like their liberal counterparts, most of the mainline critics of liberal theology do not seem to worry about this issue. The power struggle in which the modern self assumes control, while perhaps implicitly criticized, is not actually raised to the level of consciousness. Today it seems as if the tendencies to withdraw into the world of the religious texts can also be found in some manifestations of that postmodern "turn to language" which has impacted much of contemporary theology.

The full extent of the problem of the authority of the text repressing the authority of the self becomes visible only in view of the distribution of power in modernity. Without taking into account the various struggles between the modern self and its others in the present, between races, genders, and classes, the theological return to the canonical texts of the church fails to reconstruct the foundations of the modern world. While neoorthodox theology labors to connect once more with the Otherness of God, the modern self is not directly challenged to change its relation to the other. The turns to the text and to the divine Other take place largely without the turn to the human other.

In light of the cry of people at the margins, which is growing louder and louder every day, theology needs to find new ways of tying together the turn to the divine Other and the turn to the human other. In order to deal with the powers that be as faithfully as Barth did in the 1930s, at the peak of the ego's era the encounter with people on the underside of history can no longer be optional.

In North American Protestant thought, as Herzog has pointed out, the neglect of the struggle for power tends to domesticate Barth's struggle over theological authority.[68] Today Barth's struggle against heresy can be understood only in the context of the real-life confrontation between the modern self and its other. In other words, the theological struggle between faith and heresy[69] must be seen in light of actual power struggles that include race relationships, the relation of genders and, often forgotten in the North American situation, the relation of economic classes as well. The authority invested in the divine Other cannot be investigated without the struggle with the human other over power.

This is to say that a final reconstruction of the authority struggle can only be worked out through an assessment of the power struggle. Without attention to power structures, the theological distinction of God and idol, determining the location of true theological authority, misses an important element. While the texts of the church can help resist the modern liberal status quo, the lesson from the underside of history in the ego's era is that this will not happen without some relation of the texts to the repressed other.

This brings us back to our previous observation of how much theological authority and political power are interrelated at the present moment, even where theologians do not notice it. In the North American context, any critique of liberal theology that fails to relate its concern over authority to power structures might end up to be a Trojan horse, sheltering deep inside itself the powers that be.

The Texts of the Church and the Struggle for Power and Authority at the End of Modernity

What is at stake when theology turns to the authority of the text? Jacques Lacan has explored the mechanisms according to which a turn to the collective phenomena of language and text might indeed contribute to a reconstruction of the narcissistic and aggressive structures of the modern self. According to Lacan, the life-and-death struggle of the self and its other can indeed be transformed in relation to a third

---

68. See Herzog, "Reorientation in Theology: Listening to Black Theology," 240 n. 6.

69. Barth is not so much concerned about the dichotomy between faith and unbelief as between faith and heresy. The problem is faith in conflict with itself. See, for instance, Barth, *Church Dogmatics,* vol. I, 1, 31, 32.

element that he calls the "symbolic order." This third dimension introduces a new sense of otherness that goes beyond the dualism of the
self and its imaginary other. Part of the symbolic order is what Lacan
calls the symbolic Other, or the Other of language. He finds that the
encounter with the Other of language can lead to the production of a
new self that goes beyond the fixation and self-centeredness of the self
locked into the imaginary struggle with its other.[70] The much discussed
"turns to language" of postmodern and postliberal theology are based
on the processes that Lacan describes. While this shift is important, the
encounter with the underside of history is not simply an extension of
this move, but its crisis as well.

With the initiation into the symbolic order (Lacan's research starts
with the events of early childhood when the child first enters the realm
of language), the imaginary order in which the imaginary self came
into being in a first alienation in the encounter with the other is transcended by a second alienation. Language poses a twofold challenge
for the imaginary self: First of all, the imaginary self is no longer the
only center of authority. Second, language gradually takes the place
of authority, due to an alienation of the self into words. In this process, words, as one of Lacan's interpreters has put it, "gradually cease
so transparently to symbolize objects and become autonomous symbols
themselves."[71] Lacan's point is that language, dissolving the authority
of the self, finally comes to determine reality. Once put in the place of
authority, language begins to authorize itself without much need for external referents. Lacan concludes that "the symbol manifests itself first
of all as the murder of the [Kantian] thing."[72]

Lacan's reflections remind us of the power of language. This power
does not reside in the fact that language refers to outside realities. Rad-
icalizing the insights of structuralism, Lacan points out that language
is not authorized by any immediate relationship of signifier and signified, the sign and what this sign refers to. In other words, the power of
language does not depend on a referent. Where Ferdinand de Saussure,
the father of structuralism, tried to distinguish between the signifier and
the signified, pointing out their arbitrary relationship, Lacan emphasizes their radical separation. Language does not develop as reference

---

70. See Lacan, "The Function and Field of Speech and Language in Psychoanalysis."
Lacan, "The Agency of the Letter in the Unconscious or Reason since Freud," 173, understands the Other as a "third locus which is neither my speech nor my interlocutor. This
locus is none other than the locus of signifying convention."

71. Ragland-Sullivan, *Lacan and the Philosophy of Psychoanalysis,* 64.

72. Lacan, "The Function and Field of Speech and Language in Psychoanalysis," 104.

to things out there but rather in the interplay of signs in a signifying chain ("love" not being "hate" not being "power," etc.), a process that poststructuralist theoreticians call "metonymy." [73] According to Lacan, the symbolic order introduces the authority of a world of language that is nothing in itself but "a world of differences and...the value of exchange."[74] That is to say that language has the potential to become its own authority, authorizing and creating reality.

The authority of text and language in the symbolic order thus leads to a kind of "deconstruction" of the authority of the self. The initiation into a language that gradually becomes aware of its freedom from referents and signifieds poses a challenge to the narcissistic foundationalism of the modern self. Having moved into the center of the universe, language can no longer be used as a prop for the self. Here the self's imaginary possession of things, essences, or referential concepts, and its control over the other are questioned. In other words, the self is no longer in control of language but language is in control of the self. This aspect of the symbolic order is reminiscent of the early Barth's "deconstruction" of liberal essentialism. It is exactly the authority of the word of God, speaking through the "strange new world of the Bible," which brings judgment on the authority of the self. Ideally, the symbolic-order texts do not eradicate the self completely. Lacan sees a possibility that with the advent of language the self can be incorporated into the collective phenomenon of language.[75] The subject, challenged in its self-centeredness, would acquire a new identity in language, according to which language "speaks him or her just as surely as he or she learns to speak it."[76]

---

73. Cf. Lacan, "The Agency of the Letter in the Unconscious or Reason since Freud," 149ff. "One cannot go further along this line of thought than to demonstrate that no signification can be sustained other than by reference to another signification." Ibid., 150. Foucault recalls that with this discovery, a "point of rupture" took place in French structuralism that "came the day that Lévi-Strauss for societies and Lacan for the unconscious showed us that 'meaning' was probably a mere surface effect, a shimmering froth." Michel Foucault, quoted in Elisabeth Roudinesco, *Jacques Lacan & Co.: A History of Psychoanalysis in France, 1925–1985*, trans. Jeffrey Mehlmann (Chicago: University of Chicago Press, 1990), 376.

74. Ragland-Sullivan, *Lacan and the Philosophy of Psychoanalysis*, 57.

75. Language consists of "symbols [that] in fact envelop the life of man in a network so total that they join together, before he comes into the world, those who are going to engender him 'by flesh and blood.'" Lacan, "The Function and Field of Speech and Language in Psychoanalysis," 68.

76. Fredric Jameson, "Imaginary and Symbolic in Lacan," *The Ideologies of Theory: Essays 1971–1986* (Minneapolis: University of Minnesota Press, 1988), vol. 1, 91. Cf. also Jonathan Scott Lee, *Jacques Lacan* (Amherst: University of Massachusetts Press, 1990), 60.

At a time when the turn to language and the text has become a major option in theology, theological encounters with people on the underside have led to new insights into the power of language. Gustavo Gutiérrez puts it this way: "The Scriptures are not a passive store of answers to our questions. We indeed read the Bible, but we can also say that the Bible 'reads us.'"[77] The authority of Scripture is tied to its ability to transform its readers. In Herzog's words, "Before scripture leads us to creeds [as in neoorthodoxy] or to religion [as in liberalism], it invokes in us discipleship."[78] The power of the biblical texts is not confined to purely linguistic phenomena but is related to "discipleship," the Christian life as a whole.

Through the intervention of the symbolic Other, the self is potentially set free from its narcissism and can now enter into more open relationships with others where difference and otherness is finally being acknowledged. This was exactly what was missing in the imaginary order. The symbolic order introduces a ternary relation among language, self, and other that opens up the dual opposition of the imaginary dyad of self and other circling around the self.[79] In this process the imaginary split between self and other is not dissolved, or "healed" as in ego psychology, which seeks to reaffirm the self,[80] but recognized. Thus, the self is radically decentered and its authority is redistributed.

A similar transaction can be observed in Barth's focus on the "Other" (both, in rereading the biblical texts in their Otherness and in pointing to God as "wholly Other") that is not at the disposal of the self. Yet Barth stresses the Other to such an extent that the relation of self and other seems to be neglected. The ternary relationship of language, self, and other slides back into a binary relationship of language and self. Dialectical theology, stressing the dialectic of the wholly Other and the self, ultimately leaves out the other. Herzog sees this as the major problem in the context of southern culture religion in the United States. Here, "religion is ... defined as status before a morally righteous

---

77. Gustavo Gutiérrez, *We Drink from Our Own Wells: The Spiritual Journey of a People,* foreword by Henri Nouwen, trans. Matthew J. O'Connell (Maryknoll, N.Y.: Orbis, and Melbourne: Dove, 1984), 34.

78. Herzog, GW, 48.

79. This is the point of Lacan's "Seminar on 'The Purloined Letter'" (original: 1956), in *Yale French Studies* 48 (1972), which marks the climax of his emphasis on the symbolic order. At this time, Lacan is still hopeful that all "imaginary incidences" can be "related to the symbolic chain which binds and orients them." Ibid., 39.

80. Not surprisingly, psychoanalysis in the United States of the ego's era has most commonly taken the shape of ego psychology. This form of psychoanalysis, developed by Heinz Hartmann and others, seeks to strengthen the self by restoring its autonomy.

God [Other]. Somehow Christ [bringing together the Other, the other, and the self] does not function very clearly in this relationship." Herzog reminds us of the difference an encounter with the underside makes: "Jesus is not the Christ without the poor, the needy, the outcast, the oppressed. In facing him, we also face them, not just a lonely God."[81]

Unfortunately, the neoorthodox and many postliberal critics of liberal theology have not followed through in reconstructing the re-lationship of self and other. Their way of dealing with the turn to language has more or less led to a repression of both the self and the other. A closer look at possible distortions of the symbolic order exposes the dangers of this position. Lacan describes two anomalies, psychosis and normalcy, the latter of which is of interest here. In the situation of "normalcy" the subject gives way to the objectifying discourse of the symbolic order. In Lacan's words, "here the subject is spoken rather than speaking."[82] The textual reality of the symbolic order, stressing the self-sufficiency of language, takes over the self. Normalcy is determined by a free-floating signifying chain that leaves no trace of the imagi-nary self. Signifiers rule supreme, a phenomenon that poststructuralism has called metonymy, a situation in which the power of the text does not depend on the relation to any signified or referent but is produced within the domain of the text itself, in the differential relationship of signifiers with other signifiers.[83] According to Lacan, the only way to deal with this delusion would be to recover once more the imaginary relationship of self and other and to search for that which has been repressed from the texts.[84]

---

81. Frederick Herzog, "Liberation Theology or Culture Religion?" *Union Seminary Quarterly Review* 29:3/4 (Spring and Summer 1974), 237; also included in *Theology from the Belly of the Whale: A Frederick Herzog Reader*, ed. Rieger.

82. Lacan, "The Function and Field of Speech and Language in Psychoanalysis," 71. For the use of the term *normalcy* see Ragland-Sullivan, *Lacan and the Philosophy of Psychoanalysis*, 285.

83. Lacan expresses the structure of metonymy in the formula $(S \ldots S')$, which indi-cates the unrestricted flow of the signifiers detached from any signifier or referent. See Lacan, "Agency of the Letter in the Unconscious," 164. The poststructuralist concern for metonymy contrasts with the structuralist emphasis on the relation of signifier and signi-fied. Metonymy gets rid of the signified in structuralism's famous formula $\frac{S}{s}$ ("the signifier over the signified") and retains only the signifier.

84. In "The Function and Field of Speech and Language in Psychoanalysis," 70, La-can puts it this way: "If the subject did not rediscover in a regression — often pushed right back to the 'mirror stage' — the enclosure of a stage in which his ego contains its imaginary exploits, there would hardly be any assignable limits to the credulity to which he must succumb in that situation." This process of recovering imaginary groundings ap-pears to be closely related to Lacan's recovery of the notion of metaphor as a balance to metonymical processes. Metaphor is that which "buttons down" the free metonymi-cal flow of the signifiers, in a repression of one signifier by another. The structure of

If this cannot be accomplished, the textual realities of the symbolic order may end up perpetuating the power structures of modernity in their own ways. Even where the power of the text is celebrated, traces of the self, repressed but not reconstructed, are still at work below the surface; the other is not really set free. In this case, the "ego's era" is not effectively overcome, but (unconsciously) reinforced in its own way through a repression from which derives this "credulity" in which the subject is dissolved into the dominant discourse. As Ellie Ragland-Sullivan has pointed out, "Normalcy means accepting messages already in the Other and repressing well.... Such normalcy... demands blind submission to the social order and eschewal of unconscious truth."[85] In this way a new set of blinders is created, similar to the self's resistance to self-knowledge in the imaginary order. In fact, ideology manifests itself here in an even stronger sense than in the imaginary order because repression works less well in a *neurotic* structure than in a *normal* one.[86] Lacan surmises that "here is the most profound alienation of the subject in our scientific civilization."[87]

The view from the underside of history prevents us from joining any easygoing celebration of the power of language. This is one of the most important insights of Lacan's own work with the underside of consciousness.[88] Unless the turn to language takes into account its repressions and the tensions between self and other, it will simply reinforce the way things are. For this reason, language itself cannot be the ultimate authority.

Unlike some neoorthodox and even postliberal thinkers, Barth knows that the power of the Bible lies not in its inherent or "intratextual" authority but in the fact that God makes use of it and makes it alive. In the second edition of his commentary on Romans, Barth rejects any foundationalism based on either the self or the guarantees of the text, explaining that "the importance of an apostle is negative rather than positive. In him a void becomes visible.... *Possessing nothing,* he has nothing of his own to offer."[89] Even though, as we shall see,

---

metaphor is clarified by the formula $\frac{S'}{S}$, meaning that in a metaphorical relationship certain signifiers are repressed from the flow of the signifying chain, in the substitution of one signifier for another. See Lacan, "Agency of the Letter in the Unconscious." For further discussion of metaphor and metonymy, see chapter 3.

85. Ragland-Sullivan, *Lacan and the Philosophy of Psychoanalysis*, 285.
86. Ibid.
87. Lacan, "The Function and Field of Speech and Language in Psychoanalysis," 70.
88. Cf. also Jameson, "Imaginary and Symbolic in Lacan," 88.
89. Barth, *The Epistle to the Romans*, 33. Emphasis mine.

the poor have more to offer than meets the eye, "possessing nothing" they remind us that the place of authority needs to remain open.

Power and the Text

These insights can now be applied to the discussion of power and the text. The oppressed remind us that focusing theological attention on the authority of the texts of the church without attention to the tensions of self and other produced by modernity may in fact reinforce established structures of power. Herzog hit on this problem in the southern United States. In the seventies he points out that without the support of conservative Protestantism, "southern culture in its present form could not continue."[90] Here the Bible has been, and still is, used in supporting the way things are. Whether the biblical texts are read in literal, allegorical, or even historical ways does not seem to make much of a difference if they are read without concern for those who are left out.

According to Lacan, when the authority of the text takes over completely in situations of "normalcy," no reconstruction of the modern self takes place. Yet if the authority of the text merely represses the question of the modern self it ends up condoning, however unconsciously, the modern self's conquest of the other according to the dominant structures of power in the modern world. The fact that the churches are still among the most segregated places in the United States should give us pause. Racism, to name only one structure of oppression and marginalization, does not necessarily have to be preached in order to survive. The constant repression and cover-up of the ongoing struggle between black and white appears to be enough. Once again, the encounter with the underside of history reminds us that authority and power are related, leading us to wonder whether the announced shift in authority makes any difference in terms of power. Without addressing the self's conquest of the other, the authority of the text in itself does not seem to be able to overcome the ego's era.

Herzog's observation of the mid-seventies that "southern religious leadership is hard at work 'to establish orthodox religion as the basis for a ... culture religion' "[91] consolidates my suspicion that even the authority of the religious text can be used by the powers that be for its own purposes. Culture religion, the legitimation of the status quo on

---

90. Herzog, "Liberation Theology or Culture Religion?" 238.
91. Ibid., 236, quoting Samuel S. Hill. The notion of "culture religion" is Herzog's term, since he considers neither Hill's "culture-ethic" nor Bellah's "civil religion" to be appropriate.

religious grounds, can thus be a consequence of both liberal or conservative Protestantism. Recent years have shown the growing political
power of conservative Protestantism in service of the now global modern capitalist system and its confidence that anybody can make it. Here,
the powers of the text stand in for the powers of the self.

In other words, the focus on the authority of the text can be just as
effective as the focus on the authority of the self in shutting out the
voice of the other on the underside. Ironically, although the critics of
liberal theology oppose the authority of the modern self, they end up
supporting its powers. Despite its critical potential, the focus on the
texts of the church ultimately might conceal rather than challenge actual power structures. The real challenge to which encounters with the
underside of history direct us has, therefore, not simply to do with the
relation of the self to the divine Other, but with the relation of the self
to the human other as well. These blinders of the power of the text can
only be addressed, according to Lacan, by rediscovering (and restructuring) the self's "imaginary exploits." The encounter of the self with the
other, the encounter of those in power with the underside of history,
will make all the difference.

Postmodern Developments

Many have felt that the orthodox and neoorthodox tendencies of recent decades have simply been a step back into the premodern. But this
misses the real challenge. The affinities to the postmodern are striking.
Jameson's famous interpretation of "postmodernism" (as the "cultural
logic of late capitalism") is closely related to what Lacan describes as
"normalcy." Here the symbolic-order texts take over the modern self
and the neuroses of high modernism. One of the main characteristics of
the new situation is an "occultation of the present,"[92] whereby "cultural
production is ... driven back inside a mental space which is no longer
that of the old monadic subject but rather that of some ... collective
'objective spirit.' "[93] The theological move from the powers of the self
to the powers of the text and other recent shifts to language are closely
related to these postmodern developments, turning modern authority
structures on their head. In its broadest sense, these turns to the text
include turns to discourse in general; in theology represented, for in-

---

92. Fredric Jameson, "The Cultural Logic of Late Capitalism," in Fredric Jameson,
Postmodernism; or, The Cultural Logic of Late Capitalism (Durham: Duke University Press,
1991), 21.
93. Ibid., 25.

stance, by the much promoted turn to narrative and story, and even the turn to the textual phenomena of local traditions and popular culture. The postliberal theology project of George Lindbeck and others may serve as an example. According to Lindbeck, religion, "like a culture or language, . . . is a communal phenomenon that shapes the subjectivities of individuals rather than being primarily a manifestation of those subjectivities."[94] In Lindbeck's model, authority is relocated from the self to the communal phenomenon of a text. In this model, the modern self's authority is dethroned and folded into the text. Yet while this critique seems to take care of the problematic authority of the modern self, how can Lindbeck's model resist the tendency of the world of the text to move into the place of ultimate reality and to create its own reality? What keeps the text from merely "cannibalizing"[95] or appropriating that which, at first sight, does not seem to belong to its reality? How does the text relate to the other, people who were already excluded in modernity? This reversal of liberal theology seems to create its own set of problems. Here authority is ultimately usurped once more, this time by the "collective subject" of the power of the text.[96] This was the core of Barth's suspicion of what he saw as the usurpation of authority in the Roman Catholic and orthodox modes of theology. While Lindbeck assumes that the written texts of the Bible are the word of God,[97] for Barth the Bible is only one part of the word of God. In this fixation on the text, where everything is incorporated into the symbolic order, lies, in Lacan's estimate, the "ultimate form of mystification."[98] I will show in part II that the encounter with the underside of history might

94. George Lindbeck, *The Nature of Doctrine* (Philadelphia: Westminster, 1984), 33. Cf. Herzog's discussion of Lindbeck, "Vom Ende der systematischen Theologie," in *Gottes Zukunft, Zukunft der Welt: Festschrift für Jürgen Moltmann*, ed. Hermann Deuser, Gerhard Marcel Martin, Konrad Stock, and Michael Welker (Munich: Kaiser, 1986). An English translation will soon be available in *Theology from the Belly of the Whale: A Frederick Herzog Reader*, ed. Rieger.

95. Jameson, "The Cultural Logic of Late Capitalism," 18, talks about the postmodern drive to "the random cannibalization of all the styles of the past."

96. When Lacan talks about the collective subject of the symbolic order, he uses the French *je*. When he talks about the imaginary-order self, he uses the French *moi*.

97. Cf., e.g., George Lindbeck, "Barth and Textuality," *Theology Today* 43:3 (October 1986), 372. Lindbeck interprets the reference of Psalm 119:105 to the word of God in terms of the Bible. Accordingly, it is *the Bible* that is "indeed a guide to the feet and a light to the path, sweeter than honey and the droppings of the honeycomb." In this essay, Lindbeck argues for the close relationship of Barth's theology and the postliberal approach but seems to overlook the importance of Barth's threefold distinction regarding the word of God.

98. Jacqueline Rose, "Introduction II," in *Feminine Sexuality: Jacques Lacan and the école freudienne*, ed. Juliet Mitchell and Jacqueline Rose (New York: W. W. Norton, 1982), 50.

provide a new opportunity to take the authority of the text seriously
without making it absolute.

An earlier critique of Herzog points out the problem: "Too much
theology today begins with the assumption that basically the rhetoric is
sound."[99] Yet this overlooks the "fake factor," according to which rhetoric can easily create its own reality. "It is as though the rhetoric has cast
a spell over reality."[100] It is not difficult to see how this relates to Lacan's notion of "credulity," where the self is merely dissolved into the
dominant discourses. Not unlike liberal theologies, their postmodern alternatives are often unable to discern the self's power over the other
and do not help connecting to the other in new ways. The leap into
the world of the text skips over the power of the self. By not going to
the bottom of the modern self's genesis in a repression of the other, the
turn to the text ends up leaving intact modern structures of power. As I
will show in chapter 3, there is in fact a deeper connection between the
authority of the self and the authority of the text that ties liberal modes
of theology and their alternatives together. The authority invested in
text and language can actually end up reinforcing the authority of the
modern self.[101]

Conclusion

No doubt, liberal theology's concern for God in relation to the human
self and the neoorthodox and postliberal concerns for the texts and
traditions of the church are important building blocks for a new theological vision. Liberal theology reminds us that theology does not
happen in a vacuum. God is encountered in real life, in the world of
the modern self. The critics of liberal theology, on the other hand, have

---

99. Frederick Herzog, "The Burden of Southern Theology: A Response," *Duke Divinity School Review* 38:3 (Fall 1973), 169.

100. Ibid., 167.

101. Rose, "Introduction II," explains this in regard to Lacan's examination of the relationship of women and men in our society. In patriarchy the woman is elevated into the
place of the Other. Yet "the absolute 'Otherness' of the woman . . . serves to secure for the
man his own self-knowledge and truth." See below, chapter 3. Here a brief description
of the other distortion of the Lacanian symbolic, called psychosis, might be added, where
the sort of idealism that was already part of the situation of normalcy is increased: Psy-
chotics construct their own worlds where even the "collective objectivity" of normalcy is
gone and with it the power of the collective phenomenon of the text. In the most radical
way, "the *Other* as the seat of the Word and guarantor of Truth is compensated for in
psychosis by the *other*." Jacques Lacan, "Seminar of November 1957," 293, quoted in An-
thony Wilden, *Speech and Language in Psychoanalysis* (Baltimore: Johns Hopkins University
Press, 1981), 130 n. 102. It is like the apostle Paul says: "They exchanged the truth for a
lie and worshipped and served the creature rather than the Creator" (Rom. 1:25).

called for a new awareness of the power of the texts and traditions of the church in order to broaden the theological horizon once more at a time when theology is in danger of becoming "self-serving" in the most literal sense.

In both paradigms, however, the underside of history is not taken into account. Despite well-meaning concern, the other, the poor, the marginalized do not appear on the theological map. Neither the religious self nor the concern for the ecclesial texts leads us much closer to the repressed other automatically. Both camps share at least one thing in common: They are not able to challenge effectively our current blindness when it comes to the relation to the other.[102]

In the case of liberal theology, the abortive relation of self and other raises questions about the relation of the self and God. Already the writer of 1 John knew this: "Those who do not love a brother or sister whom they have seen, cannot love God whom they have not seen" (1 John 4:20). In the case of the critics of liberal theology, on the other hand, it seems that if otherness is not recognized in basic everyday relationships, talk about God's Otherness becomes questionable. Modifying the theme of 1 John, we could say that anyone who is unable to respect the other is even less able to respect the Other. The obvious point that liberal theology is challenged in the vertical dimension of faith while its critics are challenged in the horizontal dimension is more complex. The encounter with the oppressed other reminds us that liberal theology has trouble on the horizontal level as well, and its critics may not be as secure on the vertical level after all.

In the early encounters with people at the margins, theologians like Herzog were struck by what appeared to them as the "ghetto character" of mainline theology, which, despite affirming its concern for the world, was completely out of touch with the suffering of the other.[103] Not even

---

102. This is also Herzog's point: "Time and again American theology of experience uses the experience of God (even that of radical transcendence) as a cover-up of the false self-consciousness of the successful individual." Herzog, "Amerikas Theologie vor einem Neuanfang?" *Evangelische Kommentare* 7:9 (September 1974), 529. See also Herzog, "Responsible Theology?" in *Philosophy of Religion and Theology: 1974 Proceedings,* American Academy of Religion Section Papers, ed. James Wm. McClendon (Missoula, Mont.: Scholars Press, 1974), 164: "Not God is man's problem, but man is his own problem. His inner eyes, those eyes with which he looks through his physical eyes upon reality, need unblinding." The reference is to one of the most powerful expositions of North America's blindness by an African American, Ralph Ellison's *Invisible Man* (New York: Random House, 1953).

103. Frederick Herzog, "'Politische Theologie' und die christliche Hoffnung," in *Diskussion zur "politischen Theologie,"* ed. Helmut Peukert (Munich: Kaiser, Grünewald, 1969), 123: "The trouble with contemporary American theology is that it comes up with its top-

those who were aware of the limits of the modern self were able to see the other. Reading between the lines of the two theological camps, we are finally able to take note of the power struggle between the self and the other, which was hidden in both instances.

The encounter with the underside helps to formulate some basic challenges. In regard to a critique of the power of the self, the history of Jesus might be relevant. Herzog formulates the question: "Was Jesus as a Jew perhaps saying that the self is dual or corporate...and need not be transcended, but merely calls for acknowledgment in its true structure?"[104] As we have seen, the modern self seems to deflect any acknowledgment of the fact that the other is constitutive of the self, thus opening the door to the aggressive objectification of the other.

The discussion of alternatives to liberal theology has shown that a "leap of faith" into the world of the text will not necessarily do either. The power of the text does not automatically guarantee a reworking of the relationship of the self and its other. Here the encounter with the underside will open new perspectives as well. Herzog points out that "Jesus as member of Israel created the power balance between human beings by acknowledging the marginalized as part of the self. Power corrupts at the point where the weak, the poor, and the maimed are viewed as non-persons"[105] — or, we might add, not seen at all.

The provisional result thus far indicates that a new self, able to recognize the tense relation of self and other, would be an important step beyond the absolute location of power in the self. This self would, then, be able to do away with the illusion of its power as a self-sufficient monad and would be able to recover the truth of Lacan's statement that "I is an other." Likewise, the authority of the ecclesial texts in the hands of people not part of the control mode might lead to a new encounter with the source of all theology, God, and to a more effective deconstruction of the powers of the self.

We understand better now why, despite their importance in theological reflection, neither the human self nor the biblical (or traditional) texts must assume places of ultimate authority, for neither one is God. Theology needs to move beyond the popular options, now distilled as two "civil religions," one conservative, the other liberal. The encounter with the oppressed puts us on the way to a new theological vision, to be unfolded in the rest of this book.

---

ics in dialogue with itself, ironically often by greatly emphasizing the secular realm but with little real knowledge of it."

104. Herzog, "Jesus and Power," 205.
105. Ibid.

Chapter 2

Authority and Power in Latin American Roman Catholic Theology

NOT UNLIKE in North America, at the time when theology started to become aware of the underside of history in Latin America in the late sixties, the field was defined by the opposition of a more modern and a more traditional camp, the latter promoting the authority of the text and the former opening up to the authority of the self. At that time, both theological camps had the support of significant movements in the church, from the traditional institutions of Christendom on the one hand to the Catholic Action movements on the other. Certain semblances of a two-party system can still be found in Latin American theology, even though the oppositional forces do not always present themselves as clear-cut as in the north. This has several reasons, one of them having to do with the phenomenon that the theological vista is changing more rapidly.[1] Adding to the confusion is the paradox that the traditional party seems to have emerged victorious at a time when the reach of modernity continues to expand in Latin America.[2]

Another source of the complexity of the Latin American situation has always been its international horizon. As Enrique Dussel has shown, the context of Latin American theology is tied to the history of the theology of the center.[3] This relation of center and periphery, an example of an encounter with the underside of history on a larger scale,

---

1. See Pablo Richard, *Death of Christendoms, Birth of the Church: Historical Analysis and Theological Interpretation of the Church in Latin America,* trans. Phillip Berryman (Maryknoll, N.Y.: Orbis, 1987), 162: "As things are at present in Latin America, the factors involved in a particular kind of [ecclesial] practice can change very quickly."

2. Leonardo Boff, for example, was silenced by Rome in 1985 for his book *Church: Charism and Power: Liberation Theology and the Institutional Church,* trans. John W. Diercksmeier (New York: Crossroad, 1985), in which he addressed the problems of traditional theology.

3. See Enrique Dussel, "Sobre la historia de la teología en América Latina," in *Liberación y cautiverio: Debates en torno al método de la teología en América Latina,* ed. Enrique Ruiz Maldonado (Mexico City: Comité Organizador, 1976), 20.

will add one more dimension to our discussion of power and authority. The combination of all these factors suggests that the encounter with the underside of history will have wide-ranging implications for Latin American theology, reaching back into the European and North American centers as well.

Latin American Christendom: The Power of the Text

While modern theology did have an impact in Latin America, traditional theology, rooted in the perspective of Roman Catholic Christendom, has been more influential. Its influence in Latin America has been strong from the beginning because Spain and Portugal, the first evangelizing forces, were spared the early crises of Christendom starting with the Reformation. If Henry Commager's thesis that the Enlightenment was so effective in North America because there were no other worldviews that could pose a serious challenge enjoys some plausibility, we can put forth a similar thesis for Latin America: Christendom was much more forceful there since competing forces (both theological and economic) were initially less organized.[4] And although the Second Vatican Council has been widely celebrated as the end of the Christendom mentality, Christendom is still alive and well in Latin America and is once more gaining influence.

While postliberal and other theologies in the Protestant North today search for ways in which the texts of the church can pull the world again into their force fields and reshape it, in the Middle Ages the Christendom church actually managed to absorb the world. There was no longer any world outside the church. Here is an example of how the authority of a specific discourse, in this case the ecclesial one, can appropriate other identifications and incorporate them into the structured world of a symbolic order, described by Lacan as a structural, collective, and cultural phenomenon. The Latin American church follows this path. As the church historian Jeffrey Klaiber has pointed out, already in the first stage of evangelization in the sixteenth century the

---

4. See Henry Steele Commager, *The Empire of Reason: How Europe Imagined and America Realized the Enlightenment* (New York: Oxford University Press, 1982). My hypothesis about Latin America is supported by the observation of Jeffrey Klaiber, S.J., *The Catholic Church in Peru, 1821–1985: A Social History* (Washington, D.C.: Catholic University of America Press, 1992), 10, that "the absence of any internal or external threat was one of the characteristic notes of the colonial Latin American church and is one that distinguishes it from the European or North American churches."

church in Peru was established to such a degree that no other important religion remained that could have rivaled the Roman Catholic faith.[5]

The Power of the Text in the Center and at the Periphery

The structures that I have identified as the powers of the text are quite old in the history of Latin American theology. It is in this manner that the earliest theologians of the conquest provide a justification for the domination of the old world over the new. The thought of Juan Ginés de Sepúlveda, one of the most influential theologians of the sixteenth-century Spanish center, may serve as an example.

In regard to that much debated question of the salvation of the Indian, for instance, some of the very early "modern" theologians like Francisco de Vitoria, a contemporary of Sepúlveda, were aware of the new historical situation at least to a certain degree. Yet the theological thought of Sepúlveda shows no concern for matters of context. His work develops as close reading of, and commentary on, the dominant texts of the center. Authority is attributed to the texts themselves, and no outside perspective is allowed to interfere.[6] In Gutiérrez's judgment, Sepúlveda is "only rehearsing medieval theology."[7] Yet this act of repeating a given set of dominant discourses, far from being merely a sign of a lack of perspective, is characteristic of how the symbolic-order powers of the text work. What matters is, as we have seen, not so much the outside referent but the formation of chains of signification where signifiers establish meaning in relation to each other. Repetition is, as Lacan has pointed out, exactly the mechanism by which a signifying chain perpetuates and fortifies itself, thereby repressing and excluding other factors that might challenge its power.[8] In this model there appears to be little room for the specific needs of people at the periphery.

---

5. Klaiber, ibid., 10.

6. This approach is a manifestation of the second type of theology critiqued by Karl Barth, theology as collection of and commentary on the truths contained in the church. See chapter 1.

7. Gustavo Gutiérrez, *Las Casas: In Search of the Poor of Jesus Christ*, trans. Robert R. Barr (Maryknoll, N.Y.: Orbis, 1993), 248 (abbreviated: IS). Other modern theologians of the time, like Domingo de Soto and Andrés Vega, are even further ahead of Vitoria. Especially the latter is much more precise in his references to the situation in the Indies. See IS, 244–46.

8. This is the fundamental point of Jacques Lacan's famous "Seminar on 'The Purloined Letter,'" (original: 1956), *Yale French Studies* 48 (1972), 39: "Our inquiry has led us to the point of recognizing that the repetition automatism (*Wiederholungszwang*) finds its basis in what we have called the *insistence* of the signifying chain."

Similar mechanisms are described by Leonardo Boff. He discovers in the church "a system that lives in the inferno of terms and doctrines that are reinterpreted ideologically, again and again, in order to maintain power," producing an "endless chain of interpretations." The problem is that in this way theology loses its reference "to the one necessary element, the Gospel."[9] This observation reinforces one of the potential problems with the primacy of the text in the symbolic order: The text itself tends to swallow up the place of any outside referent, be it the self, the other, "the Gospel," or even God. It seems as if the power of the text takes care of the referent long before structuralism and poststructuralism formulate their specific challenges. It is probably no accident that Boff was silenced by Rome precisely when pointing out these matters. Pablo Richard has documented the presence of these processes in the church today, noting that this is a church "that repeats the past."[10] Yet while Richard assumes that this church will render itself obsolete, an insight into the powers of the text forces us to take this phenomenon more seriously.

The "text" that sets the stage for the sixteenth century in Latin America is that of traditional medieval Thomist theology, perpetuated in the European centers. That the historical and geographical conditions are completely different in Latin America is not necessarily a concern for the synchronic world of the symbolic order maintained by the free flow of signifiers where, in its premodern as in its postmodern manifestations alike, diachronic and historical dimensions such as matters of context or social location are less important. In this mindset, a consideration of the difference between center and periphery is unnecessary as long as the metonymical flow of the text can be secured.[11]

While the more modern Vitoria at times corrects the normative Thomist position on grounds of political authority, Sepúlveda proceeds the other way around.[12] Political authority is subordinated to religious authority. Not in the least worried about the validity of the dominant texts of the church, Sepúlveda is concerned solely about possible resistance to those texts as put up, for instance, by the Indians of the

---

9. Boff, *Church: Charism and Power,* 86; see also 14.

10. Richard, *Death of Christendoms, Birth of the Church,* 164.

11. Fredric Jameson, "Spatial Equivalents in the World System," in Fredric Jameson, *Postmodernism; or, The Cultural Logic of Late Capitalism* (Durham: Duke University Press, 1991), 98, notes that postmodernism in principle abolishes the modern distinction between outside and inside.

12. See Gutiérrez, IS, 129.

periphery. In cases of resistance to its texts, he argues, the church may rely on the political powers of the center. Although power cannot be applied in order to make the Indians believe (this would nullify the authority of the ecclesial texts), it can be applied in order to subdue possible resentment to the text, those "obstacles…that could hinder the preaching and propagation of the faith."[13] From the perspective of the Indian other the distinction of power and authority breaks down at this point, but what ultimately justifies and promotes the application of colonializing power is the authority of the text, the Christian faith understood as a system of beliefs and regulations, determined by the center.[14]

The crucial role of the authority of the text in the encounter between center and periphery, between Spain and the new world, is also acknowledged by the influential study of the conquest by Tzvetan Todorov, a Romanian thinker writing in France. Todorov's analysis supports my suspicion that Sepúlveda's way of affirming transindividual values and the texts of the church is tied to an inadequacy in the "conception of the other."[15] He seems to assume, however, that the emphasis of transindividual and social values and identifications, the power of the text, is more or less restricted to a position of the Middle Ages that is overcome once and for all by modernity. Yet Sepúlveda, far from being just a defender of a vanishing premodern ideology, is providing a justification for conquest and war that will be of great value for the church, the Spanish empire, and later powers for a long time. The forces characterized by a certain configuration of Lacan's symbolic order, categorized as "normalcy" in the preceding chapter, are still prevailing in the present and have even taken on a new life lately. Even today there are examples of how the "transindividual" power of the text, as in the days of Sepúlveda, continues to serve the interests of the center.[16]

---

13. Juan Ginés de Sepúlveda, *Apología*, ed. and trans. Angel Losada (Madrid: Editora Nacional, 1975), 73. This quotation is translated in Gutiérrez, IS, 134. Sepúlveda's position is in line with the tradition. In Gustavo Gutiérrez and Richard Shaull, *Liberation and Change* (Atlanta: John Knox Press, 1977), 27–34 (abbreviated: LC), 187 n. 34, Gutiérrez gives an outline of the long history of this issue, beginning with the Imperial Edict of 405 through Augustine, Bernard of Clairvaux, Bruno of Querfurt, and Thomas Aquinas.

14. For a description of the close connection of authority and power see Sepúlveda, *Apología*, 69: "It is the property of human custom and nature that the vanquished readily adopt the customs of the victors and dominators, imitating them in their works and words." Translation in Gutiérrez, IS, 135.

15. Tzvetan Todorov, *The Conquest of America: The Question of the Other*, trans. Richard Howard (New York: Harper & Row, 1984), 157.

16. Klaiber, *The Catholic Church in Peru*, 310–11, names two of the most prominent groups that perpetuate the Christendom model today and push pre–Vatican II models of

How the powers of the text reaffirm themselves throughout the history of the church in Latin America can be seen after the wars of independence in the nineteenth century. In a sort of "ecclesiastical 'colonial treaty'" the Latin American powers of the text are reconstituted in relation to the center. Gutiérrez describes it this way: "Latin America was to supply the 'raw materials': the faithful, the Marian cult and popular devotions." On the other hand, the keepers of the text, "Rome and the Churches of the northern hemisphere were to supply the 'manufactured goods': studies of Latin-American affairs, pastoral directives, clerical education, the right to name bishops."[17]

On this backdrop modern theology can be seen as a reaction to, and subversion of, the power of the classic tradition. As the Latin American thinker Julio Ramos points out, the modern critique leads to a "general disapproval" of the power of the text, "of the rhetorical and religious codes, the loss of prestige of the languages of the tradition."[18] In the next section we will see whether this position might help to be more inclusive of the periphery.

Christendom Theology, Authority, and the Underside of History

In contrast to modern theology, which opts for a dialogical relationship of doctrine and the modern self, Christendom emphasizes the objectivity of theological propositions. The truth of the doctrines of the church is supported by the claim that they contain divine intelligence.[19] Theological discourse in Christendom is developed as exposition and interpretation of the texts of the church. The focus is on the clarity of the exposition of tradition rather than on a creative dialogue with it.[20] In this way the texts of the church become the fundamental paradigm for the construction of theological authority. The validity of every theological discourse is to be judged on the basis of its fidelity to the texts and traditions of the church. Theology aims at gathering a collection of

---

the church: Opus Dei, founded in Spain in 1928, and the Sodalitium Christianae Vitae, founded in 1971 in Peru.

17. Gustavo Gutiérrez, "Contestation in Latin America," in *Contestation in the Church,* ed. Teodoro Jiméz Urresti (New York: Herder and Herder, 1971), 45.

18. Julio Ramos, *Desencuentros de la modernidad en América Latina: Literatura y política en el siglo XIX* (Mexico City: Fondo de Cultura Económica, 1989), 8.

19. Cf. also Gutiérrez and Shaull, LC, 49.

20. See Boff, *Church: Charism and Power,* 12. Gustavo Gutiérrez, *A Theology of Liberation: History, Politics, and Salvation,* Revised 15th Anniversary Edition, trans. Sister Caridad Inda and John Eagleson (Maryknoll, N.Y.: Orbis, 1988), 4 (abbreviated: TL), describes how, starting in the fourteenth century, the classical understanding of theology as a balance of science and wisdom was lost.

absolute, infallible, and divine truths, to be promoted and guarded by the magisterium of the church.[21]

The shape of Sepúlveda's theological discourse may serve as an example. In his debate with Bartolomé de Las Casas on whether heretics and pagans may be subjected to the power of the center, he grounds his arguments in what he considers to be the "authorities" of the church: major philosophers, canon lawyers, theologians, and, most important, the pope in Rome. According to Sepúlveda, the main problem with the arguments of Las Casas is that there are only a few "authorities" in his favor. Las Casas ends up a heretic because he is "opposed to the Gospel and the common declarations and testimonies of the sacred doctors," which, in Sepúlveda's judgment, seem to be one and the same.[22]

From the Middle Ages on, the church increasingly regards itself as the bearer and guardian of theological truth. Theological authority is now based on a collection of truths gathered in the church, and theological reflection is dedicated to the reproduction of the church's tradition. Even the spirituality of Christendom centers on the affirmation and repetition of the dogmatic content of the Christian faith. In the Counter-Reformation of the sixteenth century, the century of the colonialization of Latin America, Cardinal Bellarmine reinforces the power of the text in a way that has remained normative throughout later centuries. Theology now centers on the visible Roman Catholic Church, in which three elements come together that mutually reinforce each other on the basis of the power of the text: faith, the sacraments, and the magisterium.[23]

This ecclesiocentric perspective is a basic feature of Christendom. Theologically, it is grounded in Augustine's distinction of nature and grace. God's grace is manifest in the church; the natural realm lacks grace and thus autonomy. For this reason the authority of the church rules supreme.[24] This focus on the authority of the church, tied to its role as depository of the faith, does not leave much room for attention

---

21. Cf. Boff, ibid., 42. See also Gutiérrez, TL, 4, and Boff, ibid., 52: "Theology became pure and simple *sentire cum Ecclesia,* thinking with the Church."

22. Sepúlveda, *Apología,* 82. The whole argument can be found on 78–82. This is the conclusion of Sepúlveda's text, and he adds a long list of other theologians who support his position.

23. In response to Martin Luther's critique of the invisible church, Bellarmine puts primary emphasis on the church as visible institution, arguing that the church is as visible and tangible as the republic of Venice. Quoted in *Handbuch der Kirchengeschichte,* vol. 4, ed. Hubert Jedin (Freiburg: Herder, 1985), 445. For Bellarmine's definition of the church and an analysis of the spirituality of Christendom, see Gustavo Gutiérrez, *Líneas pastorales de la Iglesia en América Latina* (Lima: CEP, 1970), 30, 33.

24. Augustine's later statement is well known: "[I] defend grace, not as opposed to

to what is happening elsewhere. Here the texts of the church interpret the world, not the other way around. Boff goes one step further. Referring to Sigmund Freud's insight that the psyche has the tendency to substitute reality with words whenever there is a conflict, he suspects that "doctrine substitutes for life, experience, and everything from below."[25] In either case, the concentration on the texts of the church leaves little room for the oppressed, except on the receiving end as long as they don't cause any trouble. The Roman Catholic scholar Christine Gudorf captures well the idealization of the poor that is often related to this perspective when she points out that "the divinization of the church and its officers is a first step in empowering the church to romanticize other elements of reality by linking them to the divine."[26] When the oppressed are noticed at all, they are pulled into the reality of the text.

In the Christendom paradigm the primary task of theology and the church in Latin America, from the conquest on, is thus seen as the incorporation of a whole continent into the church, symbolized to the people by the reception of the sacrament of baptism and manifest in the related affirmation of the creed and certain moral rules.

A basic understanding of the way the powers of the text work helps us come to terms with the commonly held opinion that the evangelization of Latin America does not go as deep as in Europe. According to the logic of the powers of the text, evangelization is successful as long as the creed and certain moral rules are affirmed and their intrinsic authority is not questioned. From the perspective of the power of the text, there exists a de facto equivalence between reciting the faith and personal conversion. In other words, the distinction between the interior and the exterior does not really matter if the subject is, as in Lacanian normalcy, "spoken rather than speaking." The most important actor (and thus the location of authority) in the Christendom model is, therefore, not the individual but the church, represented by the parish and guided by the clergy, drawing together "a certain form of unanimity in a specific geographical area."[27]

An advantage of this approach is its connection to the lives of the common people. Christianity, understood as affirmation of certain cen-

---

nature, but as that through which nature is liberated and controlled." Augustine, *The Retractions* (Washington, D.C.: Catholic University Press, 1968), 207.

25. Boff, *Church: Charism and Power*, 42.

26. Christine Gudorf, *Victimization: Examining Christian Complicity* (Philadelphia: Trinity Press International, 1992), 58.

27. Gutiérrez, *Líneas pastorales*, 17.

tral texts of the church, is relevant for everybody. The elitist tendencies of much of modern theology are less prominent since the fundamental virtue of Christians is not their personal creativity and religious capacity, virtues of the elites, but rather their compliance with the authority of the "text" of the tradition as interpreted to them by the representatives of the church's magisterium. No doubt even the poor can fairly easily find a place in this theological universe. This may be one of the reasons why in Latin America poor people are generally less distanced from the church than in North America and Europe. At the same time, however, we need to keep in mind that the objective here is not primarily the attentiveness to the masses and their gifts and needs but their incorporation into existing church structures.

The Theology of Christendom and Power

The question of authority becomes most pressing in the light of the question of power. The theology of Christendom assumes that civil powers are subordinated to, and must serve, religious truth.[28] The reason, according to Bellarmine, is that "ecclesiastical power... is in every way divinely sanctioned and immediately from God." One of his interpreters notes how this argument is built on the power of the text since Bellarmine's arguments "run entirely in the domain of law and not in that of history."[29] We have already seen that this service must not be understood in the direct sense. The role of the state is not to impose religious truth. Its task is merely to eliminate the obstacles for the dissemination of faith — if necessary, by the use of force. Here Augustine's distinction between nature and grace has been forged into what has been called a "political Augustinianism," according to which the world, having no authentic existence of its own, is subordinated to the church. The basis for this arrangement is the church's theological authority, understood in terms of texts and doctrines, including "the institutions, writings, rites, liturgies, and sacraments."[30] In this context, religious errors have to be suppressed at all costs, even with the use of

---

28. Richard, *Death of Christendoms, Birth of the Church,* 1, defines Christendom "as a particular kind of relationship between the *church* and *civil society,* a relationship in which the *state* is the primary mediation." Emphasis in original.

29. James Brodrick, S.J., *Robert Bellarmine,* vol. 1 (London: Longmans, Green, 1950), 221, 222, concludes that this makes most arguments against Bellarmine "quite irrelevant." The Bellarmine quotation can be found on 223. It is no surprise that modern thinkers like Thomas Hobbes would attack Bellarmine precisely on this point. See Hobbes's *Leviathan* (New York: Collier Books, 1962), 399ff., esp. 417–19.

30. This list is drawn up by Enrique Dussel, *A History of the Church in Latin America: Colonialism to Liberation,* trans. Alan Neely (Grand Rapids: Wm. B. Eerdmans, 1981), 62.

political power, since such errors threaten not only the authority of the church but also the stability of the powers that be. It is quite telling that the Inquisition was never concerned about moral deviations. Such sins do not call into question power structures and truth.[31] In Christendom there is a close connection between the church's self-understanding as the depository of grace and truth and its allegiance with the powers that be.[32]

One of the basic temptations of Christendom is the confusion of religious authority and political power. Once the church requests the service of the civil powers, the idea that somehow those powers would share in the theological authority of the church is not far off, even if those powers are seen as subordinated to the church. The historical manifestation of this problem is to be found in the *patronato regio* of the conquest of Latin America, which, in transferring the main responsibility for evangelization from the Roman Catholic Church to the Spanish king, had the effect of integrating the evangelization of Latin America even more closely with the mechanisms of colonialization.[33] In the end, as Klaiber has pointed out, "religion had been the legitimizing force of order for so long that it was difficult to distinguish between order and religion."[34] This theological perspective is so closely allied with the powers that be at all levels that there is hardly any place for the poor, except as recipients of charity.

Not surprisingly, the breakup of the feudal world and the emergence of the modern nation-state in Latin America poses a major challenge for Christendom. Yet the church is able to make up for its loss of power by forging new relationships. One such attempt can be found in New Christendom, dating from the 1930s, which forms a coalition with the middle classes that emerge after independence. In contrast to the defensive reaction of Christendom to modernity, New Christendom promotes a more constructive interaction with the modern world, which

31. Cf. Boff, *Church: Charism and Power*, 42.
32. The French philosopher Maurice Blondel had seen a relation between the orthodox tendency to impose the faith and its support of a certain kind of civil power. "Regalistic and theocratic theories must be related in the thought of the conservatives." Blondel, paraphrased in Christofer Frey, *Mysterium der Kirche, Öffnung zur Welt: Zwei Aspekte der Erneuerung französischer katholischer Theologie* (Göttingen: Vandenhoeck and Ruprecht, 1969), 181.
33. Cf. Richard, *Death of Christendoms, Birth of the Church*, 28ff. But while for Richard the *patronato* shows mainly the weakness of the church, our discussion gives reason to suspect a closer interrelationship of power and authority.
34. Klaiber, *The Catholic Church in Peru*, 197. "The role the church assumed with greatest frequency was that of collaborator with the government in maintaining order" (201).

is foreshadowed by Social Catholicism in France and certain elements of French liberal Catholicism in the middle of the nineteenth century.[35] The distinction between nature and grace is now derived from Thomas Aquinas rather than from Augustine. In this model grace does not suppress or control nature but rather perfects it. Since the authenticity of the natural realm is affirmed in principle, the world achieves a certain autonomy from the church.

Yet while the world enjoys some authority of its own, a fact that makes the New Christendom less rigid in its religious mission, the basic goal is close to the Christendom model: New Christendom pursues the consecration of the world by the church and the creation of a favorable environment for the life of the church. The church participates in the political realm by means of political parties, social action groups, and, quite important for perpetuating the power of the text in the modern world, the foundation of Roman Catholic universities. In the pursuit of the ideal of a society inspired by Christian principles, authority is again squarely located in the church and the basic relation of authority and power remains the same: The authority of the church is still projected onto the world, searching for alliances with the powers that be.[36]

Nevertheless, in New Christendom the intellectual elites live up to the status attributed to them by modernity. Social action for the underprivileged becomes an important concern. A view from the underside, however, reveals that the masses are incorporated only in ideal terms, as they should be, not as they really are. While New Christendom, in part inspired by the papal social encyclicals, proclaims social concern, there is little real contact with the suffering of the poor masses and, not unlike the North American Social Gospel movement, little exchange between the self and the other.[37] The underlying causes of the situation are left unexamined.

---

35. Dussel, *A History of the Church in Latin America*, dates the period of the "New Christendom" from 1930 to 1962, whereas Richard, *Death of Christendoms, Birth of the Church*, 78, incorporates the earlier crises of Christendom and dates the "New Christendom in Latin America" from 1808 to 1960. Richard puts more emphasis on the general continuity of Christendom and New Christendom.

36. Cf. Richard, *Death of Christendoms, Birth of the Church*, 76. See also Gutiérrez, *Líneas pastorales*, 21, 37–39, and Gutiérrez, TL, 35–36.

37. See Gustavo Gutiérrez, "Liberation Praxis and Christian Faith," in Gustavo Gutiérrez, *The Power of the Poor in History*, trans. Robert R. Barr (Maryknoll, N.Y.: Orbis, 1983), 40 (abbreviated: PP). An example is the Christian Democrats in Chile. Cf. also Richard, *Death of Christendoms, Birth of the Church*, 166, and Klaiber, *The Catholic Church in Peru*, 170.

Postmodern Developments

Even at the beginning of a new millennium the theology of Christendom is far from being passé and has found new forms of corresponding to the present.[38] The fact that in Latin America the representatives of Christendom in the church are now supported by non-Christian politicians and governments shows that Christendom is not necessarily confined to traditional forms of society and political power. Pablo Richard, one of the foremost observers of Christendom in Latin America, points out that today the church has found new niches as an "ideological apparatus of the state."[39]

One example for this trend and the adaptability of the Christendom mind-set to a postmodern situation is the 1978 Preparatory Document for the Latin American Bishops' Conference in Puebla drawn up by the general secretary of the Latin American Bishops' Conference, Alfonso López Trujillo, and others.[40] The document shows well the transmutations of the powers of Christendom. Identifying modern secularism as the main problem in Latin America, the Preparatory Document argues for the creation of a Christian culture that generates a "new type of urban-industrial society." The role of the church is central in the "overcoming of modernism" and in "integrating the values it has provided."[41]

Yet while modern secularism is denounced, and with it the shift of authority to the modern self, the modern process of industrialization is affirmed. Adopting the point of view of the center, the document speaks about industrial society without even mentioning the working class and the concrete plight of people on the underside. Where the making of the modern self on the back of the other is overlooked, however, its power is not challenged. Here we have another example of how the modern blindness for the other can be perpetuated even in situations where the symbolic text is in charge but fails to effectively reconstruct

---

38. See Catalina Romero, "Iglesia y proyecto social en el Perú," *Páginas* 14:96 (April 1989), 28.

39. Richard, *Death of Christendoms, Birth of the Church*, 163.

40. Among them were the Belgian Jesuit Roger Vekemans and the president of the Roman Curia's Pontifical Commission for Latin America, Cardinal Sebastian Baggio. See Christian Smith, *The Emergence of Liberation Theology: Radical Religion and Social Movement Theory* (Chicago: University of Chicago Press, 1991), 209, 210. The document itself was sharply criticized in Latin America and, in the end, radically amended. Gustavo Gutiérrez's article "The Preparatory Document for Puebla: A Retreat from Commitment," PP, 111ff., which will serve as a guideline here, provided one of the most influential critiques. For López Trujillo's assessment of the Puebla conference see Alfonso López Trujillo, *De Medellín a Puebla* (Madrid: Biblioteca de Autores Cristianos, 1980), 287ff.

41. Preparatory Document, quoted in Gutiérrez, PP, 111, 112.

the modern self. Not unlike many North American critics of liberalism, the Preparatory Document delivers too shallow a critique of the modern world and the "center." Ultimately, the document finds a way to bring modern power structures and the authority of Christendom together. The power of the text is reasserted now on grounds of popular religiosity, which is interpreted as serving the traditional values.[42] Obviously, even popular religiosity can be used to support the powers that be and to conceal the struggle of the self against the other. The Preparatory Document finally designates its authoritative "texts" when, in the name of "Christian principles" and in defense of our "Western and Christian civilization," it is argued that "the world is unified by 'westernization' and it is with it or within it that the greater cultural diversities are found."[43] This revitalization of Christendom on the grounds of a realignment of the traditional church with late capitalist society reminds us once more of the mutual relationship of power and authority.[44]

Even though the context is different, there is some resemblance to North American theology's attraction to the powers of the text: Where the textual Other (even that of popular religion) takes over without attention to the plight of the human other, the powers that be are not necessarily overcome. Even the textual reality of popular religion, ever gaining in currency in postmodern times, can be used against the people. Gutiérrez sums up this problem in response to the Preparatory Document: "The presence of ancient indigenous cultures is curiously acknowledged, but their voices go unheard as the resounding marching notes of westernization drown out the sound of their primitive instruments."[45] The Latin American poor remind us that the current excitement about all kinds of postmodern "turns to the text" may not make much of a difference in the overall picture.

Authority and Power

It seems that even as the power affiliations of Christendom gradually change, the construction of authority in terms of the powers of the text

---

42. See Gutiérrez, ibid., 123. López Trujillo repeats his emphasis on popular religiosity in *De Medellín a Puebla*, 294–95. Klaiber, *The Catholic Church in Peru*, 218, points out a similar function of the church immediately after the independence movements.

43. Preparatory Document, quoted in Gutiérrez, PP, 113, 116. This celebration of Western and Christian civilization is based on the "revelation of the providential God." Ibid., 121.

44. The Preparatory Document speaks of the "third industrial revolution." Quoted in Gutiérrez, ibid., 112. Boff, *Church: Charism and Power*, 53, suspects that today "the Church-institution functions as if it were a giant multinational corporation."

45. Gutiérrez, PP, 113.

remains in place.[46] Obviously, the "text" is now no longer focused on medieval theology alone but includes other discourses, such as popular values or the dominant concerns of Western Christianity. Even popular religiosity of the periphery can be used as warrant for the values of the center, supporting its power. The increasing attention to popular culture in postmodernity does not guarantee that the needs of the poor become part of the picture. At a time when artifacts of popular culture enjoy a certain attraction in the center, the fact that theology makes use of the texts of the periphery does not necessarily mean that new models of authority and power are developed.

Latin American Christendom theology does not reflect much on the interdependence of power and authority. Here is a specific ideological blindness that we have discovered at several junctures in the other theological approaches as well.[47] This leads to a deeper insight into the problem. Defining this ideological blindness as the rationalization of positions already taken does not grasp the full range of the problem.[48] A more critical form of ideology is the rationalization of positions of which one is not even aware. The power of the text is always in danger of falling into this trap, especially where the symbolic "Other" of the text takes the place of the self and the repressed "other." Boff is right: "The majority of those in authority in the Church" are not people of ill will but rather "men of good faith, clear conscience, impeccable personal character." The problem has nothing to do with ill will or intentional neglect of poverty and oppression. The problem lies on the level of a "structure that to a great degree is independent of persons,"[49] the product of certain constellations of authority and power.

Two elements must be kept together in further reflections on authority and power. On the one hand, we have become aware of a reconfiguration of theological authority in terms of power that happens, for the most part, on an unconscious, structural level. On the other hand, we have found that authority is not only the product of power constellations but has a part in their genesis as well. In other words, if it is true that, as Boff says, "the unification of the symbolic order re-

---

46. Günther Lewy has pointed out that the traditional dogmatic fixations can adapt to a whole range of different power structures, from democracy to totalitarianism. Reference in Boff, *Church: Charism and Power,* 54.

47. Gutiérrez, IS, 408, puts it this way: "Paradoxically, some of the most ardent defenders of the 'purely religious' nature of the task of evangelization are often persons who hold political power in the service of the mighty."

48. This is the definition used by Schubert Ogden, *Faith and Freedom: Toward a Theology of Liberation* (Nashville: Abingdon, 1989), 31.

49. Boff, *Church: Charism and Power,* 39.

produces the cohesiveness of the social ruling classes,"[50] we can also argue that a unified symbolic order contributes to the cohesiveness of the powers that be.

Modern Theology: The Power of the Self

If the theology of Christendom is still so influential, why bother addressing the role of modern theology in the Latin American context? One reason has to do with the actual influence that modernity has already had on Latin America. Although modernity's earliest roots in Latin America stemmed from encounters with Europe, the past thirty years have seen an exponential growth in more localized modern influence. This influence is felt perhaps most strongly by the working classes, those most directly involved with the rapidly changing modes of production.[51] The migration to the cities, affecting broad sectors of society, is another indication of the ongoing "modernization" of Latin America, even though the results for the migrants often are to be found more in the loss of their traditional contexts than in their benefiting much from modernity. In other words, modern thought in Latin America is relevant because of its ongoing intellectual and economic connections to the centers of modernity and liberalism in Europe or North America, a characteristic trait of the theological currents discussed in this section.

Another reason why we need to address the role of modern theology in Latin America has to do with the fact that the structures of modernity have often been suggested as a remedy for the problems of Latin America by those who have pointed out its backwardness and traditionalism.[52] No doubt, modernity has the potential to reshape traditional Christendom theology; as Julio Ramos has pointed out, the modern functions in Latin America as "the crisis of a cultural system in which ... the *letters* ... have occupied a central place" in the organization of society.[53] But what about the poor? We will have to see whether

---

50. Ibid., 114.

51. Gutiérrez's increasing awareness of the problems of modernity, for instance, is related to the fact that, within the past thirty years, Peru has had more contact with the modern world in that its economy moved from being centered on agrarian and mining sectors to becoming more and more industrialized. Cf. also Catalina Romero, "Iglesia y proyecto social en el Perú," 17.

52. Cf., e.g., David Martin, *Tongues of Fire: The Explosion of Protestantism in Latin America* (Oxford: Basil Blackwell, 1990). Martin welcomes the rise of modern Protestantism in Latin America as being able to loosen up a rigid traditionalism and create "free spaces."

53. Ramos, *Desencuentros de la modernidad en América Latina,* 8.

modern theology in Latin America is able to deal with the challenge of
the underside of history.

The Power of the Self in the Center and at the Periphery

A basic understanding of the process of modernization in Latin America
starts with the intervention of the center into the peripheral areas, as
integration into the international market, as the attempt to Westernize,
Europeanize, and North Americanize.[54] This definition also holds true
for the church, in which modernization can be interpreted, according
to Klaiber, as "a confrontation between the church and the 'modern'
world, which in this context is defined as the western world."[55]

The Latin American experience of modernity adds another element
to the analysis of the modern self in chapter 1. Todorov has found some
form of the powers of the modern self already at work in the conquest of
Latin America in the sixteenth century, side by side with the powers of
the text. What makes the Europeans superior to the Indians, he argues,
is the ability of the modern self to relate to and communicate with the
other. At the same time, however, Todorov shows how this ability leads
not to an understanding of the other but rather to an assimilation of the
Indians to one's own world.[56] This is a good illustration of the powers
that determine what Lacan has called the era of the ego. As I indicated
in chapter 1, the conquest is an illustration of how the modern self
assumes power, not as an isolated monad, pulling itself up by its own
bootstraps as the myth of modernity would have it, but precisely in the
process of the (narcissistic and aggressive) assimilation of the other.[57]
The inability to develop mutual relationships and to fully appreciate
those who are other is somehow built into the modern mind-set.

There is a sense in which the powers of the modern self manifest
themselves very early on in Latin America, perhaps earlier than in
Europe itself and certainly more violently.[58] As early as the sixteenth

---

54. Cf. Tomás Maldonado, "El movimiento moderno y la cuestión post," in *El De-bate modernidad-posmodernidad*, ed. Nicolás Casullo (Buenos Aires: Puntosur Editores, 1991), 263. Maldonado argues for expanding this description to include the emancipatory character of modernity.

55. Klaiber, *The Catholic Church in Peru*, 26.

56. Todorov, *The Conquest of America*, 248.

57. From the perspective of the Latin American poor, Todorov's optimism that "this period of European history is . . . coming to an end today" and that "the representatives of Western civilization no longer believe so naively in its superiority" must seem surprising. Ibid., 249.

58. Richard, *Death of Christendoms, Birth of the Church*, 23, argues that "from the very beginning, starting with its discovery and conquest, Latin America has developed with a *capitalist social pattern.*" Yet while Richard's observation is correct that the forces of the

century, a theological approach crystallizes parallel to traditional Christendom theology that is influenced by the very first seedlings of modern
identity and tied to an increasing interest in colonial trade relationships. One of the first to initiate this shift to the modern is the great
sixteenth-century Spanish theologian Francisco de Vitoria. While not
immediately breaking with the theocratic medieval tradition, a new
point of view, that of the social and economic order of modernity and
of the emerging middle class, is gradually introduced into theological
discourse.[59]

From its very beginnings, modernizing theology is produced in the
European centers, and, although it profits from the exploitation of the
Latin American other, it remains tied to Europe. Close ties to the
powers at the center appear to be a common trait of all the different
manifestations of the rising modern spirit. This indicates a certain limit
of the reach of the authority of the modern. Not surprisingly, modern
theology has hardly been able to reflect from within the Latin American
people, let alone from the perspective of those at the margins. Gutiérrez
observes that the modern self "is alert to its own interests" but tends to
be "myopic when it comes to the claims of others in both the social and
the economic areas."[60] Although this self appears to have roots in the
center, its influence on (and gain from) the Latin American periphery
is considerable.

The main characteristic of modernity is that humanity (or at least a
certain section of it) learns to take things into its own hands. In Europe,
this is manifest in the bourgeois revolutions as well as in the Enlightenment. In Latin America as well, the modern self's ability to appropriate
the other for its own purposes will have a long history. The Latin American perspective reminds especially those of us in North America and
Europe that the repressed others of modernity include not only the marginalized at home but the majority of people living in what is quite
tellingly called the "third world."

---

early modern markets determine Latin America very early on, the other side, which is not
immediately modernist and capitalist, must not be neglected.

59. See Gutiérrez, IS, 342, and Gustavo Gutiérrez, "Si fuesemos Indios...," *Socialismo
y Participación* 40 (December 1987), 25.

60. Gustavo Gutiérrez, "The Truth Shall Make You Free," in *The Truth Shall Make You
Free: Confrontations,* trans. Matthew J. O'Connell (Maryknoll, N.Y.: Orbis, 1990), 113. Cf.
also Gutiérrez and Shaull, LC, 27–34. For reflection on the inability of modern theology to work from within the Latin American context see Gutiérrez, "Theology from the
Underside of History," PP, 194.

Modern Theology, Authority, and the Underside of History

The rise of the power of the modern self thus has an impact on theological reflection in both Americas. No doubt, Protestant theologians of the North are more closely tied to modernity than their Roman Catholic cousins in the South.[61] At the same time, however, there is also a liberal Catholicism that arises in the middle of the nineteenth century as a minority current in Europe and spreads abroad. In the Roman Catholic Church this triggers a long process of opening up to the modern world that culminates in the Second Vatican Council.

Modern Roman Catholic theology goes against the ecclesiocentric perspective of Christendom that took shape with Constantine in the fourth century and reached its zenith in the Middle Ages when the church had finally absorbed the world. Although this perspective, which concentrates all authority in texts of the church and in the hands of the church's magisterium, persists, gradually the horizon is widened. Already Francisco de Vitoria in the sixteenth century is part of a new theological current that, not unlike René Descartes in modern philosophy, lays the foundations for the modern turn to the self.

This epoch is of course closely tied to the conquest. Yet while the encounter with a new world in the conquest helped to pry open the narrow Christendom perspective in certain ways — boosting the self-confidence of the conquerors for instance — the modern turn to the self is still not able to truly appreciate the other of the new world. Dussel reminds us of "a special blindness" of the modern self in Latin America "for the external appearance of other cultures, people, states."[62] Deeper encounters with the other of the new world, soon to become the exploited other, are not part of the new theology.

In the early nineteenth century another theologian at the center, Félicité de Lamennais in France, while not giving up completely on the traditional idea of the church as location of religious truth, proposes a theology that appreciates the value of modern liberties and the progress of humanity. Lamennais invites theology to broaden its horizon and to pay attention to a universal human tradition. Even though he maintains a certain critique of modern individual reason, the theological

---

61. In this context the question of how the Latin American other functions, overtly or covertly, in the great authors of liberal theology in Europe and the United States would merit analysis. Schleiermacher's work, for instance, was produced at a time when Europe was under the strong influence of Alexander von Humboldt's reconstruction of the image of Latin America. On von Humboldt see Mary Louise Pratt, *Imperial Eyes: Travel Writing and Transculturation* (London: Routledge, 1992).

62. Dussel, "Sobre la historia de la teología en América Latina," 30. On, 29, Dussel talks about a second scholastic epoch that is more open to the modern world.

construction of religious authority follows the direction determined by the dominant authorities and powers of modernity.[63] Lamennais identifies a "perfect harmony" between religion and humanity in general, which "is why in all times, and all climates, man naturally drawn towards it, has felt the need of being enlightened by its dogmas." Religion is a natural ally of the modern self and available to every reasonable person because it "places in [human] minds at the first moment of their opening, the whole truth, in order that it may be their light, their good, their rule, and although all do not equally comprehend it, all equally possess it, and can love it equally."[64]

While other attempts to adapt theology to modernity followed, the twentieth century is of particular importance for modern Roman Catholic theology. Modernity's emphasis on human subjectivity is now at the center of the authority debate. Theological attention moves further away from an exclusive focus on the supernatural to a focus on the dialectic of supernatural and natural, including the dialectic of God and humanity.[65] In response to the traditional subordination of the world to the authority of the church, the French theologian Yves Congar and others work alongside what has become known as *nouvelle théologie,* suggesting a clearer distinction between church and world.[66] This distinction has a profound impact on the more progressive lay movements in Latin America in the 1950s and 1960s and provides the foundation for many of the texts of Vatican II. Its most fundamental characteristic is a fairly sharp differentiation of the realms of the supernatural and the natural, aiming at the limitation of the reach of traditional ecclesiastical authority. Here the modern world's authority to raise its own questions is acknowledged. In the transition from a perspective that puts all emphasis on the divine/supernatural to a perspective that rediscovers the

---

63. See Gutiérrez and Shaull, LC, 40f.

64. Félicité de Lamennais, *Essay on Indifference in Matters of Religion,* trans. Lord Stanley of Alderley (London: John MacQueen, 1895), 173 and 175. Lamennais finds an "inclination towards Christianity shown by all nations, as soon as it is announced to them."

65. Cf., e.g., Yves Congar, *Situation et tâches présentes de la théologie* (Paris: Cerf, 1967), 27.

66. An example is Yves Congar, *Lay People in the Church: A Study for a Theology of Laity,* rev. ed., trans. Donald Attwater (London: Geoffrey Chapman and Christian Classics, 1985). Not unlike Schleiermacher, Congar intends to fight both Christendom's dissolution of the world into the church and a more modern dissolution of the church into the world. See 420–22. This is the theological paradigm that Gutiérrez, in his early writings (TL, "Liberation Praxis and Christian Faith," PP, and "The Meaning of Development"), calls the "distinction of planes model." Cf. also Gutiérrez, *Líneas pastorales,* where the term "la pastoral de la madurez en la Fe" is used.

importance of the human/natural, the modern self continues to rise to a position of authority.[67]

Although this approach claims that both planes, the church and the world, are responsible to God, there is a tendency to see both realms as fairly autonomous and independent spheres of authority.[68] Traditional ecclesiocentric authority is decentered and reconstructed in no small part in terms of the modern (Christian) self, which is at work in the world for the sake of Christ and the church.[69] Yet to the degree to which this approach stresses the activism, success, and self-sufficiency of the self, the encounter with the poor on the underside of history cannot become part of the picture. From this perspective the advent of the poor on the theological map as a specific group that does not easily fit Congar's description of Christians as actors in the pursuit of "true humanism, sanity and serious work"[70] can only be seen in terms of a somewhat hostile takeover of theological authority by a special interest group.

But what would happen if a third element entered into the dialectic of church and world, text and self? The basic question for modern theology is once again directly related to the issue of the power of the self and the question of its basic relationship to the other: Is the human self suspended in the myth of its own autonomy that, as Lacan's analysis of the isolated imaginary order has underscored, leads to the blindness for the other? Or is the self able to take into account the question of its other that is part of this self and, ultimately, also of the Other, which it cannot control? This critique works both ways. It addresses the power of the modern self and its illusion of unlimited self-determination as well as the ecclesiocentrism and the power of the text that still leaves some residues in modern Roman Catholic theology. The theological encounters with the underside of history will introduce another shift in the location of authority. The world is no longer seen essentially as autono-

---

67. This also has consequences for a reevaluation of the importance of the laity within the church. See Congar, ibid., 118: "It would seem that according to God's design the one supreme mediation of Jesus Christ is exerted through a twofold mediation by men. . . . Christ's kingly, priestly and prophetical mediation is at work in two ways: through the apostolic hierarchy, for the formation of a faithful people; through the whole body, in respect of the world."

68. Cf. also Gutiérrez's comments in *Líneas pastorales*, 44–48, 59.

69. Congar, *Lay People in the Church*, 116, talks about the fact that, in the life of the faithful, "Christ's saving powers are made manifest within the dimensions of history and of the world, so as to bring back to God all the richness of his creation."

70. Ibid., 448.

mous but as called to communion with God and neighbor, challenged by an authority that is different from the authority of the self.[71]

Modern Theology and Power

One of Lamennais's conclusions at the end of his *Essay on Indifference in Matters of Religion* helps us understand the relation of authority and power: "Whatever is," he claims, at least in the society of intellectual beings, "is ordained."[72] Lamennais's appreciation of human intelligence and his trust in the goodness of a regime based on modern liberties are connected.[73] This combination of theological and political aspects may well account for Lamennais's tremendous influence on Roman Catholic thought. The parallel is striking to the persuasive power of Schleiermacher's theological system in German Protestantism. Yet in this connection of theological authority with the powers that be, the poor are left out once more. Their humanity does not seem to belong to Lamennais's universal humanity.

Nouvelle théologie provides a more contemporary example. The modern self's gain in authority is also reflected in a gain in power. Because in this approach the church and the role of its priests are restricted to the ecclesial sphere, it is the responsibility of the laity to act in the world. The practical mediation between the church and the world depends on the action and the faith of the individual Christian.[74] This strategy appears to be modeled on the idea of the modern self, which is capable of acting autonomously, on grounds of personal and free choices. No doubt, the elitist tendency of this perspective is amplified in the Latin American context where the great majority of the marginalized may find it difficult to live up to this ideal.

It is quite telling that one of the problems of the Catholic Action movements that made use of this model from the 1950s on is exactly the problem we have found to be characteristic of the modern self: the

---

71. Cf. Gutiérrez, *Líneas pastorales*, 61.

72. Lamennais, *Essay on Indifference in Matters of Religion*, 274. On 182, Lamennais proposes to show that religion, which leads the human being "to happiness, by establishing him in a condition in conformity to his nature, alone also preserves nations, and leads them to happiness, by placing them in a state in conformity to the nature of society."

73. Cf. Gutiérrez and Shaull, LC, 40, 41.

74. Congar, *Lay People in the Church*, 106: "The faithful soul busy in the world cannot but seek for himself a harmony of the two cities to which he belongs, he cannot but want to change the world in some measure." On 454–55, Congar points out that "Christian influence opening the way to faith at the level of human structures" is the task of "lay people, for they belong both to the world and to the Church in a way that is true neither of the clergy nor of the monks. And so the lay function as such is necessary to the Church's mission and to the economy of grace."

blindness to the roots of the oppression of the other. The problem stems not from a lack of goodwill or moral instruction but from the blindness of the modern self, unable to learn from the other. As Leonardo Boff observes, here the relationship to the poor is defined from the perspective of the rich: "The rich will be called upon to aid in the cause of the poor but without necessarily requiring a change in social class practices."[75] This model does not call into question the power structures of modernity.

Gutiérrez explains that in what he calls the "socio-Christian perspective" the dignity of the human person is defended in general terms, assuming that the marginalized can be "assimilated" by the mere improvement of modern society. In this way, Catholic Action movements were "reabsorbed by the social order they had intended to modify."[76] The same is true for the so-called theology of development, which in similar fashion fails to grasp the deeper roots of the repression of the poor, promoting instead a vision of progress that never materialized. It is quite telling that in both cases the failure to connect with the poor is related not only to an inability to establish mutual relationships but also to a failure to recognize the conflictual character of the present. The ongoing conflict in which the self uses the other to shore up its own powers, often perpetuated even where the self is trying to "help" the other person, is never realized. This was precisely the problem of Schleiermacher in Europe and liberal theology in the North American context.

The inability of modern theology to contribute to the transformation of the Latin American situation, in which most people are poor, is no longer surprising: If the modern self is the main actor and one of the basic authorities, the other who co-constitutes this self, as described by Lacan's reflections on the imaginary order, is excluded by default. Not even the theological and moral education of the modern self seems to change this basic constellation. As abortive models of development politics have shown, the other can fall prey even to structures established by well-meaning selves. The encounter with the other, poor and oppressed, exposing the self's narcissism and aggressivity, reminds us of the insufficiency of good intentions, which must be taken with the utmost seriousness, especially by North Americans, who often tend to promote modernization as the solution for Latin Ameri-

---

75. Boff, *Church: Charism and Power*, 7.

76. Gutiérrez, "Liberation Praxis and Christian Faith," PP, 40. See also Boff, ibid., 6, who realizes that this model "did not present an alternative perspective but a reformist one, acceptable to the dominant sectors of society."

cans. "Self"-critique, in its literal sense, seems to be impossible without an encounter with people on the underside of history.

Vatican II, opening the church to the modern world, must also be seen in this light. The modern myopia can be found even in *Lumen Gentium*, one of the most famous documents of the council.[77] Although *Lumen Gentium* does not preach modern individualism, the oppression and suffering of the poor are not seen as a deeper issue. While this text presents an optimistic view of the world and endorses the values of modernity, such as human rights, freedom, equality, and progress, social conflicts are touched on only in general terms. Ultimately, the power structures of the status quo are maintained because the world to which the church is opening up is the modern world, not the world of the poor. The underside of modernity, in particular the immense poverty of large sectors, is interpreted merely as a social problem, without perceiving its theological import.[78]

Against this backdrop it is perhaps to be expected that what Gutiérrez has called the distinction of planes model, the matrix for this approach, has changed hands in Latin America and today is used to support yet another status quo.[79] After initial differences, it seems that now a certain alliance of traditional Christendom with the forces of theological modernism has been instituted against theology in solidarity with the poor.[80] The advent of the poor on the theological map helps us to understand better the nature of the contemporary theological impasse.

On the other hand, there are also a number of positive accomplishments of modern theology that can be utilized for the construction of a new, genuinely Latin American theological perspective that includes the poor. Perhaps the most important element of Vatican II is the shift

---

77. *Lumen Gentium*, "Dogmatic Constitution of the Church," in *Vatican Council II: The Conciliar and Post Conciliar Documents*, new revised edition, ed. Austin Flannery, O.P. (Collegeville, Minn.: Liturgical Press, 1992), 350ff.

78. See Gustavo Gutiérrez, "Por el camino de la pobreza," *Páginas Separata* 8:58 (December 1983), 14–15, and Gutiérrez, "Theology from the Underside of History," PP, 182. Cf. also Gustavo Gutiérrez, "The Poor in the Church," in *The Poor and the Church*, ed. Norbert Greinacher and Alois Müller (New York: Seabury, 1977), 12.

79. "Until a few years ago it was defended by the vanguard; now it is held aloft by power groups... [whose] purposes are very different." Gutiérrez, TL, 41. In a 1987 address to Peruvian military leaders, Gutiérrez seems to presuppose that they are among those who now advocate the distinction of planes model. See Gustavo Gutiérrez, "La Iglesia y la problemática social," *Defensa Nacional* 6:7 (October 1987), 124.

80. Jeffrey Klaiber, interview in Lima, Peru, 8/24/93. The main point of distinction is no longer a conservative or a liberal attitude but commitment to the struggle for justice. See also Klaiber, *The Catholic Church in Peru*, 32–33.

from an essentialist and legalistic conception of the church to a historical one. Since Christ is now seen as being at work in the realm of history, theology is no longer exclusively focused on the "wholly Other" but includes the relationship between God and human beings. Critically appropriating this insight of modern theology, the encounters with the underside of history will teach theology that the modern concern for humanity needs to be transformed into a concern for humanity based in Christ that includes the oppressed other as well. This is the way in which Gutiérrez begins to reinterpret Congar's insight that theology must begin with facts and questions coming from the world and from history.[81]

Authority and Power

In sum, the question of authority, as encounters with people on the underside continue to remind us, is always tied up with the question of power. In this chapter we have encountered yet another aspect of this relationship. In the overall picture, the opening of the Catholic Church to the modern world, together with the reconstruction of authority, underscores the multiple junctures of authority and power. This relationship is obviously more complex than the often simplified relation between base and superstructure in vulgar Marxism.[82] In this light, Congar's distinction of planes, for instance, appears to be driven by a concern for the "superstructural" question of authority, related to the reconstruction of authority in modernity and trying to correct the ideological uses of the church's authority. Nevertheless, in the process certain types of power structures are promoted as well, consciously or unconsciously.

On the other hand, the theology of development seems to take its clues more directly from the actual constellation of power in modernity. Where the driving forces are actual policies of development and modernization, theological authority does of course not remain unaffected. As I have tried to show, the basic blindness of the modern self is perpetuated across the whole spectrum, and modern structures of authority and power tend mutually to reinforce and energize each other.

---

81. Congar, *Situation et tâches présentes de la théologie*, 72, quoted in Gutiérrez, "The Meaning of Development," 156 n. 34.

82. For good reasons Gutiérrez never supported this paradigm. In the Peruvian context a reinterpretation of the relation between base and superstructure was suggested in the 1930s by José Carlos Mariátegui; see, for example, his *Seven Interpretive Essays on Peruvian Reality*, trans. Marjory Urquidi, introd. Jorge Basadre (Austin: University of Texas Press, 1971). Mariátegui emphasizes the importance of religion and other elements of the "superstructure."

Conclusion

Despite their shortcomings, both Christendom's concern for the texts and traditions of the church and modern Roman Catholic theology's concern for the modern world and the self offer important impulses for a new theological vision. In light of an expanding modernity that favors the elites, Christendom's emphasis on the texts of the church might have a certain egalitarian effect in terms of its general appeal to the masses and its latest concern for popular religiosity. Modern theology's appreciation for the world and the self, on the other hand, has initiated the opening up of a set of rigid theological structures that prevent theology and the church from paying attention to God's work in the world and with humanity. The move of Congar and others from doctrine per se to its relation to the human person has helped to blaze the trail.

Nevertheless, both paradigms are unable to deal with the underside of history for various reasons. In Christendom the poor become merely the recipients of the work of theology, objects of theological teaching. They are spoken rather than speaking. While, as we have seen, the theology of Christendom displays little concern for historical events, there is even less sensitivity for the underside of history. Its focus on the texts of the church is characterized by the virtual absence of the diachronic and historical dimension. In this context (dubbed "normalcy" by Lacan), all roots and reference points, whether it be a God who is at work independently of the texts, or those who dwell at the margins of church and society, are sacrificed to the meanderings of the signifying chain. Authority is located in the texts of the church, produced and reproduced without much interference in the structural repetition of traditional texts.[83]

No doubt, for the synchronic world of European Christendom the encounter with the "other" in the New World might have been a watershed moment. Attention to the newly emerging relationship of self and other could have helped to initiate a dynamic reconstruction of the symbolic orders of Christendom. What actually happened, however, was the reverse. With the repression of the relation of the self and other in the new world situation, the symbolic order became even more absolute than before. In Lacan's terminology, the Other (the symbolic order) usurped the place of the other (the Indian, the poor). In other words,

---

83. This observation is supported indirectly by Enrique Dussel's assessment of Latin American theology: "It can be said that, even after World War II, theological production proceeds by imitating and applying European models, without historical or real knowledge of Latin America." Dussel, "Sobre la historia de la teología en América Latina," 49.

by "spiritualizing" or "symbolicizing" what happens in actual history, the church reinforces and covers up the conquest and the aggressive and narcissistic appropriation of the Indian other by the European self. At the same time, it is also covering up the difference between center and periphery.

In this regard, modern theology is off to a slightly better start. Since the concern for the interests of the self in modernity can facilitate, to a certain degree, a rereading of the traditional use of texts of the church and related ideological closures, the texts of the symbolic order do not become absolute. The self's theological vision offers a certain double check of the texts of the Christendom church that have assumed almost absolute authority. Lacan has given us some insight into the mechanisms at work. Herein lies the importance and the promise of modern theology for Latin America. A passage from Yves Congar expresses what is at stake: Reconstruction of the Christendom perspective "cannot occur effectively except on the basis of a very determined revision of the historical character of institutions, forms and structures, and of a very genuine spiritual return to the sources."[84]

Yet modern theology faces a twofold dilemma. The modern self has a tendency to overpower not only the texts of the church but also the other. The self, locating itself in the center of history, has a hard time even acknowledging the existence of an underside of this history. As a consequence, modern historical consciousness has a tendency to exclude the conflictual character of history. Even if the poor were added to modern theology's focus on the elites, this view would still not be able to deal with the ways in which they are different from the modern self. This blindness to actual conflicts is, as I have shown in chapter 1, even worse where the relationship to the symbolic Other is weakened. The modern self is at its most narcissistic and aggressive where it is left entirely to itself. It can be challenged in its narcissism up to a certain degree where it encounters the authority of the text.

A closer relation of the modern self and the texts of the church, as

---

84. Yves Congar, "Renewal of the Spirit and Reform of the Institution," in *Ongoing Reform of the Church*, ed. Alois Müller and Norbert Greinacher (New York: Herder and Herder, 1972), 47–48. Congar had a distinct impact on Gutiérrez's early theological development. Congar's "historical perspective," he writes, "got me out of an almost exclusively rational way of looking at theological work." Gutiérrez, "The Task of Theology and Ecclesial Experience," in *The People of God amidst the Poor*, ed. Leonardo Boff and Virgil Elizondo (Edinburgh: T. & T. Clark, 1984), 61. In TL, 9–10, Gutiérrez lets Congar speak: "Instead of using only revelation and tradition as starting points, as classical theology has generally done, it must start with facts and questions derived from the world and from history."

important as that might be, is not enough, however. While the rigidity of the self decreases in its encounter with the text, the ability to encounter the other is not guaranteed. On the other hand, even if the theology of Christendom might come to a more concrete understanding of God's work and admit at least that even the world and the modern self are "not unaffected" by God's grace, this would not change things much because, as Gutiérrez notes, this is "to respond more to the modern mentality... than to the poor of Latin America."[85] In other words, a theology that could guide us out of this impasse must figure how the selves, the texts, and the other all belong together. In part II, I will introduce two models, a North American and a Latin American one.

The provisional result thus far indicates that theological interaction with the texts of the church on the basis of an awareness of the relationship of self and other might be an important step forward in Latin American theology, which is still dominated by the Christendom perspective. The texts of the church can be taken even more seriously if they are not left to themselves but reread in relation to the work of God and the need of the world. Gutiérrez comes to understand that only through participating in the liberation process "will be heard nuances of the Word of God which are imperceptible in other existential situations."[86]

---

85. Gutiérrez, "The Preparatory Document for Puebla: A Retreat from Commitment," PP, 121.

86. Gutiérrez, TL, 32. The reading of the biblical text thus becomes a historical reading that no longer shuts out the underside. Gustavo Gutiérrez, *Revelación y anuncio de Dios en la historia* (Lima: Servicio de documentación del MIEC-JECI, 1977), 4–5: "God reveals Godself in the history of the people that believes and hopes in God; this leads us to rethink the Word from our own history. But this is real history, penetrated by conflicts and confrontations."

Part II

APPROACHES TO THE REAL: THE UNDERSIDE OF HISTORY TRANSFORMING THEOLOGY

I N THIS PART I will address another element in the construction of theological authority beyond theology's focus on either the modern self or the texts of the church. Throughout the histories of the people of Israel and the church, God does not meet humanity in sacred texts or personal encounters alone. God's concern for those at the margins — the strangers, the widows, the orphans, the oppressed, the blind, the lowly, the tax collectors, and the prostitutes — adds another aspect, breaking up the binary relationships of God and self or God and text that have been played off against each other for so long. In the traditions of the Bible, encountering God is often related to encountering one's neighbor.[1] The theological challenge before us is to develop a better understanding of what it is that contemporary mainline paradigms of theology cannot account for. The Lacanian notion of the real will help set the stage for reflecting on the new element that theology, against the worldwide backdrop of the increasing challenge of marginalization and suffering, can no longer afford to ignore.

In this part I introduce new paradigms for thinking about the theological challenge of the underside of history. Tracing the impact of the voices of marginalized and oppressed people on the theological reflections of Frederick Herzog and Gustavo Gutiérrez will help identify new theological vistas. Because these encounters with people on the underside are part of an ongoing process, we need an account of the genesis and the continuing development of these theologies. Examining specific nodal points and shifts in this development (somewhat in the fashion

---

1. Cf. 1 John 4:20–21, Matt. 25:31–46; Matt. 18:23–35 and Amos 5:10–15 imply that to fail one's neighbor is to fail God as well.

of a Lacanian analyst) will help mark the most significant effects of those encounters and gain further insight into the often unpredictable challenges they bring.

Since the marginalized often make their presence felt by interrupting the dominant flow of ideas, the theological challenge of the underside of history can never be quite grasped in terms of a conventional history of ideas approach.[2] In this context, theological shifts, for instance, do not necessarily have to signify inconsistencies or breaks but can also mark readjustments in an ongoing relationship.[3] In these shifts the process of theological reflection is condensed since the self of the theologian, the texts of the church, and the encounter with the other are drawn together most closely.

While mainline theology has paid little attention to these dynamics, it is surprising that even the numerous interpretations of liberation theology in North America have rarely given an account of the function of this elusive third element, the position of the other beyond the self and the text. Most interpreters seem to be caught up in the framework of mainline theology, trying to figure out either the central doctrines of a theology developed in solidarity with the underside (if they approach the matter from the theological emphasis of the text) or the new theological agents assuming positions of authority (if they approach things from the theological emphasis on the self). Yet neither a reading on the level of the texts of the church (dogmatics) nor a reading on the level of the self (systematics) can fully grasp the theological challenge of the underside of history. Here an altogether new theological paradigm emerges.

---

2. This is still the predominant way of dealing with liberation theology, and so a deeper understanding of its encounter with the poor is not possible. An example is John Ronald Blue, "Origins of Gustavo Gutiérrez's *A Theology of Liberation*" (Ph.D. diss., University of Texas at Arlington, 1989), vi, who interprets liberation theology as a "unique blend of humanism, Marxism, utopianism, and universalism."

3. In his 1988 "Introduction to the Revised Edition," in Gustavo Gutiérrez, *A Theology of Liberation: History, Politics, and Salvation*, Revised 15th Anniversary Edition, trans. Sister Caridad Inda and John Eagleson (Maryknoll, N.Y.: Orbis, 1988), xviii (abbreviated TL), Gutiérrez points out that "at every stage . . . we must refine, improve, and possibly correct earlier formulations if we want to use language that is understandable and faithful both to the integral Christian message and to the reality we experience." Yet in the numerous studies of Gutiérrez's work this aspect of the shifts and readjustments in relation to the underside, leading to the development of its original motives, has never been addressed. Where shifts are recognized, they are usually understood as inconsistencies.

Chapter 3

The Missing Link:
Searches for the Real

I T HAS BEEN SAID that "if Lacan had proposed only the Imaginary and Symbolic orders, we could fit him comfortably into the binary tendencies of Western philosophy."[1] As the previous chapters have shown, these binary tendencies have left their mark on the theological landscape as well. The two main camps in theology have long understood themselves as providing the only viable alternatives in their respective hemispheres.

Yet in the struggle of the two poles, the self and the text, something has been lost or, more precisely, repressed. Lacan's notion of the real indicates how this third element might be understood. The notion of the real is related initially to a struggle against various idealisms in the field of psychology that have covered over the more painful aspects of reality. In this context Lacan begins to develop one of the main insights of psychoanalysis, namely, that what is repressed into the unconscious has a considerable bearing on the shape of reality.[2] I will show here how an encounter with the repressed underside might move us beyond the binaries.

Reality and the Real

The increasing focus on the real in Lacan's work has to do with the insight that even though the turn to the text or the symbolic order can provide a certain relief in the ego's era, it can also be turned into

---

1. Ellie Ragland-Sullivan, *Jacques Lacan and the Philosophy of Psychoanalysis* (Urbana: University of Illinois Press, 1986), 195. Cf. also Fredric Jameson, "Imaginary and Symbolic in Lacan," in Fredric Jameson, *The Ideologies of Theory: Essays 1971–1986* (Minneapolis: University of Minnesota Press, 1988), vol. 1, 106.

2. See Elisabeth Roudinesco, *Jacques Lacan & Co.: A History of Psychoanalysis in France, 1925–1985*, trans. Jeffrey Mehlmann (Chicago: University of Chicago Press, 1990), 115.

a structure of mystification.[3] Whereas Lacan had earlier promoted the symbolic order as key in overcoming the ego's era, announcing the word as the "death" of the myth of the modern autonomous self (this is the popular Lacan on the verge of structuralism and poststructuralism), he now concentrates on the real as a "second death."

The real absolutely resists symbolization and thus breaks up the regular flow of the signifying chain and its search for stability and security. The real is what keeps disrupting any turn to language and the text, even in its postmodern (or poststructuralist) forms.[4] It stands in opposition to what is often perceived as "reality," since "reality" or "realism" is usually constructed on the grounds of some dominant symbolic order. What counts as reality in this sense is what is commonly accepted as true, the product of the social mechanisms of the text that determine the collective consciousness of society or the church. We have already seen how this type of reality, constructed by the symbolic order, is free to produce its own world because it is not necessarily bound by any referent. Nor is it necessarily accountable to the positions of the self or the other, as the state of "normalcy" shows. Traces of this powerful linguistic idealism, which often tends to understand itself as realism, can be found for instance in such diverse phenomena as certain North American alternatives to liberal theology and Latin American Christendom.

The analytic process cannot be confined, however, to whatever is defined as "reality" at any given moment, be it in premodern, modern, or postmodern terms. Analysis looks for the point where this reality breaks open in the encounter with its underside. In order to understand the shape of modern reality and its limits, for instance, one must look for its underside in the repressions of the modern self. In order to understand the limits of the construction of reality on the grounds of the powers of the text (a move now promoted not only by the neoorthodox and Christendom critiques of modernity but by many postmodern theologies as well), one must look for the repressions that are created at the underside of the metonymical flow of the symbolic order.

---

3. This later development of Lacan's work begins with his seminar "The Ethic of Psychoanalysis" (1959/60), referred to in Slavoj Žižek, *The Sublime Object of Ideology* (London: Verso, 1989), 73–75, 131–33, 162. The Lacanian notion of "normalcy" has already given us one example in which the symbolic order itself becomes a problem.

4. Lacan finds that "the real is beyond the *automaton*, the return, the coming-back, the insistence of the signs." Jacques Lacan, *The Four Fundamental Concepts of Psycho-Analysis*, ed. Jacques-Alain Miller, trans. Alan Sheridan (New York: W. W. Norton, 1978), 53, 54. All of these notions are descriptions of the symbolic order and the phenomenon of metonymy. This concern for the real, as "that which always lies behind the automaton," was, according to Lacan, also the object of Sigmund Freud's research.

Lacan thus helps us develop a deeper sense for the other and otherness. While the turn to text has already introduced a first challenge to the homogeneous world of the modern self — poststructuralism accounts for this fact by emphasizing the differential play of signifiers in the symbolic order as source of a new sense of otherness (see chapter 1) — the encounter with the underside provides a more radical challenge that goes unnoticed even by much of the postmodern celebration of otherness and difference now in vogue. When Lacan talks about this new other in relation to the real, he calls it *objet petit a*, or small other. I will talk about the "real other."

Questioning Authority

When in the following a critique of the power of the text is presented, we must not forget that in our historical context a critique of the power of the self is implied here as well. As I have shown, the power of the self is left unchallenged and even preserved by a symbolic order that fails to address the modern self's ongoing conquest of the other. This was a major problem in neoorthodoxy and Christendom, but this is also a major problem for much of the postmodern critique of modernity.

The Lacanian notion of the real brings us to a deeper understanding of what I have called the power of the text, a text that asserts its authority in the creation of its own peculiar realism. As we have seen, in the ego's era the turn to the text can serve as a corrective to the turn of the self. At the end of the ego's era, however, when the turn to the text has gained momentum in both North and South, the symbolic order itself needs to be reconstructed without reproducing once more the shortcomings of modernity. According to Lacan, the symbolic order is challenged most constructively where it intersects with the real. In other words, in an encounter with the real other, the power of the text can be reconstructed.[5] In a world in transition from modernism to postmodernism, from the power of the self to the power of the text, which nevertheless still benefits from the self's conquest, the analytic process now needs to zero in on the repressions of the symbolic order as well. The blind spot of the text resembles the blind spot of the modern self; both are unable to realize that their authority is built on a repression.

The "real other," and this is the crucial point, is put in place by a repression of the symbolic text that is not unlike the earlier repres-

---

5. See Jacques Lacan, "The Subversion of the Subject and the Dialectic of Desire in the Freudian Unconscious," in Jacques Lacan, *Écrits: A Selection*, trans. Alan Sheridan (New York: W. W. Norton, 1977), 313f.

sion of the other by the self in the imaginary order. The real is that
which is repressed from the flow of the signifying chain, made up of
those elements that are foreclosed from participation in the power of
the text. This is one of the central insights of Lacan that dampens the
postmodern excitement about the turn to language, the symbolic order,
and the metonymical flow of meaning from one signifier to the next.[6]
The repressions that put the real other in place point to deeper ruptures
than the mere flow of difference on the surface level, the kind of difference celebrated by many postmodern thinkers.[7] The exclusive focus on
the meanderings of the text misses this moment of an interference with
the repressed real that always goes unrecognized by the symbolic order
itself. While, as we have seen, modernity had missed the point of the
power of the text, many postmodern critics of modernity miss the real
other, that which is repressed even in postmodernity, which prides itself
on having done away with the modern self.

In this context Lacanian thought can help us create new conceptual
openings for a concern for the underside of history and identify new
locations of authority. One of the central insights of psychoanalysis is
that authority structures, like desires and drives, are not preordained
but created in specific constellations, as products of repression.[8] The
imaginary other and the real other, produced by either the repressions
of the self or the text, are both guides to alternative authority structures
that are hidden.

The discussion of sexuality in Lacan's later work illustrates what is
at stake and helps us to broaden our encounters with the underside

---

6. Let me recall briefly that in exploring the symbolic order Lacan was interested
not only in the (postmodern) concern for "metonymy," the free flow of signifiers, but in
another phenomenon as well, tied to the notion of metaphor. Metaphor, defined as the
replacement of one signifier by another, interrupts the free-floating chain of signification
and, by repressing another signifier from the surface, "buttons down" the free metonymical flow at various places. For the definition of metonymy and metaphor see Lacan, "The
Agency of the Letter in the Unconscious or Reason since Freud," in *Écrits: A Selection*,
164.

7. Cf., e.g., Paul de Man's preference of metonymy to metaphor, "Semiology and
Rhetoric," in *Critical Theory since 1965*, ed. Hazard Adams and Leroy Searle (Tallahassee:
University Presses of Florida, Florida State University Press, 1986), 229. In theology cf.
also Charles E. Winquist, "The Silence of *The Real*: Theology at the End of the Century,"
in *Theology at the End of the Century: A Dialogue on the Postmodern with Thomas J. J. Altizer,
Charles Winquist, and Robert P. Scharlemann*, ed. Robert P. Scharlemann (Charlottesville:
University Press of Virginia, 1990). Winquist assumes that, since the Lacanian real is
silent, the structural play of metonymy is left as the only way to go. We have good reason
to suspect, however, that this may lead once more into the repressions of yet another
symbolic-order "normalcy."

8. See on this point Slavoj Žižek, *Looking Awry: An Introduction to Jacques Lacan
through Popular Culture* (Cambridge: MIT Press, 1991), 6.

of history in a patriarchal society. The basic point is that authority, that which authorizes and creates identity, is constructed in different ways for those who are confined to the dominant powers (in patriarchal society the majority of men) than for those who, due to their repression by the powers that be, are closer to the repressed real (women in patriarchal society, as well as the poor and all those others on the underside of history). In a patriarchal context, Lacan points out, one cannot even speak of "*The* woman" since "there is woman only as excluded by the nature of things which is the nature of words."[9] That is to say, unlike *man* and other signifiers of privilege, *woman* is not an ordinary part of the dominant symbolic order. Women, Lacan argues, exist only as repressed from the dominant symbolic order, as displaced by more powerful signifiers. The limited advantage of this position is that as such they are not simply functions of the power of the text. Women participate in what Lacan calls a certain "surplus enjoyment" that escapes the authority and control of the formative powers of the symbolic order at certain points.[10]

This does not necessarily mean that every man has to be a function of the powers that be. Lacan tells men that solidarity with women is possible: "You can also put yourself on the side of not-all," the repressed.[11] In this sense his discussion of sexuality is not an argument as to what women or men essentially are, but an analysis of existing identifications and structures of authority and power, and an invitation to see beyond the position of those in power. Let me add, however, what Lacan does not say explicitly, namely, that it is not easy to put oneself on the side of the other and that real solidarity with those who are oppressed will most likely lead to a sharing in their repression.[12]

Beyond Romanticizing the Underside

Staying with the example of the construction of gender identity, we find that man in patriarchal society is vested not only with the authority of

9. Jacques Lacan, "Seminar 20, *Encore*" (1972–73), in *Feminine Sexuality: Jacques Lacan and the école freudienne,* ed. Juliet Mitchell and Jacqueline Rose (New York: W. W. Norton, 1982), 144.

10. Lacan, ibid., 143–44. Žižek, *The Sublime Object of Ideology,* 52, follows up on the notion of "surplus enjoyment."

11. Lacan, ibid., 147.

12. For an assessment of the sheer impossibility of such solidarity in a classic colonialist situation see Albert Memmi, *The Colonizer and the Colonized,* trans. Howard Greenfeld (New York: Orion, 1965), and his discussion of the dilemma of the "colonizer who refuses." Nevertheless, since Memmi, like Lacan, is talking about a specific situation, there is hope that in other situations relations of solidarity may be more likely.

the dominant symbolic text (having been woven into its fabric and thus having become a function of it) but also with the reality of the powers that be. In order to preserve his power he needs to make sure that all others are integrated into existing power structures as well.

One way of doing this is by playing down the repressed status of women by elevating "*the* woman" to the status of an absolute category. Unlike real women, "*the* woman" can thus be incorporated into the dominant symbolic order as one more signifier among others.[13] In this way the repressed real other is made, against her will, into one of the pillars of the symbolic order and the powers that be. The romanticizing of the marginalized by those in power exemplifies this problem: Here stereotypes are created that often not only prevent real contacts with actual people at the margins but also play down the challenge that real suffering poses to the powers that be. This way of dealing with people at the margins necessarily leads to further mystification (closely resembling the mystification of the imaginary self's other), thus creating a vicious circle that can only be broken by the recognition of the marginalized as real other — in other words, as something that is not completely subordinated to the authority of the dominant symbolic structure and therefore able to challenge it.

These reflections are summarized in Lacan's often misunderstood statement that "*the* woman does not exist,"[14] which means, as Jacqueline Rose has pointed out, "not that women do not exist" but that women's status as "an absolute category and guarantor of fantasy" for those in power is false.[15] To put it differently, the generalizations and idealizations of women (or the marginalized) by those in power are smoke screens that do more harm than good since oppressive structures of authority and power preserve themselves in these ways.[16]

---

13. Cf. Jacqueline Rose, "Introduction II," in Mitchell and Rose, *Feminine Sexuality*, 50: "As negative to the man, woman becomes a total object of fantasy (or an object of total fantasy), elevated into the place of the Other and made to stand for its truth . . . this is the ultimate form of mystification." Cf. also Teresa Brennan, "History after Lacan," *Economy and Society* 19 (August 1990), 302.

14. Jacques Lacan, "Seminar of 21 January 1975," in Mitchell and Rose, *Feminine Sexuality*, 167.

15. Rose, "Introduction II," ibid., 48. Cf. also Jacques Lacan, *Television: A Challenge to the Psychoanalytic Establishment*, ed. Joan Copjec, trans. Denis Hollier et al. (New York: W. W. Norton, 1990), 38: "But the fact that she doesn't exist doesn't stop me from making her the object of one's desire."

16. Albert Memmi, *The Colonizer and the Colonized*, 85, observes the connection between the power of the colonialist and the depersonalization of the colonized, who are always referred to in the plural. "The colonized is never characterized in an individual manner; he is entitled only to drown in an anonymous collectivity ('They are this.' 'They are all the same.')."

For my project this serves as a reminder that to assess the theological challenge of people on the underside of history means to walk a fine line; the danger of romanticizing the oppressed, those without power, is always very real. At the same time, the fact that the position of people at the margins cannot be grasped by the universalizations of those in power does not, of course, mean that they exist only as individual entities, separated from each other. On the underside of history new models of solidarity are produced that differ from the totalitarian tendencies of the text.

Since it can control the real only to a certain extent, the symbolic order must constantly try to integrate it and ultimately explain away its power. The *"excessive* power" of the symbolic status quo, its striving for control, can be understood "as the very form of appearance of [this] fundamental *impotence*."[17] Even where the challenge of the underside is not recognized explicitly, there seems to be a deep fear of those who are different. The powers of the text have developed their own means of assimilation of those who are different. Charity, for instance, not unlike the welfare reform in the United States of the 1990s, is often used as a way to make the other into our own image. Only those who are well adjusted, the ideal types, deserve it.

What is neglected in most neoorthodox, Christendom, and postmodern celebrations of the symbolic order and the power of the text are precisely these mechanisms of idealization and repression. In other words, the main problem is not their involvement with the power of the text — it has been the genius of those theologies to remind us once more that theology cannot be done without serious attention to the texts of the church — but that they are not able to see the moments of repression and distortion that are part of the world of the text and deal with them self-critically.

A general epistemological blindness makes it impossible for those who identify with the powers that be, and here the power of the text and the power of the self are very much alike, to cut through the illusions of the reality they have constructed. At the same time, however, and this is most significant to understanding the challenge of the underside of history, this form of blindness does not apply in the same way to those at the margins. Using once more Hegel's terminology of master and slave we can put it like this: In being forced to serve the master's desire, the slave comes to learn about the "underside" of the master's consciousness and power, while the master is, as Fredric Jame-

---

17. Žižek, *The Sublime Object of Ideology*, 53. Emphasis in original.

son has observed, "condemned to idealism — to the luxury of placeless freedom"[18] and the idiosyncrasies of his (or her) own position.

In the final analysis, the power of the symbolic text, accustomed to being in charge of reality, is limited precisely by an encounter with its underside, the repressed real. It is only in the real that the oppressive forces of the power of the text become visible. The position of the real other exposes the (unconscious) truth about the symbolic order that has, thus far, been hidden between the lines. According to Lacan, this is a significant difference between oppressed and oppressors: "the enjoyment of the woman does not go without saying, that is, without the saying of truth," while for the man "his enjoyment suffices which is precisely why he understands nothing."[19]

The encounter with those pushed into the position of the real leads, however, not only to a better understanding of the mechanisms of repression but also to a new account of authority beyond the text and the self. In patriarchy, only women and those who adopt their point of view are able to point beyond the reach of the symbolic order.[20] In creating the real, the symbolic order cannot help but prepare the conditions that eventually will undermine its absolute power.

Those who are not completely subjected to the forces of the symbolic order (e.g., women who are excluded from participation in patriarchal power) escape the symbolic order and its totalitarian myth in some ways and are, therefore, able to introduce new perspectives. Lacan sees a parallel to certain mystics who have found their own ways of escaping the complete control of the symbolic order by putting themselves on the side of that which is not in control. Clarifying that "the mystical is by no means that which is not political,"[21] he underscores in his own way the close relationship of authority and power that people on the underside are helping us understand. New authority structures, for instance, are tied to awareness of political repression, and new political challenges grow out of the reconstruction of authority structures.

In this light we begin to understand what it means when some liberation theologians talk about the poor as those who are the teachers. The marginalized have potential access to aspects of truth that escape

---

18. Fredric Jameson, "Third-World Literature in the Era of Multinational Capitalism," *Social Text* 15 (Fall 1986), 85.

19. Lacan, unpublished Seminar 21, *"Les non-dupes errent"* (1973–74), quoted in Rose, "Introduction II," in Mitchell and Rose, *Feminine Sexuality*, 53.

20. Lacan, "Seminar 20, *Encore*," in Mitchell and Rose, *Feminine Sexuality*, 152.

21. Ibid., 146. Lacan counts his own *Écrits* as part of the body of mystical literature. See 147.

those in power. Two interconnected aspects need to be seen together here: One is the openness of the marginalized to something beyond the power and authority of the text and the self, which can, as Lacan says, be experienced but not immediately known and owned. The other aspect that must be noted is that this function is closely connected to the fact of their oppression by, and exclusion from, the established powers.

Reconstructing Authority and Power

The way authority is redistributed in the real can best be seen in the analytic process. Lacanian analysis takes place in terms of a recognition of, and identification with, the repressed real other. This step is, of course, impossible for those who never leave the totalizing influence of the power of the text, unable to recognize even the fact that there is repression. In this connection Lacan notes, rather shockingly, that there is no sexual relation between man and woman.[22] Even if everybody means well, a relationship between the marginalized and those in power is not possible since those in power (authorized by either the power of the self or the power of the text) are unable to relate to anyone but their own kind.

In order to preserve themselves, the realisms of the text must constantly cover up those actual (and "real") tensions that surface in the form of symptoms and interpret them away as simple, insignificant accidents. This way the repressed others are retained as part of the system. The myth of the relation between the marginalized and those in power is simulating a unity that denies factual divisions.

In this context Lacan gives credit to Karl Marx for reinventing the notion of the symptom because he showed how existing conflicts are not merely accidental and essentially insignificant deviations from a normal state, as the powers that be would have it. Conflicts and tensions are the products of the prevailing system itself, and as such point to its unconscious truth that must be constantly repressed in order to preserve the way things are.[23] As the German thinker Walter Benjamin, a victim of Germany's Third Reich, has realized, it is exactly "the tradition of the oppressed" that "teaches us that the 'state of emergency' in which

---

22. Lacan, "Seminar of 21 January 1975," in Mitchell and Rose, *Feminine Sexuality*, 170.

23. See Jacques Lacan, "Seminar 22 R.S.I." (1974–75) in *Ornicar?* 4 (1975), e.g., 106. The historical context of Marx's discovery is the transition from feudalism to capitalism. Cf. Žižek, *The Sublime Object of Ideology*, 23ff., and Lacan "Seminar of 21 January 1975," in Mitchell and Rose, *Feminine Sexuality*, 166, for examples of how Lacan himself draws parallels between the "social" interpretation of the symptom and the "private."

we live is not the exception but the rule."[24] Only the identification with the symptom, the repressed or real other, leads to an understanding of the mechanism of the powers of the dominant system of which one is a part and the authority structures that hold it in place. This is the first step to transformation.

At this point it must be noted that the real in the form of the symptom or the real other is nothing in and of itself. The real does not have its existence independently from the powers that be, just as the oppressed as such never exist independently from the oppressors. The real grows out of repression by those in power, even though it can never completely be restrained by them and eventually transcends them. Lacan reminds us that the proper place of the real itself must ultimately remain open. It is occupied only in specific situations and only temporarily. The real other functions as a guide to truth but is not itself the truth. One of the greatest challenges growing out of actual encounters with people on the underside of history is knowing that even the real other, the marginalized person, is not the "thing in itself." The place of the real must always be kept open.[25]

This ultimate openness creates problems not so much for the marginalized themselves, who have a sense that the stereotypes created by the oppressors are false. While the marginalized can in fact benefit from an understanding of the multifaceted nature of life on the underside of history, an understanding that leads to new solidarities across the lines of different forms of oppression,[26] this openness poses a major challenge to the powers that be, which are unable to face the void and must therefore always try to cover it up, for instance, by elevating those disturbing real others into the place of "the dignity of the Thing."[27] In this

---

24. Walter Benjamin, "Theses on the Philosophy of History," in Walter Benjamin, *Illuminations: Essays and Reflections,* ed. and introd. Hannah Arendt, trans. Harry Zohn (New York: Schocken Books, 1969), 257.

25. As the Latin American Subaltern Studies Group has pointed out in its founding statement, the subaltern, the repressed, is "not one thing" but rather a "mutating migrating subject." Latin American Subaltern Studies Group, "Founding Statement," *boundary 2* 20:3 (Fall 1993), 121.

26. bell hooks, "Postmodern Blackness," *Postmodern Culture* 1:1 (September 1990), 9–11, notes that the critique of modern essentialism — creating the openness that I am talking about — may pose a challenge to people on the underside struggling with their own identities. But she goes on to explain the usefulness of a deconstruction of the old myths of racism, for instance, constructed on the basis of ideas about essential blackness.

27. Jacques Lacan, Seminar on "L'éthique de la psychanalyse" (1959–60), quoted in Jonathan Scott Lee, *Jacques Lacan* (Amherst: University of Massachusetts Press, 1990), 165. With this observation, we are now able to make the connection back to the imaginary order. Lacan's concepts of the imaginary order and the real are related in that the imaginary other and the real other are both products of repression, produced and kept

way the marginalized are romanticized, idealized, and become objects of charity while at the same time their true challenge of the status quo is lost.

The process of defeating the stereotyping by those in power, uncovering the location of the real other, and identifying with her is therefore also a process of redistributing authority and power. Yet both the authority and the power of the real cannot be absolute; they are always produced on the underside of history. As such the real is engaged in a constant "self-critique" in a most literal sense, constructively rewriting imaginary as well as symbolic identities and the corresponding authority and power structures. As Lacan discovered early on, "I is an other." Not being the "thing in itself," the authority of the real other is always related to those concrete situations in which it functions as a stand-in for the real. In this sense "*the* woman" does not exist and neither do "*the* poor" or "*the* oppressed." The place of the real can never be filled on a permanent basis.

Here is an intriguing parallel to the Protestant principle of *ecclesia semper reformanda,* which is rooted in the insight that the church is also not the "thing in itself." In that sense both the Reformation and modern Roman Catholic theology can be understood as a "decentering" of the church that clears the way for an encounter with the real. Yet, as we have seen, the real can never be had as a possession. Its position can only be occupied on a temporary basis. And anything that occupies the place of the real at any given moment must point away from itself.[28] In this process, the tradition of the church is constantly shaped and reshaped in the most constructive way.

We are dealing here with an inversion of the "realism" of the powers of the modern self and the powers of the text. Lacan's notion of the real involves a reconstruction of the self and the text from the bottom up that includes a retroactive movement. The truth cannot be known a priori. Both the self and the text must be reconstructed on the basis of the presence of the real other; authority is reconstructed in relation to those who were thus far excluded.[29] This implies the

---

in place by relations of power. The similarity of the cases lies in the fact that both the imaginary other and the real other are being used by either the self or the text to sustain their absolute authority and, by extension, to support their respective status quo.

28. The apostle Paul was aware of this. See 2 Cor. 4:7: "But we have this treasure in clay jars, so that it may be made clear that this extraordinary power belongs to God and does not come from us." Ultimately, "the place of Power must always remain an empty place; any person occupying it can do so only temporarily, as a kind of surrogate, a substitute for the real-impossible sovereign." Žižek, *The Sublime Object of Ideology,* 147.

29. A changed relation to the other and a new relation to the (symbolic) Other are

possibility of a constructive transformation of those imaginary-order identifications of the modern self and the symbolic-order texts of the tradition that are already in place in which, due to the integration of the aspect of the real as limit (which can only be approached asymptotically), power identifications can now be analyzed and subsequently transformed.[30]

This moment of realizing the (real) symptom is what characterizes a truly revolutionary situation. For Lacan, the analyst in touch with the underside is the true revolutionary, which is why he cautions the revolutionary students of the late sixties that the overthrow of oppressive systems is not sufficient in itself and will necessarily lead to the replacement of the old masters with new ones, a prediction come true.[31] It is only in the encounter with the underside of history, encountering the real other and realizing the truth of one's symptom, that new ways of projecting and practicing human relationships become possible.

It is important to remember at the end of these reflections that Lacan has discovered these structures in his practical work as analyst. He is not trying to develop a "universal Law of humanity,"[32] another romanticization and idealization of the underside on the basis of abstract philosophical insights, but he shows the distortions of power and authority in a specific historical era, in the vicinity of the era of the ego, which is preserved through both imaginary-order and symbolic-order identifications. Lacanian analysis is useful only where

---

connected. Jonathan Scott Lee, *Jacques Lacan,* 186, argues that "women's *jouissance* may provide something that the sexual relation as determined by the phallic function cannot deliver: namely, a genuine relation to the Other."

30. Terry Eagleton, *Ideology: An Introduction* (New York: Verso, 1991), 57, points out that the textual reality of the symbolic order (e.g., in the construction of class consciousness and universalizations) does not necessarily have to be ideological in revolutionary times. It becomes so, however, "when it needs later to conceal contradictions between its own interests and those of society as a whole."

31. Cf. Jacques Lacan, "L'envers de la psychanalyse: Les Quatre Discours" (1969–70); printed seminar, no publisher, 176, and Mark Bracher, "Lacan's Theory of the Four Discourses," *Prose Studies* 11:3 (December 1988), 45, 47.

32. This is the misunderstanding of Mikkel Borch-Jacobsen, *Lacan: The Absolute Master* (Stanford: Stanford University Press, 1991), cf. 225. See Lacan, "Seminar of 21 January 1975," in Mitchell and Rose, *Feminine Sexuality,* 166: "nothing I say to you comes from anywhere else [than my practice], which is precisely its difficulty." Cf. also Shoshana Felman, *Jacques Lacan and the Adventure of Insight: Psychoanalysis in Contemporary Culture* (Cambridge, Mass.: Harvard University Press, 1987), 6: "Lacan was first and foremost a clinician, and not — as is mistakenly believed and as the myth would have it — a pure theoretician." Alice A. Jardine, *Gynesis: Configurations of Women and Modernity* (Ithaca: Cornell University Press, 1985), although critical of Lacan, protects him against similar misinterpretations by some of his own students.

it is understood that Lacan does not describe the way things are and always will be, but rather the way power and authority are structured in specific social contexts, laying the ground for transformation and change.

As the discussion of this chapter has shown, the Lacanian real functions as a limit structure. It limits the excessive powers of the self and of the text and initiates their constructive transformation, putting to new use the basic building blocks of those two camps whose opposition is often seen to be all-determinative in contemporary theology, and reconstructing their various repressions. In this process authority is not abandoned, but its structures are changed. At stake is not another "flight from authority" but a constructive reinterpretation.[33] A reconstruction of the power of the self and of the texts can now take place that is geared to the conflicts and tensions of the present.

This dynamic helps to structure my evaluation of the specific characteristics of theological encounters with the underside of history. Having examined two basic forms of corruption of authority and power, we are now able to discern more closely the movement of the real in the nodal points and shifts in the development of a theology that takes seriously the voices of marginalized people. Consequently, an important focus here will be the examination of those symptomatic elements that initiate the transformation of fixed power and authority structures. In this manner I am following an analytic process in which elements of truth are uncovered, as a path not "marked out in advance in its every detail [but] a way that is established in the very going."[34]

In the following, critical transition points will be marked in the context of their development and their consequences. At each of these points, specific encounters with the real can be located, taking the form of specific relationships to people on the underside of history. The marginalized, the poor, the oppressed always have names, stories, and specific social locations. Lacan has reminded us that any generalizing reference to "the poor" or "the marginalized," if it is produced by those in power rather than by those on the underside themselves, may

---

33. Here is a basic difference between liberal theology and liberation theology that is often neglected. For one narrative of the modern rejection of traditional authority see Jeffrey Stout, *The Flight from Authority: Religion, Morality, and the Quest for Autonomy* (Notre Dame: University of Notre Dame Press, 1981).

34. Gustavo Gutiérrez, *We Drink from Our Own Wells: The Spiritual Journey of a People,* foreword by Henri Nouwen, trans. Matthew J. O'Connell (Maryknoll, N.Y.: Orbis, and Melbourne: Dove, 1984), 3, quoting the poetry of Joaquín María Machado de Asís.

end up reinforcing the status quo. While these encounters with the real cannot be easily universalized, therefore, without betraying their genesis and specific truth, they cannot be relativized as a passing fad, either. The strands of transformation they effect do not fade out but are constantly interwoven and reformulated in new encounters with the real.[35]

---

35. This phenomenon can be observed in Lacan's own work, where the orders of the imaginary, the symbolic, and the real, developed in practical settings, are not surpassing each other in a dialectical *Aufhebung*, but, as distinct vectors intersecting in various ways, enter into a relationship that is mutually corrective.

Chapter 4

New Encounters in "God's Own Country"

IN THE ENCOUNTER with marginalized people, theology is faced with that twofold challenge introduced in the preceding chapter. First of all, in placing ourselves on their side, we begin to understand the hidden truth about the current state of affairs and about ourselves. The view from the underside provides a mirror for those on the upper levels. Second, there is a potential openness beyond the confines of the powers that be. The self of the theologian or the sacred texts are no longer the exclusive points of reference for theological authority. In order to share in this openness, selves and texts need to be transformed in an encounter with what they have repressed so far: the other. The work of Frederick Herzog shows what happens when in North American theology a third element enters the theological binaries of self and God and text and God.

In this chapter, I will examine the implications of the encounter with the underside of history for North American theology. In order to develop a vision for the future of theology, I will take a look at the past three decades and where we are now.

A First Encounter with the Other

Even though the theological gains of the initial encounters with the other are fairly limited, a significant shift is introduced early on. Becoming aware of the claim of the other on the self and on the theological task as a whole is a major step in a theological world whose attention is focused mainly on the religious self or the sacred texts of the church.

Serving People at the Margins?

The church has a long history of serving people at the margins. The modern church in particular, probably more so than at any other time

in the history of the church, has been involved in the exercise of charity through special programs and activities. At the same time, however,
an older problem has been intensified in modernity. The modern self's
blindness to the other as part of the self has led to an increasing perception of charity as a one-way street, something that originates with
the charitable self and leads to handouts for those in need. Here the
challenge that the other poses to the self is lost. The primary focus of
charity in modern times has become, implicitly or explicitly, making the
other into the image of the self.[1]

In this connection, fresh encounters with people on the underside
of history introduce a critical change. In solidarity with the marginalized, the modern one-way street gradually begins to bear traffic in both
directions. One of the fundamental insights of those early encounters
is that the modern understanding of service needs to be turned back
from its head to its feet. Herzog realizes that in a context where "too
often the 'rich' and 'healthy' Christian has condescended in 'diaconic
paternalism' to the less fortunate," a fundamental restructuring needs
to take place. The point is that "primarily the poor and the sick does
not need me, but I need him."[2] This is a new insight in mainline North
American theology of the sixties. The modern self needs to relearn that
it is inextricably connected to the other. The other is part of the self.

The theological challenge, recognized early on, is that in the encounter with those at the margins we are somehow confronted with
God. This insight does not imply any identification of God and the marginalized. The point is simply that service and worship can no longer be
separated since, as Herzog discovers, what lies at the heart of service is
worship of God rather than activism motivated by the modern self.[3] The
encounter with the marginalized other is crucial, therefore, not only in
regard to service but also in regard to worship. There is a connection
between the concern for persons and the source of personhood which
Herzog finds already in the New Testament.[4]

Out of initial encounters with the struggle of African Americans and
others grows, therefore, not only the theological task of reforming the

---

1. Cf., e.g., George E. Tinker, *Missionary Conquest: The Gospel and Native American Cultural Genocide* (Minneapolis: Fortress, 1993), who tells the story of the modern
church's missions to Native Americans.

2. Frederick Herzog, "Diakonia in Modern Times: Eighteenth–Twentieth Centuries,"
in *Service in Christ: Essays Presented to Karl Barth on His 80th Birthday*, ed. James I. McCord
and T. H. L. Parker (Grand Rapids: Wm. B. Eerdmans, 1966), 150.

3. See ibid., 136.

4. Frederick Herzog, *Understanding God: The Key Issue in Present-Day Protestant
Thought* (New York: Charles Scribner's Sons, 1966), 115 (abbreviated: UG).

modern self but of reforming the church (and the powers of the text) as well: "*Ecclesia semper reformanda est!* The belief and cult of the church has to be examined ever anew relative to God's involvement in man's plight."[5] Theology encountering the other cannot stop at making a few cosmetic adjustments.

All these moves are examples of the theological challenge introduced by Herzog's growing awareness of suffering and oppression and an initial sense of their importance for theology. Even before coming to Duke University in 1960, where he would become involved in the racial tensions of the South, Herzog gradually became alert to the dynamics of oppressive power within the context of the church.[6] Only in North Carolina, however, did the encounter with the marginalized take on more specific forms. Herzog talks about a "mutation," closely connected to the civil rights struggle, which was an "encounter with the resurrection that did not have an antecedent."[7] In the seventies he would talk about this process as "becoming black," a phrase that dropped into the theological scene like a bombshell.

Getting in touch with the people and out into the cotton fields, he learned about their struggles. One of the most crucial figures was an African American firefighter, William Edwards, whom Herzog met in the hospital after Edwards became disabled.[8] Through Edwards, struggling with his bad health and an equally bad economic situation for more than ten years, Herzog became deeply aware of the suffering and the struggle for liberation of the African American other. Edwards taught Herzog what he later called the "Bible-in-hand approach," a rereading of the biblical texts from the perspective of the underside of history that

---

5. Frederick Herzog, "The Montreal 'Crisis' of Faith and Order," *Theology and Life* 6:4 (Winter 1963), 318.

6. One of the early encounters with this phenomenon took place when, as a seminary teacher in Wisconsin (at Mission House Theological Seminary in Plymouth), Herzog observed during the Kohler strike, one of the longest and toughest in North American history, that the church, while not taking sides publicly, did not remain neutral either when it accepted a gift from the industrialist. In response, Herzog comes up with the suggestion to draw together the "reorganization of society" with the "reorganization of the soul." Already at this point Herzog begins to deal with the activism of the modern self that neglects the need to reconfigure itself. See Frederick Herzog, "A Christian Approach to Decency in the Social Order," *Social Action* 26:3 (November 1959), 4.

7. Interview with Frederick Herzog, 4/12/92, at Duke University.

8. Frederick Herzog, "Let Us Still Praise Famous Men," *Hannavee* 1 (April 1970), is an article in memory of William Edwards. It is also included in *Theology from the Belly of the Whale: A Frederick Herzog Reader*, ed. Rieger. For a brief account of Edwards's history see Herzog, "After Civil Rights — What?" *Duke Divinity School Review* 32 (Fall 1967), 233. See also Frederick Herzog, "Doing Liberation Theology in the South," *National Institute for Campus Ministries: Southern Regional Newsletter* 1:2 (January 1976), 6.

he did not learn from his theological teachers. His later book *Liberation Theology* would be just that: a rereading of the Fourth Gospel in the light of oppression that at times displaces even the struggle with the theological state of the art.[9]

While these might have been rather small steps initially, it is here, in a new encounter with the biblical text in the context of actual moments of oppression, that we can locate these elementary encounters with the "real" that account for a broadening of Herzog's critique of mainline theology of which he himself is a part. What liberal theology and neoorthodox theology, unaware of the structures of power at play in these settings, have in common in their construction of theology, is not a lack of social concern, charity, or goodwill, but rather their de facto inattentiveness to the suffering of the people and their struggle for liberation.

New Theological Impulses

While the theological impact of these early encounters with the underside is limited — Herzog notes that in this early period "praxis anteceded theory by miles"[10] — a first broadening of the horizon takes place. The encounters with the marginalized push for a more contextual theology. Theology can no longer afford to lock itself up in its academic ivory towers. But in the midst of a growing number of contextual theologies in North America, most of them driven by the concerns of the modern self in one way or another, not just any context will do. Since contextual theologies can easily end up perpetuating the dominant context closest to home, the question is which contexts will challenge mainline theology to open up to both the human other and the divine Other.[11]

In the midst of the struggle of black and white in the south, Herzog finds a powerful impulse that might create such an opening. One of the major tasks of theology will be to reinforce these openings and to confront ideological closures, defined at this point as "doctrines felt

---

9. In writing *Liberation Theology: Liberation in the Light of the Fourth Gospel* (New York: Seabury, 1972) (abbreviated: LT), Herzog left out much of the extensive research on the theological reception of the Gospel of John that he had conducted over a number of years, including in-depth discussions of the work of Rudolf Bultmann.

10. Interview with Frederick Herzog, 4/12/92.

11. For further reflections on the implications of the term *contextual theology* see Joerg Rieger, "Developing a Common Interest Theology from the Underside," in *Liberating the Future: God, Mammon, and Theology,* ed. Joerg Rieger (Minneapolis: Fortress Press, 1998).

as facts" — the deification of what I have called the power of the text — or "the premises which are never mentioned" — referring to the mechanisms that help promote the myth of the autonomous self.[12]

In the encounters with the African American other, the rigid dualism of the two camps of mainline North American theology of the time, one liberal and the other neoorthodox, becomes more and more questionable. Herzog agrees that the liberal emphasis on the self might help to restrict the neoorthodox overemphasis of the power of the text by claiming a fundamental (presymbolic) awareness or openness of the self to God, but he also realizes that there are limits to the position of the self that are not understood by its liberal proponents.[13] Both aspects need to be kept together, therefore: basic human openness and the textual elements of the Christian tradition. Along these lines, Herzog argues that "it is the first hermeneutical step to show how language is related to reality."[14]

There is a third element that enters the relation of text and self. Initial encounters with the other seem to have taught Herzog that theologians do not know automatically what "reality" is all about. Theology is faced with a fundamental impasse: Liberal theology must admit that there is no "clear-cut awareness" of God. Theology is up against a profound paradox, for "man's understanding of God presupposes a complete lack of understanding."[15] Obviously, Herzog's idea of human openness to God is constructed in diametrical opposition to liberal theology. Assuming to grasp some basic aspect of reality, the liberal trust in the self's openness to God is in danger of forgetting about its limits. In the liberal paradigm the modern self, more or less able to access God,

---

12. Herzog, referring to Arnold Nash, in UG, 171, 172 n. 23. This issue is at the heart of Herzog's broad theological debate with contemporary European and North American theology in this book.

13. Herzog, UG, 101, gives credit to Paul Tillich for "stressing deliteralizing." On the other hand, Herzog reminds liberal theology that "in its procedure" systematic theology can never escape "the very language it investigates." Ibid., 137.

14. Ibid., 97. In 162 n. 30, Herzog suspects that theological linguistics (developed by Frederick Ferré and others) and the new hermeneutic (as worked out by Ernst Fuchs and Gerhard Ebeling) "perhaps assume that the language is the understanding" — the classical misunderstanding of a fixation on the symbolic order. What they forget, however, is that "the '*Sitz im Leben*' of the language has to be taken into account, too." In basic agreement with the philosopher Hans Jonas, Herzog points out that "the question is not how to devise an adequate language for theology, but how to keep its necessary inadequacy transparent for what is to be indicated by it." UG, 160 n. 41.

15. Ibid., 40, 41, and 43. This is called the ontological *aporia*. In the same manner, Herzog stresses the historical *aporia*, since history does not directly speak of God either; 155 n. 55.

is put in a position of control. The fundamental difference in Herzog's model is that this openness is tied not so much to a capacity of the modern self to connect successfully to both God and reality as to the (initially very limited) openness of the human being to the presence of the Holy Spirit, breaking through into the present in unlikely places.[16]

In the development of Herzog's theology, the concern for the openness of the self will be more and more related to the awareness of oppression on the underside of history and to the concern for the excluded other. Herzog senses that it is in the involvement with his or her neighbor, "rather than in any experience of the transcendent," that the modern self participates in the "pre-awareness of what the Gospel affirms, though he might show a complete lack of understanding at this point."[17]

If this initial openness to God and the other is related to what the Bible tells us about Jesus' history, we hit, according to Herzog, on "a concern for the neighbor that shows itself especially in a regard for the marginal figures of life."[18] This process leads to a reconstruction of that basic awareness of the other through a rereading of the texts of the Gospel. Such a rereading is a creative process because, even though Jesus' acts as portrayed in the texts of the Gospel provide us with a "central image,"[19] they are not acts to be slavishly imitated. They must always be related to the actual location of the "marginal figures."

These are only the beginnings. Many aspects of the theological challenge of the marginalized still have to be worked out. Yet at this point a triangular relationship is gradually emerging that ties together God, the self, and the other, without identifying them. The advent of the other loosens up the close identifications of God and self that can be found in modern theology, leading to new theological reflections both on the nature of God and humanity.

---

16. At this point Herzog distinguishes himself from Jürgen Moltmann, who, as a result of his emphasis on the "radical rupture between God's Word and the Logos of man," has trouble embracing this presence and thus switches to the future. UG, 86. This basic difference will be decisive in the later development of theology from the underside in both Americas.

17. Ibid., 133.

18. Ibid., 119. Cf. also "Diakonia in Modern Times," *Service in Christ*, ed. McCord, 135f. It must be kept in mind that the relationship to the other has its negative aspects as well, where, for instance, "secular man deifies the peer group or his position in the peer group." Herzog, UG, 133. This problem is further illuminated by Lacan's observations on imaginary narcissism.

19. Herzog, UG, 124.

Lessons of the Civil Rights Struggle

In the first encounters with the underside of history the awareness increases that "ignorance of the problem of power contributes a major share to our social dilemma."[20] The encounter with marginalized people raises new theological questions, based on the growing sense that "any theology today that does not think through its questions relative to the agony of Vietnam, the plight of the sharecroppers, the riots of our cities, or even the ecstasy of the hippies, can lead to an equally meaningless theological narcissism."[21] Reflections on authority in theology need to be related to reflections on power. Theology in North America is learning to take its first steps out of its modern self-centeredness.

Human Power and God's Power

As that question is worked out more fully, Herzog introduces a theological distinction between human revolution and God's revolution. In this way he restricts modern theology's confidence in the power of the activist modern self that is at the center of other radical theologies of that time, including such diverse approaches as the theologies of development and revolution. Theology must maintain a critical distance from the modern self's efforts at revolution, which often end up where they started if authority and power are not shared. Nevertheless, Herzog finds, theology must become deeply involved in revolutionary change. What sets the pace for this revolution, however, is God's own revolution, which makes all things new, a revolution that introduces new models of power, such as the "power of powerlessness," a conception of power that includes those on the underside.[22]

The concern for mapping out power structures and identifying the site of God's revolution grows out of deepening encounters with the underside. At the end of the sixties Herzog reports that "many of my theological words have broken to pieces."[23] On the occasion of a protest by a group of African American students at Duke University and a standoff with the administration, he comes to the conclusion that we "need to take a new look at each other." The extent of the problem

---

20. Herzog, "After Civil Rights—What?" 235.
21. Frederick Herzog, "God, Evil, and Revolution," *Journal of Religious Thought* 25:2 (Autumn–Winter 1968/69), 5.
22. Ibid., 21, 26, 28.
23. Frederick Herzog, "Black and White Together?" *Duke Divinity School Review* 34 (Spring 1969), 115; also included in *Theology from the Belly of the Whale: A Frederick Herzog Reader,* ed. Rieger.

that poses itself for theology is seen only now: "White Christianity has not identified with black history at any significant point."[24]

In this context a major challenge for theology is formulated. Herzog finds that the way in which many well-meaning white theologians have tried to deal with the African American other, namely, to become "color-blind," only reinforces the modern self's blindness to the plight of the other. Integration must not lead to that misrecognition of the difference between oppressor and oppressed that is so characteristic of the modern self and the powers that be.

In personal encounters with the struggle of African Americans in light of the Gospel, theology learns that the contemporary situation is determined by the political. Theology can no longer close its eyes to structures of political power. Here a specific type of "political theology" takes shape that understands that its task is not to politicize the Gospel but to realize how much everything is politicized already.[25] Two things come together: "Over against those who stress man's limitless capacity for transformation, political theology points to man's limitedness. But over against those who stress man's limitation, it speaks a strong word about the power for transformation in Christ."[26]

Liberation Theology

These challenges posed to theology by encounters with the underside of history are condensed in Herzog's call for a theology of liberation, the first one to be published in the United States, appearing slightly earlier than James Cone's *A Black Theology of Liberation* and even before Gustavo Gutiérrez's *A Theology of Liberation*. Toward the end of this article Herzog argues that liberal theology, in its pluralism and relativism, "needs to make way for liberated theology, a theology in which the initiative and power of God's liberation unite the theologian more fully with the lot of the disadvantaged."[27] The catalyst for this vision has

---

24. Ibid., 116, 117.

25. See Frederick Herzog, "'Politische Theologie' und die christliche Hoffnung," in *Diskussion zur "politischen Theologie,"* ed. Helmut Peukert (Munich: Kaiser, Grünewald, 1969), 124, 125. "The notions of justice, freedom, and peace in the New Testament are important, but I feel they do not clarify sufficiently why the political dimension is so predominant in theology today." Ibid., 132.

26. Frederick Herzog, "Political Theology," *Christian Century* 86:30 (1969), 978. Note that "theology cannot become the servant of politics and politics cannot become the servant of theology, but both must become servants of God." Herzog points out that political theology, unlike the Social Gospel movement, "makes no claims to redeeming society." Ibid., 976.

27. Frederick Herzog, "Theology of Liberation," *Continuum* 7:4 (Winter 1970), 524; also included in *Theology from the Belly of the Whale: A Frederick Herzog Reader,* ed. Rieger.

been the martyrdom of Martin Luther King Jr. Herzog later compares
the moment when King was shot to the situation of the disciples after
the Crucifixion. "Up to that point we were all pretty optimistic. Then
it dawned on me that something was going on."[28]

The encounter with the martyrdom of the African American other
raises new theological questions, reaching all the way into the doctrine of God. The main question is no longer whether God is dead
or alive, the focus of the discussion of much of modern theology, but
whether God is black or white. At stake is, in Herzog's words, whether
God is "independent of the white man's value structure of prestige
and success." For this reason theology needs to assess whether it is
"*authorized* — brought into being — by a reality 'other' than itself."[29]

Two aspects are involved in reshaping the self-centeredness of mainline theology. First of all, Herzog points out that "it is the living power
of the 'otherness' of the Word that theology needs in order to make
sense at all." The self, as Lacan has shown, can be opened up in this
encounter with the biblical texts. Without inviting a new biblicism,
Herzog calls for a "new high regard for the *liberating power* of the Word
of God."[30] It is striking how closely the notions of authority and power
are intertwined at this point.

Equally important, and this is the other element that helps to open
up the modern self, is a new step in the encounter with the other. In
agreement with black theology born at the same time, Herzog formulates the question for theology in the seventies: "What happens to the
spectrum of Christian doctrine if the theologian seriously makes this
identification" with the oppressed?[31] To say, in this context, that "God
is black" does not mean to confine God to the control of yet another
context but to question "white theological supremacy which, however
subtly, evades identification with the wretched of the earth."[32] Little did

---

Herzog strongly goes against any liberal "references to contemporaneity in general." Ibid.,
516.

28. Interview with Frederick Herzog, 4/12/92. Cf. also Frederick Herzog, "Liberation
and Process Theologies in the Church," *Prism* 5:2 (Fall 1990), 61: "It was April 4, 1968,
6:00 p.m. Suddenly it dawned on me: here was not just the liberation process in the death
of King, but the theology of liberation. It was martyrdom that made the difference." This
essay is also included in *Theology from the Belly of the Whale: A Frederick Herzog Reader*,
ed. Rieger.

29. Herzog, "Theology of Liberation," 518, 520.

30. Ibid., 520, 522.

31. Frederick Herzog, "God: Black or White? The Upshot of the Debate about God
in the Sixties," *Review and Expositor* 67:3 (Summer 1970), 308; also included in *Theology
from the Belly of the Whale: A Frederick Herzog Reader*, ed. Rieger.

32. Ibid., 313.

Herzog suspect that this would still be a key question way into the new millennium.

Here a North American liberation theology is conceived, pulling together the self of the theologian and the sacred texts of the church in new encounters with God and people on the underside of history. The concern for the reconstruction of the content of theology in light of the encounter with the other distinguishes it not only from mainline theology[33] but also from other theologies that see themselves as calls to action (e.g., the Social Gospel movement). A new theological project is born. In the encounter with the underside of history, as the location where God returns, the issue of theological authority is raised once more in connection with the power struggle.[34]

In these new encounters with the word of God and the marginalized, the modern self and its powers are reconstructed. The point for white theologians is not to write theology for African Americans but to reshape their own approaches. In the encounter with the African American other Herzog admits, "I do not know how they feel, but I know how I feel: as if I have been disemboweled of what I thought was my inmost being."[35] As mainline theologians become aware of that radical emptiness, the other as warrant for the power of the self can be gradually released. Easygoing optimism will no longer do.

Reshaping the Power of the Self

The encounter with the other is leading to new insights into the power of the modern self.[36] In 1970 Herzog is only able to point away from the identification of modern humanity with the *imago Dei* to another humanity as *imago futuri*. The implications are still open, and a more

---

33. In my interview with Herzog, 4/14/92, he points out that in his early work it never occurred to him that there could have been anything wrong with the content of theology.

34. Cf. Frederick Herzog, "Befreiung zu einem neuen Menschenbild?" *Evangelische Kommentare* 5:9 (1972), 520.

35. Frederick Herzog, "The Political Gospel," *Christian Century* 87:46 (November 1, 1970), 1380, 1381; also included in *Theology from the Belly of the Whale: A Frederick Herzog Reader*, ed. Rieger. See also Frederick Herzog, "Between Ignorance and Arrogance," *Theological Education* 7:1 (Autumn 1971), 73: "Instead of now trying to point out where we find black theology self-contradictory, mistaken, or fuzzy in logic, we might fruitfully concentrate on our white self-contradictions."

36. In a preface to the German translation of James Cone's *Black Theology*, Herzog points out that, unlike in Germany, the search for a new human being has been at the center of the civil rights struggle and the youth rebellions in the United States. See James H. Cone, *Schwarze Theologie: Eine christliche Interpretation der Black-Power-Bewegung* (Munich: Kaiser, Grünewald, 1970), 6.

concrete vision of the new human being will have to be worked out in the community of a liberation church.[37]

The initial questions are fairly simple. Herzog wonders, for instance, what it says about his own humanity that in 1969 an African American woman still has to work eleven hours for six dollars. In a world where human beings are classified in large part by their economic value, theological anthropology can no longer be done without attention to economic structures. The relationship of self and other, repressed in much of modern theology, must now be broadened to include not only race but class and ultimately gender issues as well. Adam Smith's image of "economic man" looms in the background.[38]

Two essential elements for a new theological anthropology emerge at this point. One is the consideration of the other at the point where he or she is most oppressed. The encounter with the *other* helps Herzog to initiate that reconstruction of the modern self that is still missing in the concentration on the wholly *Other* of his teacher Karl Barth. Theological authority must now be reconfigured in light of the power struggle.[39]

The second element is the reflection of the interconnectedness of one's own life with the oppressed other, which can only come as a gift.[40] In this interconnectedness the oppressed other sets a limit to the repressive powers of the self, a phenomenon whose mechanisms Lacan has interpreted for us. Slowly the insight develops that "I is an other." Herzog indicates how this encounter with the other transforms theology when he rereads the biblical commandment "Love your neighbor as yourself" as "Love your neighbor as [being] your self."[41] While the old liberal interpretation, repeated many times, emphasized the primacy of the love of self, theology needs to take another look at the way self and other are related. Unfortunately, even today modern theology still preaches that in order to love others, one must first love oneself.

Here the two critiques of the first chapter come together: It is not that modern or postmodern theologies, or any other theology on the market today, would need to be invited to become more involved in service to people at the margins. The problem is that the encounter with

---

37. Herzog, "The Political Gospel," 1383.

38. See ibid., 1381.

39. See Frederick Herzog, "Ein neuer Kirchenkonflikt in den USA?" *Evangelische Theologie* 32:2 (March/April 1972), 179, 180.

40. Cf. Frederick Herzog, "Die Kirche als Befreiungskirche," *Evangelische Kommentare* 5:2 (1972), 70.

41. Herzog, "Befreiung zu einem neuen Menschenbild?" 518.

the other in terms of service or charity does not lead to self-critique in its most literal sense, leaving theology without a reconstruction of the modern self. Thus the old opposition of liberal and conservative theology has become invalid at a time when this opposition is in full swing, when the liberals accuse the conservatives of the (symbolic-order) fallacy of worshiping the status quo, while the conservatives maintain that the (imaginary-order) trust in the powers of the self and in progress is the real idolatry.[42] Losing sight of the other makes theology prone to fall for the claims of the powers that be.

In this connection heresy is more than just a distortion on the doctrinal level. Heresy, as Herzog defines it, is an error concerning "the essence of the human being and his or her relation to its context"; it is the question of the truth about the human being, manifest most concretely in racism, where power over the other is rationalized and the other is commodified, made into a thing.[43] The first step in theology's encounter with the underside of history in the United States is thus the elaboration of a new view of the human being, the construction of a "corporate self" in which the oppressed other becomes a part of the self.

Reconsidering the Power of the Text

The encounter with the other also clears the way for new approaches to the authoritative texts of the church. Herzog's interpretation of the Fourth Gospel intends to be an example of "an exercise in the discipline of new listening," both to the other and to the text of the Gospel.[44] It is in the notion of "becoming black" that the importance of the other for theology is stressed most drastically: "To 'think black' means to be able to think from the perspective of the underdog."[45] In the encounter with the power of the Gospel, the self is able to realize its relationship with the oppressed other more clearly: "*The oppressed self as part of the self,* this is a compelling factor because of the power of the originating event of Christianity over us."[46]

---

42. Cf. Herzog, "Die Kirche als Befreiungskirche," 72. Cf. also Herzog, "Ein neuer Kirchenkonflikt in den USA?" 164.

43. Herzog, "Ein neuer Kirchenkonflikt in den USA?" 176, 177.

44. Herzog, LT, 26.

45. Ibid., 15. This notion has often been misunderstood by Herzog's critics. Its importance is not even seen in the positive reception in Benjamin Reist, *Theology in Red, White, and Black* (Philadelphia: Westminster, 1975), 175–85. Reist is correct that ultimately whites need to become white, but this can only happen where the black person is seen as part of the self.

46. Herzog, LT, 14; emphasis in original. This is one of the basic differences between theology of liberation and the Social Gospel movement: Walter Rauschenbusch "theologically aligned himself with the liberal tradition . . . his notion of the self . . . did not include

Herzog, aware that he is not in a position to write a black theology, is searching for "the truth the black knows just because he is black,"[47] the truth of the repressed real other of modern North American society and the church. Admitting that we cannot represent the oppressed, he recommends that we at least "get off their backs and give up our white pride."[48] "Becoming black" for whites, then, means that theology needs to start with radical *metanoia*, a change of our view of the self, grounded in Jesus' selfhood, not only a change of mind but change of those "old white ways" as well.

The trouble with white Christianity, and this is essential to the new theology, "is not that it does not do enough (remember how many of us rushed off in the sixties to find 'where the action is'!), but that it does not have power enough to do effectively whatever it does."[49] "Becoming black" has, therefore, to do with participation in that real power in which people are "born again," the latter expression being perhaps as humorous as the former one in referring to something that is not humanly possible.[50] The theological conclusion is that "the blackness or redness of the man reborn is always related to *Jesus'* blackness or redness." Christ's own identification with the oppressed as manifest in the biblical texts makes all the difference.[51]

Deeper encounters with the text and the other have made theology more conscious of the existence of several factors in the struggle for power that include national, racial, and class distinctions as well as the oppression of women; and even though Herzog does not yet quite understand how these issues are interconnected,[52] he realizes that all those questions have to do with the power of the modern self. He now finds that "in some respects the God-question is not primary. The Gospel, first of all, compels us to acknowledge a new view of the self."[53] While religions are basically very much alike, as "man's way of making a profit from his sense of transcendence, sanctioning the status quo of exploitation with the divine," Herzog stresses the difference of the

---

the wretched of the earth as part of the self." Cf. Herzog, "The Burden of Southern Theology: A Response," *Duke Divinity School Review* 38:3 (Fall 1973), 160.

47. Herzog, LT, ix.

48. Ibid., vii.

49. Ibid., ix.

50. Ibid., x: "Must not the man who compelled Nicodemus to wonder whether he could get back into his mother's womb have had a sense of humor, and a poetic one at that?" Cf. John 3:1–21 and ibid., 61–67.

51. Ibid., 65.

52. See ibid., 73. Women's liberation, for instance, is still subordinated to "color liberation."

53. Ibid., 94.

Christian faith: "Jesus does not bring a new religion, but the experience of corporate selfhood."[54]

Here a new theological starting point is formulated: "What God is all about one learns...only by what man in Christ is all about."[55] Two things come together: the decentering of the modern self and the creation of a corporate self in the identification with those on the underside. It is God's liberating presence with the oppressed other in Jesus that poses the crucial challenge to the powers of the modern self. In this constellation the authority of the biblical text, read on the basis of an encounter with the other, plays an important role, for "the discovery of the presence of God where the pain is, is impressed on us by the biblical story."[56] Theology thus arrives at an "interpretive focus" that signals a basic openness and the refusal to create another closed system.[57]

The reactions to Herzog's rereading of the Gospel of John range from complete puzzlement to emphatic agreement. One reviewer in particular, however, understands the fundamental challenge of the book when he compares it to Karl Barth's work on Romans: "Like Barth, Herzog is not content to play according to the going rules of the theological and ecclesiastical game."[58]

At the Intersection of the Self, the Other, and the Text

Herzog formulates the challenge: "Let us see what happens if *on grounds of the biblical Word* we radically bring theology in confrontation with the concrete sufferer, the concrete oppressed."[59] The encounter with the other does not have to lead to a reduction in the authority of the texts of the church. If anything, the authority of the text becomes more

---

54. Ibid., 147.

55. Ibid., 150.

56. Ibid., 259.

57. Ibid., 261. As Gerald A. Butler, "Karl Barth and Political Theology," *Scottish Journal of Theology*, 27:4 (November 1974), 456, has observed, this is one of the decisive points where Herzog's theology differs from Johann Baptist Metz's as well as from Jürgen Moltmann's political theologies, since the latter tend to give political theology a more important role by making it function as the hermeneutical norm rather than as an "interpretive focus."

58. James C. Logan, review of *Liberation Theology: Liberation in the Light of the Fourth Gospel*, in the *Review of Books and Religion* (Mid-May 1973), 1. For a serious misunderstanding, cf. Patrick J. Leonard, review of *Liberation Theology*, in *Review for Religious* 32:2 (1973), 446, 447.

59. Frederick Herzog, "Liberation Theology or Culture Religion?" *Union Seminary Quarterly Review* 29:3/4 (Spring and Summer 1974), 243. Emphasis mine. This essay is also included in *Theology from the Belly of the Whale: A Frederick Herzog Reader*, ed. Rieger.

effective as a critique of the deeply ingrained authority structures of the ego's era.

In the North American context, this interrelation of the biblical text with the oppressed other has the potential to overcome not only the self-referential nature of the modern self, since the oppressed are less in a position to usurp the text, but also the restrictive focus on the ecclesial texts in certain forms of orthodoxy (and perhaps even in fundamentalism) that fail to address the deeper dilemmas of the modern world.[60]

Herzog argues that in reading the biblical text in relation to the other "a new reality is being created" that, in interfering with the control of the self, is located "not *behind* this world, but *in* this world."[61] This contrasts both with an understanding of biblical language in terms of symbol, based on the self's connection with the divine,[62] and with an understanding of biblical language in terms of dogmatic concepts, which is text centered. The metaphorical character of language, according to Herzog, offers an alternative since it "does not transfer meaning to a deeper or higher reality," the level of the religious at which many modern symbolic theories of language function, "nor does it primarily conceptualize reality," as do certain orthodox approaches to the Bible that aim at constructing a comprehensive worldview. Biblical language, understood in terms of metaphor, "creates new reality."[63] This new reality often contrasts with existing realities and initiates transformation.

In this encounter of the biblical text and the other, theology finally is able to transcend the tug-of-war of the text and the self in modern theology that often ends up turning the text into reflective images of oneself. At the same time, theology can also transcend some of the

---

60. Cf. Frederick Herzog, "Amerikas Theologie vor einem Neuanfang?" *Evangelische Kommentare* 7:9 (September 1974), 532: "Adaptation of the biblical message to modern humanity dictates what that message is allowed to say and does not interfere with the successful American. The literalism of fundamentalism also dictates what the message may say, namely only that which has been said in former times. Here the successful American is not challenged either." Both the power of the self and the power of the text do not really challenge the present. Cf. also Frederick Herzog, "Liberation Theology: Continuing the Discussion," *Christianity and Crisis* 34:17 (October 1974), 226.

61. Frederick Herzog, "Liberation and Imagination," *Interpretation* 32:3 (July 1978), 241.

62. According to Paul Tillich, *Systematic Theology* (Chicago: University of Chicago Press, 1951), vol. 1, 239, the power of a symbol depends on "the correlation between that which is symbolized and the persons who receive it as a symbol."

63. Frederick Herzog, *Justice Church: The New Function of the Church in North American Christianity* (Maryknoll, N.Y.: Orbis, 1980), 4, 5 (abbreviated: JC).

orthodox camp's fixation on the text as sufficient in and of itself. According to Herzog, the metaphorical powers of the biblical text open
us up for a "reorientation to the action of God."[64] In other words, the
biblical text, for all its importance, does not take up the place of ultimate authority either. In the encounter with the other, both text and
self learn to point away from themselves to the authority of God.

The theological task is therefore not primarily to fight the battle
for the oppressed, the dream of modern theologies as represented by
the Social Gospel movement and various theologies of development
and revolution. The fundamental question for theology is first of all
"whether the theologian himself is free at all to see the true character of the biblical texts as long as he disregards the plight of the poor."
Since, as we have seen, embedded structures of power and authority are
least obvious from the top, the theologian needs "to take the poor into
account so as not to turn his work into a mere legitimation of the high
and the mighty — the affluent."[65] One of the basic claims that arise
in the encounter with the underside is that "text-criticism needs to be
accompanied by self-criticism."[66]

Uncovering the Truth of One's Symptom

The encounter with the other has led to new insights into theological authority. The new interpretive focus, finding God at work where
the pain is, does not do away with the fundamental authority of Scripture and the Christian tradition but contributes to a profound rereading
that, contrary to the idiosyncratic closures of the imaginary order self
and the symbolic order text, is open-ended.

New challenges emerge. If it is true that, as Latin American liberation theologians have said, the poor are the teachers, they seem to
be teaching different lessons in different situations. Broad reflections
on the general situation or on the underside of history as such will no
longer do. Herzog calls for a "specific analysis of the cities and towns
in which we live in terms of their socio-political dynamics."[67] In a response to the claim that universality of religious experience is a better
guide than historical particularity, he puts it quite drastically: "We are
not employed as children of God but as black garbage collectors or red

64. Herzog, "The Burden of Southern Theology," 156.
65. Frederick Herzog, "Liberation Hermeneutic as Ideology Critique?" *Interpretation*
28:4 (October 1974), 393.
66. Ibid., 396.
67. Herzog, "The Burden of Southern Theology," 154. See also 157 n. 9.

fieldhands or white-collar workers, as male bosses or female secretaries, and so on."[68]

The encounter with the underside of history must now be developed further in its theological meaning. Having established the poor as part of the Gospel, the "praxis text analysis" is now followed by what Herzog calls "praxis context analysis."[69] The fundamental issue still has to do with the relation of self and other: "I have often heard it said in debates about liberation theology that first of all we must define oppression and who the oppressed are. I believe it's the other way around: the oppressed define us."[70] Redefining ourselves in relation to the other, we need to learn "theological decontrol."[71]

Christological Self-Critique

In a next step, the encounter with the other leads to a deeper understanding of the Christ event. We can no longer think about Christ's person in abstract terms, without considering his close connection with the marginalized people of his day and with a God who may be more black than white. At stake is the question of how Christology can be more than transcendental anthropology, Christ fashioned in the mirror image of the normative humanity of the modern self. How does Christ challenge the modern self and reconstruct our anthropological assumptions? Herzog now adds another layer to theological self-critique when he defines it as *"christological* self-critique," something that "is much more than *self*-examination."[72] Only in this way can the specific situation of the southern United States be addressed, which is characterized by the fact that "there is hardly a region left in Western civilization where culture and Christianity are so much of one cloth."[73]

The fundamental issue for theology in the south is how to arrive at a new awareness of the relationship of self and other in Christ's own person, covered up by the symbolic-order fixations of traditional theology. Here the question arises whether in the life, death, and resurrection

---

68. Frederick Herzog, "Liberals versus Liberationists," *Christian Century* 93:24 (July 21–28, 1976), 666, response to Deane William Ferm.

69. Herzog, JC, 6: "I believe that it is fair to say that the first stage of liberation theology is behind us."

70. Frederick Herzog, "From Good Friday to Labor Day," *Journal of Religious Thought* 34:2 (Fall–Winter 1977/78), 22. Here is, once more, a fundamental contrast to the Social Gospel movement, whose "liberal premises seemed to be legitimating doing good for others while not changing oneself." Herzog, JC, 137 n. 9.

71. See Herzog, JC, xiii.

72. Herzog, "Liberation Hermeneutic as Ideology Critique?" 396.

73. Herzog, "The Burden of Southern Theology," 151.

of Jesus Christ "a radical mutation of human selfhood" took place. Or, more precisely: "Was the human self constituted anew in this history as a corporate self, so that also we are enabled to become a new self?"[74] In light of a long history of Christology being interpreted exclusively in terms of the relation between God and self, what would the import of Jesus be for the relationship among human beings? In contradistinction to "southern culture-religion," for instance, which at best understands the corporateness of life in Christ as referring to one's own group,[75] the new selfhood includes the oppressed.

Lacan's thought helps clarify the challenge. One of the basic lessons for theology in the ego's era is that the repressed other is a part of the self. Only in this way can the power of the self and its aggressive and narcissistic tendencies be transformed. At the same time we must keep in mind that identification with the oppressed is not something that the modern self can make happen. It is a gift. Our eyes need to be opened in actual encounters that are spurred by Christ's own solidarity with the oppressed. Here the whole framework of theology is redefined: "Understanding God begins in the experience of God's reconstitution of human selfhood as social selfhood including the oppressed."[76]

In regard to the theological claim that God in Christ meets us in people at the margins, the Lacanian notion of the real offers a model to understand better the crucial position of the marginalized within the parameters of power and authority, without immediately identifying them with Christ. The ultimate place of authority is kept open for God.

Christopraxis

It is common knowledge that theology has often failed to pay sufficient attention to practical matters. The bigger problem, however, is that even where it did pay attention, the relation of theory and praxis has often been interpreted as a one-way street, starting with theory. Theologies from the underside of history were among the first to reclaim a more constructive relation of theory and praxis, dealing with the inter-

---

74. Herzog, "Liberation Theology or Culture Religion?" 244.
75. See Frederick Herzog, "United Methodism in Agony," *Perkins Journal* 28:1 (Fall 1974), 10 n. 28, referring to *Religion and the Solid South*, ed. Samuel S. Hill. Herzog's essay is reprinted in *Doctrine and Theology in the United Methodist Church*, ed. Thomas A. Langford (Nashville: Kingswood, 1991).
76. Frederick Herzog, "Responsible Theology?" in *Philosophy of Religion and Theology: 1974 Proceedings*, American Academy of Religion Section Papers, ed. James Wm. McClendon Jr. (Missoula, Mont.: Scholars Press, 1974), 166.

dependence of action and reflection. Today, the relation of theory and praxis has become more widely asserted.[77]

While much of theological reflection has started with theory, theology in touch with the underside finds that praxis comes first. Theology is built into it as a second step. According to Herzog, this is already true for the writings of the New Testament since all of them grew out of particular praxis situations. For this reason he can say, for instance, that "to begin again with the Bible means to begin again with praxis."[78] In the basic interdependence of doctrine and life, word and action cannot be separated: "word is deed (worddeed) and deed is word (deedword)."[79] The fact that this relation between word and deed is found most clearly in the Gospels does not eliminate the significance of the rest of the Bible. It does point, however, to the central importance of the shape of Jesus' ministry.[80]

Even more important than the basic recognition that praxis gives rise to thought is its definition as "Christopraxis." Herzog discovers the new paradigm in Jesus' own story: "What happened in Jesus was that a hermeneutic of Christology was turned into a hermeneutic of Christopraxis. We need to explain to the church that in this praxis God entered history, so that thought finally could rise from praxis and we too could act our way into thinking."[81] What really moved people was not only

---

77. The term *praxis* itself is defined as action-reflection. Frederick Herzog, "Doing Liberation Theology in the South," 7. Herzog quotes David Tracy's definition in *Blessed Rage for Order: The New Pluralism in Theology* (New York: Seabury, 1975): "Such praxis, of course, is not to be identified with practice. Rather praxis is correctly understood as the critical relationship between theory and practice whereby each is dialectically influenced and transformed by the other."

78. Frederick Herzog, "Birth Pangs: Liberation Theology in North America," *Christian Century* 93:41 (December 15, 1976), 1121.

79. Herzog, "United Methodism in Agony," 8. Cf. also Frederick Herzog, "Reorientation in Theology: Listening to Black Theology," in *The Context of Contemporary Theology: Essays in Honor of Paul Lehmann*, ed. Alexander J. McKelway and E. David Willis (Atlanta: John Knox Press, 1974), 235f.

80. Herzog, JC, 3.

81. Herzog, JC, 50. Cf. also Frederick Herzog, "Dogmatik IV," in *Theologische Realenzyklopädie*, vol. 9, ed. Gerhard Krause and Gerhard Müller (Berlin: Walter de Gruyter, 1982), 113; a translation is included in *Theology from the Belly of the Whale: A Frederick Herzog Reader*, ed. Rieger. The term *Christopraxis* occurs in Herzog's work for the first time in 1976, in "Doing Liberation Theology in the South," 7, and in Frederick Herzog, "Introduction: On Liberating Liberation Theology," in Hugo Assmann, *Theology for a Nomad Church* (Maryknoll, N.Y.: Orbis, 1976), 18. Herzog is the first to use this term and not Ray S. Anderson, who, in his book *Ministry on the Fireline: A Practical Theology for an Empowered Church* (Downers Grove, Ill.: InterVarsity Press, 1993), 212–13 n. 2, claims that he invented the term in 1984. Already in 1974 Herzog had raised the question whether "Christology offers some cogent reasons for a praxiology not oriented in middle-class values." Herzog, "United Methodism in Agony," 8.

Jesus' message but his particular praxis, in touch with those at the margins: The lame walked, the blind saw, the oppressed went free, and the poor had good news preached to them.

Reestablishing the importance of praxis is, therefore, not enough. Theology needs to be clear as to which particular praxis it is talking about. The praxis of Jesus serves as a guideline, not something to be slavishly imitated, to be sure, but setting the framework, keeping in mind that Jesus is also acting in the present. Herzog often wondered, "What is Jesus doing now?" Following Jesus, theology needs to remember and work through concrete history from the perspective of the margins. For theology in the southern United States this means that "today we need to keep alive the Southern insights of the sixties in matters of liberation. In the beginning was the black struggle. That itself had been tied into our Judeo-Christian heritage from Exodus to Resurrection."[82] In that situation, paralyzed Christians began to walk again on the way to life, blind mainline theologians started to see, the oppressed became freer, and good news was preached again to the poor.

Over against other approaches that immediately stress Christian action or "orthopraxis," the notion of "Christopraxis" reminds us that theology is reborn first in God's own praxis. This shift in emphasis is crucial in North America, where praxis is often defined in terms of the self-propelled activism of the modern self whose motto is reflected in the motto of the Nike Company: "Just do it." Herzog's notion of Christopraxis, on the other hand, shows how our modern understanding of praxis is reshaped by God's praxis in Christ with those who suffer: *praxis passionis divini*,[83] the praxis of God's own suffering. The point is not to glorify suffering and weakness but to come to a better understanding of God's power, which is, as the apostle Paul knew, "made perfect in weakness" (2 Cor. 12:9). In the encounter with the underside theology begins to realize, once more with Paul, that "God's weakness is stronger than human strength" (1 Cor. 1:25).

---

82. Herzog, "Doing Liberation Theology in the South," 7.

83. See Frederick Herzog, "Praxis Passionis Divini," *Evangelische Theologie* 44:6 (November/December 1984). A translation of this essay can be found in *Theology from the Belly of the Whale: A Frederick Herzog Reader*, ed. Rieger. In a response to Herzog's work from the German perspective, Gerhard Sauter underscores the importance of the redefinition of the notion of praxis over against modernity's emphasis on activism. See Gerhard Sauter, "'Leiden' und 'Handeln.' Frederick Herzog zum 60. Geburtstag," *Evangelische Theologie* 45:5 (1985).

God and Ideology

While the encounter with people on the underside of history has presented a significant challenge for theology, this does not mean that all
theology now needs to be written for the other. Herzog is fully aware
that as a white theologian he cannot write a theology for black sharecroppers. Nevertheless, the plight of the sharecroppers can no longer be
excluded from mainline theology: "The real question for whites is not,
What should we do about black theology? It is rather, What are we going to do about white theology?"[84] What would a theology look like in
which the powers of the self and of the text come to understand better
their own limitations and tasks? In this process, Herzog begins to realize
that "we need first of all to think *historically*, rather than to pontificate
categorically, about our societal realities."[85] Applied to theology and the
church, this means that *"we need to be keenly aware of the shift from theologizing about an ideal church,"* the focus of many liberal and traditional
theologies, *"to analyzing the actual church."*[86]

Theology that takes into account the context of the sharecroppers and others gradually begins to understand that "all doctrine today
which is not explicitly also a critique of the present economic system
eo ipso also becomes a justification of the system, and opium for the
people."[87] At stake are not just the mystifications of neoorthodoxy's and
southern culture religion's reliance on the texts of the church. The false
consciousness of liberal theology must also be considered since modern
theologians, promoting various types of critical reflection, often assume
to be on top of ideological distortions.[88]

This leads to a fundamental theological shift. By introducing the notion of God's "unconcealment," Herzog turns away from the problem of
revelation as formulated by those who consider the texts of the church
as ultimate authority.[89] On the other hand, God's immediate presence

---

84. Herzog, "Liberation Hermeneutic as Ideology Critique?" 388. To speak of "white
theology" is to realize that theology as it is usually done brings in its own perspectival
angle. Cf. Herzog, "Responsible Theology," 159.

85. Herzog, "Doing Liberation Theology in the South," 7. Emphasis in original.

86. Herzog, JC, 11. Emphasis in original. This, as Herzog recalls at the end of the
seventies, is probably "the most elementary understanding we have discovered in North
Carolina." Herzog, "From Good Friday to Labor Day," 15. Cf. also Robert T. Osborn,
"Jesus and Liberation Theology," *Christian Century* (March 10, 1976).

87. Herzog, "United Methodism in Agony," 6.

88. Herzog, "Responsible Theology," 161.

89. Herzog, "Liberation Hermeneutic as Ideology Critique?" 403 n. 51. Cf. also
Herzog, "Responsible Theology," 163, 164. Herzog is surprised that even sympathetic interpreters like James D. Smart have not seen the significance of this move, introduced
initially in LT.

to self-consciousness, as in liberal theology of the Schleiermacher type, must also be questioned on the grounds of the ideological blinders of the modern self. Arguing that "not God is man's problem, but man is his own problem,"[90] Herzog directs attention to the problem of North American theology in its various forms. The main theological problem is no longer the availability of God but the availability of the human being. Both liberal theologies and their critics may have kept God from breaking through by concentrating on the availability of God in relation to the authority of selves and texts, often to the exclusion of a reflection on the availability of the human person. The real challenge is to find ways to become open to God's "unconcealment," to what God is doing all along. North American theology faces its most fundamental challenge in rethinking the authority of the self and the text and reshaping established structures of control, thus creating new openness for God and the other.

On the basis of its growing encounter with the other, the marginalized, and oppressed, theology needs to limit those powers that direct our attention away from God's own work. Theology from the underside counters the distortions of the imaginary and the symbolic identifications and, in touch with the other who restricts the powers of both self and text, provides us with a new vision of God. In this process, the self and the text are put to new use. At the same time, however, as Lacan helped us understand, the other does not need to become the source of ultimate authority. The other points to the truth, helps identify the truth, without being truth itself. In the encounter with this other, neither the self nor the text can be absolute authorities anymore. In constant interrelation of the three elements, the place of authority can be kept open.

One of the main tasks of theology from the underside is to keep the view open for what God is doing.[91]

From Development to Liberation

Much of the civil rights struggle of the fifties and early sixties was influenced by a philosophy of development, driven by the belief that things would gradually improve and guided by the vision that the African American other could somehow be made to fit into the structures

---

90. Herzog, "Responsible Theology," 164.

91. Herzog shows how Stanley Hauerwas's critique of liberation theology, for instance, despite arguing convincingly that "what charity requires is not the removing of all injustice in the world, but rather to meet the need of the neighbor where we find him," leaves out precisely this issue: "A subtle shift takes place here that is foreign to New Testament thought: away from God's battle for justice to our love of neighbor wherever we find the neighbor." Cf. Herzog, JC, 87.

created by white America. Over time, however, a shift takes place in some sectors, sparked by closer encounters of blacks and whites. The insight into the seriousness of the situation grows, including a deeper understanding of the nature of oppression first in terms of political and later in terms of economic conflict.

While toward the end of the sixties the confrontation in the political realm became a central issue, it was only in the seventies, according to Herzog, that people began to "grasp the seriousness of the revolutionary struggle." At this time, deeper encounters with the plight of the other made even theologians aware of deep tensions in society, including class divisions and the exploitation of one class by another.[92] Realizing in the dialogue with the oppressed that "in capitalism today there is an 'oppression explosion,'" this insight is hammered out from the mid-seventies on. Theology in touch with the underside gradually begins to broaden its horizon, and the former emphasis on politics shifts to economics.

Looking back, Herzog summarizes the early history of theology encountering the underside in North America in this way: "God's claim in the poor Christ was felt anew. The experience was not triggered by the kind sentiments of do-gooder white theologians. Rather, 'objective' claims made on us by God and by the poor on the margins of society turned us around."[93]

As white theologians were entering into new relationships with the black community that no longer co-opted blackness,[94] the shooting of Martin Luther King Jr. led to the painful insight that the racial problem was not something society would be able to cure easily, but was a symptom (in Lacan's sense of the term) that pointed to the truth about the deeper roots of the problem and the truth about the white establishment. The challenge of the encounter with the African American other for white theology is thus not first of all a moral imperative, a call to begin fighting for black freedom. Rather, the challenge has to do with an awareness of the mechanisms of repression perpetuated by the white system. As Herzog puts it, liberation theology requires "paying attention to the silences in the church."[95]

Along the way there were of course also moments of frustration, and

---

92. Frederick Herzog, "Which Liberation Theology?" *Religion in Life* 44:4 (Winter 1975), 451.
93. Herzog, "Birth Pangs: Liberation Theology in North America," 1120.
94. These new relationships are acknowledged by the AME bishop Philip R. Cousin, "Black Identity and White Identity," *Dialog* 15:2 (Spring 1976).
95. Lecture to a Duke-UNC Working Group on Religious Change in Latin America, 10/15/93.

Herzog's work is perhaps distinguished most by the fact that he takes them up productively and self-critically. One of the first of these moments occurred after the Vietnam War when disappointed activism led to a new repression of the symptoms of society: "It was not at all surprising that after the activist sixties, in the seventies we reverted to the old piety, only now wrapped up in the excitement of so-called charismatic movements."[96] But within this disappointment there was also new hope. In the early seventies Herzog noticed a "corporate accountability in the Christian community" he "had not known before."[97]

Initially, theology in touch with the underside of history was shaped in oral rather than written discourse.[98] In these conversations theology unfolds in trying to listen to the people. Here the biblical texts find their true location. The genesis of liberation communities that identify with the oppressed is crucial for further theological development. Herzog comments, "Without such a community in North Carolina I could not act, think, or write theologically." The formation of liberation communities may well signal the dawn of a new era for the churches in the United States.[99]

Reconstructing Authority

The early encounters with the other in North America have guided theology back to the Bible. It is only later that, in conjunction with the growing awareness that "the 'nonpersons' have had no place in dogmatics,"[100] the doctrinal heritage of the church as a whole comes into view.

96. Herzog, "Which Liberation Theology?" *Religion in Life,* 450.

97. Herzog, JC, 1.

98. Herzog, "Birth Pangs: Liberation Theology in North America," 1120. For a reproduction of such a dialogue see the *Perkins Journal* (Summer 1976). See also Frederick Herzog and J. Deotis Roberts, "Contextualization of Theology in the New South," *Journal of Religious Thought* 36:1 (Spring–Summer 1979), Frederick Herzog, et al., "Theological Education and Liberation Theology: An Invitation to Respond," *Theological Education* 16:1 (Autumn 1979), and the appendix of Herzog, JC. Some other documents that reflect oral discourses are reproduced in *Theology from the Belly of the Whale: A Frederick Herzog Reader,* ed. Rieger. Names of other white theologians involved that appear over and over again are M. Douglas Meeks, Robert T. Osborn, Theodore Runyon, and Robert McAfee Brown.

99. Herzog, "From Good Friday to Labor Day," 19. Herzog, "Amerikas Theologie vor einem Neuanfang?" 531. Herzog points out that in the United States there were no leaders like August Hermann Francke or Johann Friedrich Oberlin, who laid the foundations for a strong diaconic tradition in Germany. The North American Social Gospel movement, influenced by liberal theology, did not pay enough attention to solidarity with the poor.

100. Frederick Herzog, "A New Spirituality: Shaping Doctrine at the Grass Roots," *Christian Century* (July 30–August 6, 1986), 681.

Herzog's initial sense that "the seventies will probably compel American theology to a complete reconstruction of its material" and that "it will have been black theology that has called the shots"[101] is thus extended. Broadening the scope of theological reflection and expanding the challenge of the underside of history by including various other struggles for liberation by women and people of the "third world" will take us into the twenty-first century.

"Do Not Trust a Thought Discovered While Sitting in Your Chair"

The encounter with the suffering of people at the margins marks one of the deepest crises of theology in the United States.[102] Theological words fall apart in the face of reality. Herzog puts it this way: "You don't understand what theology is unless you have looked in the face of suffering, unless you have become an atheist in the presence of pain."[103] In this context it is not enough merely to update a limited number of aspects of mainline theology. Theology needs to be reconstructed from the bottom up.[104] Here is another step in the transformation of theology as it relates to the encounter with the other. As Lacan has found, the encounter with the real other allows for a reconstruction of the textual reality of symbolic order. In this reconstruction, the fixations of the self locked up in the imaginary dyad are also challenged.

At a time when the relation of the self and the text is still at the center of theological attention, whether starting with the self and moving to the text, as in liberal theology, or starting with the text and moving to the self, as in postliberal theology, the encounter with the repressed other opens up new vistas. The binary relationships give way to a ternary relationship. At the intersection of all three elements, a new theology emerges. This new theology is not primarily a call to action, appealing to the moral integrity of the modern self. In the United States, liberation theologies have often been misunderstood in this way. But, even though it does take the texts of the church more seriously than modern theology, neither is the new theology just another turn to

---

101. Herzog, "God: Black or White?" 313.

102. The title of this section comes from Friedrich Nietzsche, quoted in Herzog, *God-Walk: Liberation Shaping Dogmatics* (Maryknoll, N.Y.: Orbis, 1988), xx (abbreviated: GW).

103. Herzog, "Let Us Still Praise Famous Men," 6.

104. "A whole superstructure of theological words has to collapse." Herzog, JC, 125. In retrospect, Herzog feels that in the seventies he did not elaborate thoroughly enough the implications of this superstructure in terms of the distinction between God and idol. See Herzog, GW, 204 n. 35.

the text. Interrelating the self, the other, and the text, the new theological impulse is able to compensate for what is lacking in the turns to the text and in the activisms of the modern self. Authority is restructured in regard both to the self and to the text. The encounter with the other introduces an openness that opens up new ways of listening to God's own Otherness.

Truth and Method

In the encounter with the other it is becoming increasingly clear that the unilateral foundations of mainline theology break down. While modern theology, for instance, could be grounded in the stability provided by the modern self, theology in touch with the other has to come to terms with the fact that in the world of oppression and marginalization there are no Archimedean points anymore. Immediate reliance on the texts of the church in order to create stability is also not an option.[105] Reconstructing theological method against this backdrop, Herzog combines four elements that I will discuss in the following, resembling what has come to be designated as the "quadrilateral" of Scripture, tradition, experience, and reason.[106]

In the search for a location where all of these elements come together, Herzog hits on the Eucharist as the point where "we most holistically express who we are as Christians individually and corporately," and where "we share most concretely in the life of Jesus, the realpresence of God in Christ as God continues to struggle with humankind in history."[107] In the celebration of the Eucharist the elements of reading Scripture, immersion in the traditions of the church, and reflection on these things in the light of a communal experience that includes "the least of these," people at the margins, merge. In this sense the Eucharist is where the Christian's social location in the world can be

---

105. Against Terrence Tilley's suggestion that in a postmodern world telling stories would help calm our terror. Terrence Tilley, *Postmodern Theologies: The Challenge of Religious Diversity* (Maryknoll, N.Y.: Orbis, 1995), 150, referring to John Shea.

106. Developing most of his theological reflections at the United Methodist Duke Divinity School where he has taught since 1960, Herzog implicitly seems to provide a rereading of the United Methodist "quadrilateral," whose elements of Scripture, tradition, reason, and experience (first brought together by Albert Outler and taken up into the United Methodist *Book of Discipline* in 1972) guide theological reflection. In the Methodist tradition the elements (whose interrelation goes back in certain ways to John Wesley himself) are not sharply determined as far as their historical context, contemporary interpretation, and interrelation go.

107. Herzog, GW, 4, 5. In "Kirchengemeinschaft und Eucharistie," *Berliner Theologische Zeitschrift* 8:1 (1991), 116 n. 2, Herzog explains his preference for the term Eucharist since it keeps together proclamation and Holy Communion. A translation can be found in *Theology from the Belly of the Whale: A Frederick Herzog Reader*, ed. Rieger.

related to God's own location with people on the underside of history, as witnessed in both the Old and the New Testaments.

Social Location: Experience

Describing how Christian thought arises in community settings, not simply as "God-talk" but always in the context of "God-walk," Herzog suggests three dimensions, a socio-critical, a historico-critical, and a psycho-critical one, taking up some of his earlier investigations and providing a more coherent framework. Each of these dimensions implies a self-critical moment missing in the liberal and neoorthodox concentrations on the self and the text as primary authorities.

The *socio-critical aspect* analyzes who Christians are in terms of their social relations. This analysis cannot be worked out in isolation, on neutral grounds. In biblical times, Herzog argues, "only those who as disciples were involved with Jesus in the struggle could work out the analysis correctly."[108] Out of the participation in God's own walk in the world, which does not bypass the struggle of those on the underside, grows an awareness of the conflictual nature of contemporary society.[109] This step is crucial since it is precisely this awareness of conflict that is constantly covered up, not only by the modern self (owing to its neglect of the other as part of the self), but by the critics of modern theology as well. Contrary to a common suspicion, conflict does not need to be produced systematically by turning classes, races, or genders against each other.[110] Conflict is simply a fact of life in modern society in which the church participates, but it is a fact that can only be noticed from the perspective of those on the underside who are the victims of it. From the view of the top floors, it hardly exists.

In contrast to modern historico-critical methods, the *historico-self-critical dimension* is aimed at realizing one's *own* involvement in history. Here the thrust of historical critique is reversed: The study of history is no longer about the critical historical study of the texts of the church and their historical dimensions alone; it now also includes a critical study look at the role of the modern self, the reader. In this process the

---

108. Herzog, GW, 7.

109. Ibid., 6. This is the subject of Herzog's 1985 article "God-Walk and Class Struggle," also included in *Theology from the Belly of the Whale: A Frederick Herzog Reader*, ed. Rieger.

110. Actual encounters with the underside leave no doubt that conflict as such is a painful reality in the lives of those without power and not, as some critics have suspected, an ontological necessity for liberation theology. This often repeated critique is also perpetuated in a more sophisticated way by John Milbank, *Theology and Social Theory* (Cambridge: Basil Blackwell, 1990).

texts of the church occupy a new function. They are no longer just objects to be questioned; they also raise questions. Herzog puts it this way: "We are not reading the texts of the early church as much as the texts are reading us. We need to be shaken in our modern self-security."[111] Yet, as the discussion of the Lacanian symbolic order has also shown, texts in themselves do not necessarily reconstruct the power of the modern self if they are allowed to cover over the conflictual history of self and other, and if no attention is paid to their own mechanisms of repression. For this reason, the postmodern "turn to the text" does not necessarily solve the problems of the modern self. The critical forces of the biblical text are only effective when they are applied within the actual context of concrete involvement with the other. This process is most clearly visible in the light of the Eucharist, where the authoritative texts are read and both the self and the marginalized other meet at the table, and text, self, and other illuminate each other in the context of Christ's presence.

The *psycho-critical dimension,* finally, serves as a reminder that religion has often provided opium for the people, generating the type of authority structures that cover up and preserve existing power structures. In the psycho-critical dimension it becomes most clear that the new concern for praxis, located on the underside of history, is not at all interested in the reduction of theology to action. What ultimately counts is not "what you *do.*" The point, and in this both Freud and Lacan suggest themselves once more as crucial interlocutors for the project of a theology from the underside, is to find out where one's desire is located, what authors the Christian life, in Herzog's words, "where your head is and where your heart is."[112] What is at stake is a conversion in which the converts, learning the truth about themselves in the double encounter with Christ and the marginalized, join in a transformation of authority structures that includes a transformation of their innermost desire. This calls for a constant process of conversion that includes not only the self but also the structures of the texts of the church.

The Struggle for Truth: Reason

Reflecting on Christian faith in light of the underside of history, the doctrines of the church gain new importance. In this setting, Karl

---

111. Herzog, GW, 7.
112. Ibid., 10. Herzog quotes Matt. 6:21: "Where your treasure is, there is your heart also."

Barth's concern for true doctrine still provides an important theological paradigm. But in Barth's *textual* struggle the *contextual* questions, having to do with social location and the power of the self over the other in concrete historical situations of oppression, are not adequately addressed. The relation of classism and racism, for instance, to the distortion of church doctrine is not yet part of theological reflection.[113]

In the encounter with the underside a new understanding of the task of theology emerges. According to Herzog, theology is no longer motivated by "the need for a coherent worldview" but by "the battle between truth and untruth in God's struggle for justice."[114] In other words, the theological search for the truth of the doctrines of the church is less interested in replacing one worldview with another than in finding ways in which God's truth can break through into the present. Herzog warns that "ideas are dangerous illusions unless they are rooted for Christians in the God-walk that lies at the base of all Christian unity."[115] Becoming aware of the repressions of the underside, we understand better than ever before that it is easy to fool oneself in matters of God and theology.

This approach amounts to a fundamental reconstruction of modern reason. While reason in North American theology has often been understood on the grounds of a philosophical tradition that, based on trust in the powers of the modern self, affirms the power of the knowing subject over the object of knowledge, Herzog suggests that "reason does not have to be grounded in the knowing subject. It can also mean the perception of an Other which is not controlled by the subject."[116] As I have argued throughout, the perception of the divine Other cannot be separated from the perception of the human other who cannot be controlled by the self. In the relation with the repressed other, modern reason is reconstructed from the bottom up.

Here reason is no longer in control, no longer authoritative in the sense that it alone authors and authorizes Christian thought. Reason becomes "co-reason," judging Christian praxis in light of the otherness of God's praxis. Herzog's conclusion, which can be found also in the work of Gustavo Gutiérrez, is that "reason can think God. But it

---

113. Herzog, GW, 36: "Barth does see the power struggle going on all the time. But he does not make it central in God's own God-walk."

114. Herzog, JC, 97. Cf. also Herzog, GW, 36f.

115. Herzog, GW, 36. An epistemological issue is involved here as well: "If we do not struggle together with God..., we do not notice God at all. That is why God is so dead for many." Herzog, JC, 117.

116. Herzog, "Dogmatik IV," 113.

limps after God's self-realization."[117] Rather than grasping God, reason is grasped by God.

The Authority of Scripture

Theology from the underside is aware of a double movement in which we read the Scriptures and they read us. In Herzog's words, "The primal function of the Bible is its power, which, together with the realpresence of Messiah Jesus in the eucharistic meal, brings the corporate Christian community into being."[118] In creating a community of readers from all walks of life, the Bible initiates encounters with the oppressed other in which authority can no longer be separated from the question of power. If authority is relocated, therefore, at the point where the Bible reads us, so as to include the other as well, this will have implications also for a relocation of power.

As Herzog learned early on in his encounters with African Americans in North Carolina, the Bible needs to be read *in via*, on the way. Christian thought does not start with an ominous "leap of faith," or a leap into the texts, but with the call to follow Christ, the call to align ourselves with God's own praxis, which includes a special concern for those on the underside of history.

The authority of the Bible, and the traditional claim to its primacy among the four elements of the quadrilateral, becomes most obvious where it reshapes the lives of its readers. Scriptural authority has to do with the power to redirect the social location of the followers of Christ. It is for this reason that Herzog can claim that "the authority question is turning more and more into the social location question."[119] Herzog's constant emphasis on social location might in fact be better expressed by a term such as *social relocation,* which makes clear the nomadic character of social location in following Christ and avoids the static character of the notion of "location." The church, the "ecclesia," those who are "called out," is made up of those who are called to relocate, to give up the secure location of their own self in the encounter with the human other and the divine Other.

Scriptural authority in the interplay with the other dimensions, the power of the Bible to "read us," is therefore not aimed first of all at the revelation of doctrine or at the distillation of ethical principles but at authoring the Christian way of life.

---

117. Ibid., 114. Herzog coins the term *co-reason* in GW, 33.
118. Herzog, GW, 38.
119. Ibid., 41.

Accountable Teaching: Tradition

The inversion of mainline theological methods in the encounter with the underside locates what is often seen as the proper theological endeavor, the development of Christian teaching and the formation of Christian tradition, at the end of the process. Yet the fact that theology is a second step does not mean that it is a secondary step.

Doctrines, the teachings of the church, no longer arise primarily in theological committees that work at the symbolic-order level where, especially when its ties to both social location and Scripture are weakened, tradition can easily function "as a 'free-floating' authority base."[120] Doctrine can no longer be developed on the synchronic levels of the text alone, as postliberal theology and others seem to argue today. Neither can it be grounded in the pulsations of the modern self. In touch with the underside of history, Herzog realizes that "the true 'creeds' of today are bled out of the sufferings of the martyrs in the church of the oppressed."[121] This constructive move implies a critical one as well since, in the encounter with people on the underside of history, the process of the formation of doctrine is constantly reminded of its limits. Authority cannot ultimately be secured by the constructs of the text alone. Tradition is no longer sufficient to grasp God.

Theology must not give up on the ongoing formation of Christian tradition. This is of particular importance in the United States, where theological structures are not as clear-cut as elsewhere.[122] Herzog discerns two traditions especially relevant to North American Protestantism: the Reformation tradition and a tradition of liberation, the latter taking shape in both Americas. The liberation tradition, shaped by the oppressed, thus is acknowledged as part of the spectrum of authority, one authorizing factor in the development of new doctrine. Theology needs to pay attention, for "traditions different from our own help us come to a healthy self-critique."[123]

---

120. Ibid., 45.

121. Frederick Herzog, "Reformation Today," *Christian Century* 99:33 (October 27, 1982), 1079.

122. Cf. Frederick Herzog, "Kirchengemeinschaft im Schmelztiegel — Anfang einer neuen Ökumene," in *Kirchengemeinschaft im Schmelztiegel*, ed. Frederick Herzog and Reinhard Groscurth (Neukirchen-Vluyn: Neukirchener Verlag, 1989), 67. Explaining the North American situation to German readers, Herzog refers to Sidney E. Mead's observation that the great failure in North American Christianity is its lack of theological structure.

123. Frederick Herzog, "Kritische Spiritualität," *Evangelische Kommentare* 17:10 (October 1984), 567. Cf. also Herzog, "Kirchengemeinschaft im Schmelztiegel," 66, and Herzog, "Praxis Passionis Divini," 565.

A crucial shift has taken place. Encountering the marginalized, theology is no longer the property of specialists, whether they operate "from below" or "from above." Formation of church traditions happens in communities of Christians that no longer exclude the other. Theologians need to understand that "no single person can hope to turn the tide. This is the time for the whole people of God to stand up and move church and society in a new direction."[124] The lay movements in the church are a sign of great hope.

The Liberation and Relocation of Authority

How do all these elements go together? Herzog concludes that there is no "neat formula for arranging scripture, tradition, experience, and reason in sequence." What matters is "that these factors work together in a particular empowerment of human beings."[125] It is not in philosophical frameworks but in basic Christian communities that the fundamental dynamics in which these elements are tied together are discovered. The base communities that Herzog has in mind "tend to root themselves in the eucharist, take Bible study seriously, examine tradition critically in terms of the option for the poor, and shape experience within the dynamics of these factors, so that reason knows what it needs to doublecheck."[126]

A brief summary of the four elements of theological authority — Scripture, tradition, experience, and reason — in terms of their interrelationship will help us lay the ground for a concluding reflection on theological method and authority. The authority of Scripture is central, but implies a critique of the notion of authority as domination. Authority becomes "authority as partnership,"[127] in the interplay with the other criteria, drawn together at the Eucharistic table where the self and the other, rich and poor, oppressors and oppressed, meet. In the sense that the Scriptures are not only God's "Wordpresence," authoring Christian praxis, but also the human reception of God-walk, there is no absolute distinction between Scripture and tradition. Between Scripture and tra-

---

124. Herzog, "Reformation Today," 1080. Herzog suggests a change in perspective: While the priesthood of all believers was discovered in the Reformation, today we are discovering the layhood of all ministers, the self-understanding of all Christians as *laos*, people of God. Frederick Herzog, "Pfarrer als Laien Gottes," *Evangelische Kommentare* 15:10 (October 1982), 537.

125. Herzog, GW, 50.

126. Ibid., 52.

127. Ibid., 215 n. 60. Herzog refers to Letty M. Russell, "Authority and the Challenge of Feminist Interpretation," in *Feminist Interpretation of the Bible*, ed. Letty M. Russell (Philadelphia: Westminster, 1985).

dition a continuing process of mutual correction is going on in light of
God's own identification with those at the margins. Experience, therefore, no longer stands on its own as the property of an individual, the
modern autonomous self. Having itself been shaped in the encounter
with Scripture and tradition, it stands in creative tension with these
"texts" by relating to that conflictual relationship of self and other in
the modern world that is often covered up. This kind of experience "directs us back to *scripture* in order to change certain *traditions.*"[128] The
last element, reason, is no longer the place from which theology is generated or where it is grounded, but simply the place where the other
criteria are interpreted and sorted out.

From this a number of circular relationships emerge that can be
seen as spirals and in which the different elements are authorizing each
other: Starting with Christian experience of God's praxis with the poor
and oppressed at the Eucharist and the enlistment in that praxis, Scripture and tradition are reread and interpreted. Reason keeps the process
in balance, indicating that the reading of Scripture and tradition are
not just addenda to experience but, in turn, motivate, shape, and inform experience and praxis. Another spiral could be imagined that is
somehow intertwined with the former and captures the primary authority of Scripture: Scripture's authorizing of Christian praxis is confirmed
and historically described in tradition. Both are then screened by the experience of God's work of liberation, and the whole process is examined
by reason for consistency.

Nevertheless, these spirals must not be seen as evolutionary models.
What keeps them moving is not the universal spirit of progress, which
guarantees the success of the modern self, or the metonymical flow of
the sacred texts, which covers over real-life suffering, but God's revolutionary involvement on the underside of history, which engages human
sin, thus constantly reconstructing structures of power and authority.

If in the participation with God's praxis on the underside of history
something like a "canon within a canon" emerges in which God's option for the poor and God's justice are highlighted, this is not to be
understood in the sense of yet another systematic principle in control
or a set of dogmatic concepts elevated to a higher level. Any such focus
must be inextricably connected with, and springs from, the Christian life
in the continuing process of self-correction within Scripture, tradition,
experience, and reason.

The relationship of praxis and theory, an important impulse generated

---

128. Herzog, GW, 32. This is the element that is largely missing from Barth's theology.

in the encounter with the underside of history, runs right through the criteria themselves. Experience implies the practical solidarity with the poor
and oppressed on the underside of history, social relocation according to
God's social location. The resulting theory part has to do with the critical analysis of church and society in socio-critical, historico-self-critical,
and psycho-critical terms. The practical element of reason concerns the
participation in God's own praxis and struggle for truth in history. It is
only on these grounds that the theoretical challenge, the discernment
of truth in double-checking the other criteria, can be approached. The
authority of Scripture is established in communal reading, in solidarity
with the marginalized, and in the Eucharist and its power to relocate
Christian praxis. Out of this practical involvement with Scripture grows
a dynamic understanding of its heart. Finally, the formation of tradition
grows out of the historical praxis of the church in tune with God's praxis.
In regard to its theoretical function, it is the construction of a framework,
determining the boundaries within which theology and praxis move.

This relationship of praxis and theory, rediscovered on the underside of history, is not structured as a hierarchy. No doubt, praxis enjoys
a much more prominent role here than in many traditional theologies. Yet even affirmations of the "primacy of praxis" refer not to a
temporal distinction, which would elevate praxis to the status of an absolute starting point, but to a logical distinction, according to the logic
of God's own praxis, discovered in the formation of theology and the
church from the bottom up. Still, there is never "pure praxis" in a priori
fashion. Praxis is always informed by, and interdependent with, theory.
Ultimately, the practical element helps to overcome the closures of the
text and of the self: "Because of the new praxis we will have to learn
a new language,"[129] writes Herzog. We have seen how his own theology
was transformed in the encounter with the African American struggle
for liberation.

A reconstruction of authority occurs "on the road" that cannot easily be fitted into the old theological dichotomy of from below and from
above: "Whenever we fix our eyes on this God, we see also the poor."
And, vice versa, when we encounter the poor, we also become aware
of God's holiness.[130] In other words, the affirmation of God's Otherness
is somehow tied to the affirmation of the otherness of people on the

---

129. GW, xx.
130. The first point is emphasized in Frederick Herzog, "Luther and Liberation," *Christian Century* 97:33 (October 29, 1980), 1036, and the second aspect is central in Frederick
Herzog, "Hat die reiche Kirche ein Gewissen?" *Evangelische Kommentare* 13:10 (October
1980), 571.

underside of history. Both perspectives must not be played off against each other. The Lacanian analytic process shows how that balance might be kept. Even more important, Lacan also shows how to resist the constant temptation to conflate the Other and the other, that process in which the other is romanticized and integrated into the powers of the text, releasing in turn the powers of the self from their responsibility for the other (see chapter 3). In Herzog's own words: "The new thing does not burst upon us as 'a step of logical thought.' Liberation theology begins as the poor begin to listen to each other before God. Liberation theology continues as we listen to the poor before God."[131] Theology will not encounter the Other without the other, but neither will it encounter the other without the Other.

In the end, Herzog's project remains humble, realizing that "dogmatics obviously can deliver only a few things." What dogmatics can do, however, is "make clear the mandate of resistance to empire-domination over church and society at the point where God is used to bless America — as empire."[132] In clarifying the misuse of Christian authority in justifying unjust power structures, theology is redirected to a reinterpretation of authority that, ultimately, leads to a new understanding of power, where power is taken away from the selves and texts and, in surrendering to God's power, redistributed to those at the margins with whom God freely identifies.

Conclusion

Discussing the Lacanian real, we have observed its function as a limit which helps reconstruct the authority of the universe of the text as well as the universe of the self. The place of the real needs to remain open; it can only be filled temporarily. In similar fashion, theology as reflective enterprise needs to become aware of its limits in order to remain open to God's work. As we have seen, these limits become clearest in the encounter with those at the margins about whom Jesus cared. Ultimately, as Herzog reminds us, Christian self-limitation has to do with God's own self-limitation in Jesus Christ, who joined humanity on the underside.[133]

Theology in touch with the oppressed does not need to end up as one more special interest theology built on the claim that oppressed

---

131. Herzog, GW, xxii.
132. Ibid., 216 n. 65.
133. Frederick Herzog, "Vernunft der Weisheit," *Evangelische Kommentare* 18:10 (October 1985), 553.

people now own God, no matter what. While there is always the danger that those who are used to being in control appropriate God and Christ for their own purposes, things look somewhat different on the underside of history. In one of his last articles Herzog rendered this more explicitly: "What the theologian needs most is to see God. Yet God will not be seen where the divine can be controlled." Here people on the underside introduce a different perspective. "The poor, as such, do not demonstrate God, and yet they are the place for us to 'see' God. How can this be?" A partial answer to this fundamental question is that "the poor cannot be controlled."[134] In the encounter with the marginalized, a new window into the work of God opens in unexpected ways. Theology is transformed in a new encounter with God beyond the control of the powers that be. It is in this sense that the oppressed function as teachers, being aware at the same time that their authority is only a borrowed one. We are now able to appreciate the crucial position of the marginalized without immediately identifying them with Christ.

Theology in touch with the underside, deconstructing the securities of other theological approaches and refusing to develop more hegemonic solutions, is all about a new openness of the human being to God rather than about yet another attempt to appropriate absolute power and authority. In the encounter with the margins, Herzog learns the truth of Karl Barth's insight that "the revolutionary must...own that in adopting his plan he allows himself to be overcome of evil. He forgets that he is not the One, that he is not the subject of the freedom which he so earnestly desires."[135] Here is the fundamental difference between a theology of revolution and a theology in touch with the position of the marginalized. Only where our own limits are clear can the power of Christ be identified.

At the same time, a theology that limits the authority of the texts of the church and the modern self does not have to end up in relativism. Herzog suggests a new understanding of authority in which the Scriptures are still the primary source, but tied to listening to God's own praxis on the underside of history, a process identical to the dynamics that have produced the biblical texts themselves. Lacan has given us a model that helps understand some of the dynamics at work in the encounter with the underside of history. At a time when postmodernism celebrates relativism and the end of the authority of the self, he has

---

134. Frederick Herzog, "Athens, Berlin, and Lima," *Theology Today* 51:2 (July 1994), 274.

135. Herzog, LT, 213, 214.

shown how alternative structures of authority might work. Lacan sees no need to completely abandon the notions of truth and a referent, which otherwise seem to have become obsolete with postmodernity. Authority is now restructured in relation to the real, related to those who have thus far been excluded from the powers of the self and of the text. Truth is relational rather than relativistic. The notions of referent and truth are now tied to that which is repressed, the underside of history.

All would go wrong, however, if those who are currently in the place of the real other, the marginalized, would start to develop yet another system and provide absolute guarantees for truth. The only situation that would, in fact, be worse than what we have at present would be if the powers of the text or the self were able to use the other, the oppressed themselves, as a token for their own systems. The place of the real must, ultimately, remain open. Yet since opening up the place of authority seems close to impossible for theologies based on the power of the self and the power of the text, there is a very real danger that the oppressed are adapted once more as warrants of theological systems. When modern theology is pushed to deal with the oppressed, there is the constant temptation to put them in the place of the authority of the modern self. Many orthodox and even postliberal models often reinforce rigid forms of textual authority by dealing with poor people as recipients of charity or as objects to be integrated into the world of the text.

Herzog's work leads beyond the impasse in contemporary theology due to his willingness to listen to the lessons from the periphery and the various liberation traditions, black, feminist, and "third world." In broadening the circles of the liberation dynamic beyond the southern United States, a constant reorientation of theology has been initiated, affirming the classical purpose of theology: the rereading of the biblical and doctrinal traditions of the church, its symbolic appearance, in light of new encounters with the Spirit (cf. John 16:12–14). Redistributing authority and power within the church in these ways, a new self emerges that begins to realize the mutual interdependence of self, human other, and divine Other. As Lacan has shown, only where the mechanisms of the oppression of the other are clear is a nonhegemonic identification with the other possible and, the theologian might add, with the Other as well.

Regarding the binary opposition of modern theologies and their critics, addressed in the first chapter, the view from the underside of history adds a new perspective. Opening up the rigid authority structures of the self and of the text, the other does not assume final authority but points away from itself, exposing the structures that put her in place, and pointing to the place of ultimate authority, which belongs to God and can, therefore, never be filled out permanently. Here both the text and the self can be taken more seriously in their actual theological authority since they no longer have to bear the weight of ultimate authority. In this process, North American Protestantism might have to face its first Reformation yet.[136]

---

136. Dietrich Bonhoeffer's description of Protestantism in the United States as a "Protestantism without Reformation" is well known. See Dietrich Bonhoeffer, "Protestantismus ohne Reformation," in *Gesammelte Schriften*, vol. 1 (Munich: C. Kaiser, 1958), 323–54.

Chapter 5

Encountering the Poor in Latin America

THE COMMITMENT to the poor of Latin American liberation theology is well known. Some elements of its terminology, for instance, the "preferential option for the poor," have become widely used in theology and the church, although frequently without much sense of their implications. In North America, for example, this option has often been misinterpreted as favoring a certain kind of special interest theology, a theology mainly of interest to people on the underside and their friends. Others use it in terms of charity. In order to understand the meaning and significance of the Latin American encounter with the poor for North American theology, we need to see it first of all as it emerged in its own context.

In this chapter I will outline the implications of the encounter with the underside of history for Latin American theology. Once again, the vision for the future will need to grow out of a look at those encounters throughout the past three decades up to the present.

Approaches to the Poor

Between the Text and the Other

It is often overlooked that a theology that takes the poor seriously does not have to fall into the common trap of liberal and modernist theologies, which tend to subordinate the study of the sacred texts of the church to the experiences of the modern self.

While the encounters with the underside of history lead to new insights into the biblical text, the study of biblical texts remains a crucial factor in its own right.[1] In fact, biblical texts provide the

---

1. Cf. Gustavo Gutiérrez, *Caridad y amor humano* (Lima: UNEC, 1966), later taken up in Gustavo Gutiérrez, *A Theology of Liberation: History, Politics, and Salvation*, Revised 15th Anniversary Edition, trans. Sister Caridad Inda and John Eagleson (Maryknoll, N.Y.:

framework for the initial encounters with the other in Latin America. Early on, Gutiérrez's reflections on texts of both testaments lead to the conclusion that "to be Christian is to love," that "to love is . . . to change the center, to establish as center the other, the thou" and that "encountering the neighbor I encounter God."[2]

In Gutiérrez's work, another framework for his initial encounters with the poor of Latin America is provided by modern European theological paradigms. The Christocentric perspective of the Second Vatican Council is the general backdrop.[3] As the council has argued, and this is crucial for all subsequent encounters with the poor, the love for the divine Other and the human other come together in Christ. The theology of Yves Congar goes one step further and provides another clue when he talks about the relationship to the other in sacramental terms, determining what he calls the "sacrament of our neighbor" as a "paradoxical sign of God." Along those lines, Gutiérrez refers also to the philosopher Emmanuel Levinas, who puts things most strongly when he says that in the neighbor we encounter "God who is deep down in the heart of each person."[4]

What is lacking in most of those modern theological and philosophical paradigms, however, is a closer understanding of the actual character of this encounter with the other. Writing in Peru rather than in Europe, Gutiérrez slowly becomes aware that the neighbor is not only the individual "thou" but "a person situated in economic, social, cultural, and racial coordinates." He begins to understand that the neighbor "refers to the exploited social class, the dominated people, the marginated."[5] The conflictual character of the "real," one of the major insights of a theology that enters into the actual contact with the oppressed, is noticed only gradually. Modern theology, even where it creates an opening for the other, is never quite able to get rid of the blindness of the modern self for the tensions that are produced in its relation to the other.

Gutiérrez's insight into the conflict between the self and the other signifies a crucial step beyond the modern mind-set. What has been a nonissue in modern theology and philosophy is not necessarily the

Orbis, 1988), 106–16 (abbreviated: TL). The discussion of a great number of biblical texts in *Caridad y amor humano* from the outset dispels the suspicion, often repeated, that liberation theology would be grounded only in a few token texts, such as Matt. 25:31–46.

2. Gutiérrez, *Caridad y amor humano*, 31.

3. Cf., e.g., Gutiérrez, TL, 30.

4. Congar is quoted in ibid. 230 n. 39; for Levinas, see ibid., 116.

5. TL, 116.

person of the other as such, but the actual struggle between self and other in which (as Lacan has shown) the self assumes its powers by repressing the other.

Beyond Elitism and Populism

Modern theology initiates a reconstruction of the ecclesiocentrism in which the church was caught up for centuries. According to modern Roman Catholic theology, the power to save is no longer with the church but with Christ. And, since Christ cannot be restricted to the church, the realm of salvation is extended into the world. Theology now includes the reflection on, and evaluation of, what is going on in both church and world.[6]

While the perspective of modern theology allows for the insight that God can be encountered in the other, actual encounters with poor people introduce a new perspective. In the Latin American setting the impoverishment of the masses can no longer be overlooked. More specific encounters with the plight of the masses soon call into question modern theology's rather unspecified reference to the "other." Which other are we talking about? This fundamental concern for the common people on the underside, rather than for just anybody whom the modern self happens to choose as its conversation partner, is at the basis of Gutiérrez's debate of the possibility of salvation inside and outside of the church. Reflecting on God's work outside the church among the common people, Gutiérrez sets himself apart from modern theology, which tends to get stuck in a certain elitism. At the same time, he also sets himself apart from a certain type of concern for the masses found in Christendom that, while reaching out to the people, fails to listen to them, since theological authority is exclusively located in the hands of those within the church who have access to the texts.

It is with the Latin American masses in mind that Gutiérrez appropriates the opening of the church to the world that the Second Vatican Council promotes. Two things are related in this process: a process of personalization and a collective process of socialization.[7] Both elements are directly opposed to the ongoing objectification of the other, perpetuated in different ways by the modern self and the power of the text.

A new element that distinguishes theology in touch with the poor from other theological approaches, whether traditional or modern,

---

6. Gustavo Gutiérrez, *Líneas pastorales de la Iglesia en América Latina* (Lima: CEP, 1970), 57–61.

7. Cf. ibid., 68, 62.

arises early on in the process. While modern theologies have developed
effective critiques of the church establishment where traditional theologies often tended to offer little critique, the encounter with the poor
calls for a *self-critical* look at the church.[8] Theology itself and the self of
the theologian, encountering the other on the underside of history, are
now included in the critique.

Discovering the Theological Challenge of Poverty and the Poor

At the same time, another crucial impulse takes shape. Broad segments
of society and even entire continents are becoming aware of their poverty. In this new situation poverty can no longer either be spiritualized
or, with a certain fatalism, be left to the merciful acts of the church.
Theology begins to understand that actual poverty refers to a subhu-
man condition that produces, in Gutiérrez's words, "a sundering both of
solidarity among persons and also of communion with God."[9]

In this context Gutiérrez begins to reexamine the special concern
for the poor in the Gospel. Going back to the biblical texts, he finds
that the poor hold a special place in God's economy. The well-known
passages in Matthew 25 are joined by many others of both testaments.
In the Lucan version of the Sermon on the Mount, for instance, the
poor are called blessed. They are blessed because with the coming of
Christ the kingdom of God and the reversal of their situation have already begun.[10] In other words, the option for the poor is not grounded
in the goodness of the poor but in the goodness of God. To call the
poor blessed does, therefore, not mean elevating them into a status of
absolute authority. Any theological authority attributed to them at all
rests in God's own authority. It does not compete with it.

Theology is transformed where the poor are no longer either romanticized or misrecognized, mechanisms through which the modern

---

8. See ibid., 26.

9. Gutiérrez, TL, 168. Gutiérrez, ibid., 171, distinguishes three meanings of poverty:
real poverty, spiritual poverty, and poverty as "a commitment of solidarity and protest."
The most important reference to this distinction on an official level can be found in
the documents of the Medellín conference, for example, in the section titled "Poverty of
the Church," English translation in *The Church in the Present-Day Transformation of Latin
America in Light of the Council*, official English edition of the documents of the Latin
American Bishops' Conference in Medellín (Bogota: General Secretariat of CELAM,
1970). Despite the support of Pope John XXIII, the theme of poverty did not get into the
documents of Vatican II. Gutiérrez finds support in the works of Pie-Raymond Régamey,
O.P., R. Voillaume, Paul Gauthier, and Jacques Dupont. See TL, 251 n. 6 and 252 n. 12.
The work of the latter will be influential also later on in Gustavo Gutiérrez, *The God
of Life*, trans. Matthew J. O'Connell (Maryknoll, N.Y.: Orbis, 1991), chapters 6 and 7
(abbreviated: GL).

10. See Gutiérrez, TL, 170, 171. Reference to Luke 6:20.

self gained much of its identity and power. Gutiérrez begins to realize that "the 'poor' person today is the oppressed one, the one marginated from society, the member of the proletariat struggling for the most basic rights; the exploited and plundered social class, the country struggling for its liberation."[11] Here a fundamental shift takes place. The poor are no longer merely objects of charity, as in traditional theology. As oppressed and marginalized, they challenge established structures of power and authority. But, as we will soon see, they do not establish their position according to the model of the modern self.

At this point the modern mind-set, exemplified by the Second Vatican Council, which talks about the church in a world that is coming of age "and describes it in a way designed to reduce tensions and smooth down rough edges," breaks down.[12] In solidarity with the oppressed, theology realizes for the first time the conflictive character of the relationship between the modern self and the subdued other, gradually understanding the truth of Gutiérrez's statement that "to be with the oppressed is to be against the oppressor."[13]

The newly found solidarity with the oppressed initiates two things: a better understanding of mechanisms of oppression and a process of transformation. As Lacan has taught us, those who are oppressed are instrumental in unveiling the truth about oppressive forces, a truth that is not available any other way. Even the analyst does not have access to truth apart from solidarity with whatever is repressed in a given situation. This is why the poor are the teachers, as Latin American liberation theology soon discovers. Second, solidarity with the oppressed also leads to a rewriting and reconstruction of the hegemony of oppressive powers, tied to either the self or the text or both, initiating a process in which the powers of the self and the text are put to new use. Other forms of relating to the other that do not give an account of the other as oppressed will no longer do.

The concern for the other of modern French theology and philosophy does not give enough attention to this issue. Neither Congar nor Levinas, despite all the inspiration each seems to have provided for Gutiérrez, pays much attention to the question of who put the other in place. By the same token, the support of rich "first world" churches for the churches in the poor countries is always in danger of toning down

---

11. Ibid., 172.
12. Gustavo Gutiérrez, "Contestation in Latin America," in *Contestation in the Church,* ed. Teodoro Jiméz Urresti (New York: Herder and Herder, 1971), 41.
13. Gutiérrez, TL, 172.

the challenge of the underside of history if it shuts out the question of how the poor are still calling the rich to account.[14]

Relating to the other by means of charity or sympathy ultimately leaves unchallenged those deceptive realisms of the self or the text. By turning the poor into objects of charity, their challenge is lost. At the same time, romanticizing and idealizing the poor will not reinstate their challenge either. If it is not seen that the oppressed point to what is fundamentally wrong with the current construction of power, no real transformation will be possible. Equally important, increasing solidarity with people on the underside of history will have a profound impact on the reconstruction of theological authority as well.[15]

Liberation Theology

Gutiérrez introduced the term *theology of liberation* in 1968, a couple of months prior to the Latin American Bishops' Conference in Medellín. The basic problem is formulated in this way: "As Christians come in contact with the acute problems that exist in Latin America, they experience an urgent need to take part in solutions to them," yet if they do this without "a reexamination of their own basic doctrinal principles," they are left with a form of action that is "ultimately sterile."[16] We have seen that modern theology can easily end up this way. The distinction of planes model, the theology of revolution, and the theology of development all display similar problems since they do not offer a theological reflection "*from within* the liberation process."[17] Christian commitment

14. Cf. Gutiérrez, TL, 255 n. 50.

15. Gutiérrez, ibid., 173, points out that "only authentic solidarity with the poor and a real protest against the poverty of our time can provide the concrete, vital context necessary for a theological discussion of poverty." This sentence, however, cannot be found in an earlier version of this text in Gutiérrez, "Pobreza Evangélica, Solidaridad y Protesta," *Víspera* 5:24–25 (December 1971), 3–14. Osvaldo Mottesi, "An Historically Mediated Pastoral of Liberation: Gustavo Gutiérrez's Pilgrimage towards Socialism" (Ph.D. diss., Emory University, 1985), 61, is not quite correct when he concludes that up to this point one cannot find any strictly original thought in Gutiérrez's work. Mottesi, ibid., 62, is right, however, that "the increasing historification of [Gutiérrez's] reflection is the result, not the cause of his growing option for the poor as victims of injustice."

16. Gustavo Gutiérrez, "Toward a Theology of Liberation" (1968), in *Liberation Theology: A Documentary History*, ed. Alfred T. Hennelly (Maryknoll, N.Y.: Orbis, 1990), 62. This talk, delivered in Chimbote, Peru, has made history. In it the basic definition of liberation theology is given that Gutiérrez will pursue in the following decades. From here, the notion of liberation makes its way also into official documents of the church, most notably the Medellín documents. Cf. the account of the development of the "liberation theme" in Hugo Assmann, *Theology for a Nomad Church*, trans. Paul Burns (Maryknoll, N.Y.: Orbis, 1985), 45–56.

17. Gutiérrez, "Liberation Praxis and Christian Faith," in Gustavo Gutiérrez, *The Power of the Poor in History*, trans. Robert R. Barr (Maryknoll, N.Y.: Orbis, 1983), 44 (abbreviated: PP).

can no longer stand on its own but needs to be seen together with theological reflection.

We need to realize that the activism of the autonomous self of modernity and its motto "Just do it" is not able to settle the power and authority crisis in Latin America, especially if basic theological principles are not reexamined. Remember Lacan's warning that no real change can take place on this basis since the activism of the self is not able to transcend its own purview. In other words, old masters will only be replaced by new ones. The fact that the new masters, the current neoliberal tendencies in Latin American politics and economics, have not improved the lot of the poor supports my argument. The modern self's gain in power and authority is not designed to trickle down. The opposite phenomenon, however, is equally problematic where, as in traditional Christendom, theological decisions seem to hover above praxis and the Christian life. Although deeming itself in control of praxis, this mode of theology is never completely unaffected by the praxis that dominates at a given time and, thus, often ends up unconsciously perpetuating established structures of power and authority. The shortcomings of a theology based on the activism of the self cannot be overcome, therefore, by returning to the realm of theological truth claims developed on seemingly neutral ground.

For these reasons, Gutiérrez suggests new ways of interrelating theology and praxis. While Christian praxis in solidarity with the poor helps to open up the rigid world of Christendom, such praxis "must be accompanied by a reflection to orient it, to order it, to make it coherent, so that it does not lapse into sterile and superficial activism."[18] Theology is now redefined as "critical reflection on Christian praxis."[19] This definition includes a self-critical moment since the activist self, where it participates in theological reflection on praxis in solidarity with the poor, can no longer avoid taking a good look at itself.

In this way, theology "fulfills a liberating function for humankind and the Christian community, preserving them from fetishism and idolatry," on the one hand, the problem of theologies grounded in the power of the text, "as well as from a pernicious and belittling narcissism," on the other, the perennial problem of modern theology based on the mod-

---

18. Gutiérrez, "Toward a Theology of Liberation," 64.

19. The definition of theology as critical reflection on praxis is first formulated by Gutiérrez in "The Meaning of Development," a talk presented in Cartigny, Switzerland, in 1969, published in *In Search of a Theology of Development* (Geneva: SODEPAX, 1970), 116–79, and later renamed "Notes on a Theology of Liberation." A shorter essay under this name can be found in *Theological Studies* 31 (June 1970), 11–16.

ern self. As a consequence, the identity of the theologian will have to
change, from being the ideologue either of the modern self or the ecclesial texts, to becoming an "organic intellectual" whose reflection is tied
to specific social locations and historical contexts on the underside of
history.[20] Only then will theology be able to integrate the powers of the
self and of the text in more constructive ways, making room for God's
own praxis.

The Lacanian analysis of authority further puts things into perspective. At stake is not the abandonment of the established elements of
theology — concern for the self and the texts of the church — but
a new way of interrelating them. The proponents of the texts of the
church need to understand that leaving the texts to themselves has
often led to the formation of realisms in tune with the status quo. By
"sinking roots where the pulse of history is beating at this moment," the
ecclesial texts are reconstructed and, in turn, put to new use in "illuminating history with the Word of the Lord of history."[21] In this sense
the texts of the church exercise their authority most constructively at
the point where they give up absolute control and tie into the present
reality of Christian praxis. In this process, the powers of the text are
reconstructed.

What is still not quite clear at this point, however, is the notion of
Christian praxis and how it differs from the praxis of the modern self.
No wonder that liberation theology could easily be misunderstood in
the United States and other "first world" contexts as one more version
of modern theology, proposing yet another method of correlation.[22] We
need to reflect further on the difference of praxis in general and the
praxis that grows out of the underside of history. The basic challenge
is slowly becoming clear. The encounter with the poor leads first of
all to a "serious self-examination...occurring in the very midst of the
Church."[23] Critical reflection is on the way to self-critical reflection.
The self is no longer in control.

The first insight into the challenge of the poor grows out of an
awareness of economic, social, and political processes. This is what
Gutiérrez calls the "first level of liberation." On this level the poor make

---

20. Gutiérrez, TL, 10. For further reflections on the notion of organic intellectual see
below, chapter 9.

21. Ibid., 12.

22. Craig L. Nessan, *Orthopraxis or Heresy: The North American Theological Response
to Latin American Liberation Theology* (Atlanta: Scholars Press, 1989), 13, compares Latin
American liberation theology to Paul Tillich's method of correlation and, on 39, to Rudolf
Bultmann's "famous...insight that exegesis without presuppositions is not possible."

23. Gutiérrez, TL, 79. This is the purpose of the final part of TL, 79–173.

a real difference, for liberation "has to be undertaken by the oppressed themselves."[24] In regard to the second and third levels of liberation, however, having to do with humanity and the religious aspect, things are not yet as clear. The second level, somehow lacking Gutiérrez's critique of modern developmentalism, which seems to apply only to the first level, draws a rather general picture of human emancipation, starting with René Descartes. It is not clear how the reality of marginalized Latin Americans figures in. Even the focus of the third level is mostly about what the church and theology can do for the poor rather than on what the poor can do for the church.[25]

Reshaping Theology from the Underside

From the Viewpoint of the Poor

The Latin American Bishops' Conference in Medellín in 1968, where Gutiérrez served as a theological adviser, marked a major turning point in the encounter with the poor. Here the Latin American Church started to get more closely in touch with its own context. While the Second Vatican Council spoke about underdevelopment, playing down the conflicts of the modern world, Medellín dealt with the problem from the viewpoint of poor people and their actual struggles.[26]

The year 1968 was also a watershed moment in a broader sense for Latin America. In the structural crisis of the capitalist system in Latin America, which many date around 1967, popular movements gained momentum. Pablo Richard recalls that while up to that time the middle class was the agent of change (for instance, through the Roman Catholic Social Action movements), around 1968 "the popular classes as a whole began to make themselves felt: proletariat, subproletariat, peasants, and Indians."[27] What happens to theology once it starts to listen to the voices of the people?

Gutiérrez's work with the dynamics of popular movements in the church places him in a new context where, even many years later and despite this being a reencounter with his own roots, he still feels as if he

---

24. Gutiérrez, TL, 57.

25. For this paragraph cf. ibid., 24, 19–20, and 68–71.

26. Pablo Richard, *Death of Christendoms, Birth of the Church: Historical Analysis and Theological Interpretation of the Church in Latin America*, trans. Phillip Berryman (Maryknoll, N.Y.: Orbis, 1987), 145, points out that while the First Plenary Latin American Council in 1899 was still nothing more than the application of the First Vatican Council to Latin America, in Medellín the issue was no longer the application of the Second Vatican Council but its interpretation in the light of Latin American reality.

27. Ibid., 148.

is taking his first steps. Here he learns that "the first thing to do is to listen. Listen endlessly to the human and religious experiences of those who have made the sufferings, hopes and struggles of this people their own."[28] The methodological reversal of theory and praxis that is born here is not the intellectual discovery of any particular theologian but arises out of the encounter with the underside itself.[29]

In this process the "evangelizing power of the poor" is gradually discovered. If this is taken seriously, theology becomes, as Gutiérrez says, "a hermeneutic of the hope of the poor in the God of life."[30] This statement needs to be seen on the background of my earlier discussion of the redistribution of power and authority on the underside of history, keeping in mind that this is not a reversal in which poor people move into the place of ultimate authority and become the measure of all things. Quite the opposite: A hermeneutic of the hope of the poor teaches to reshape power and authority and to give up their absolute and ultimate forms.

While Gutiérrez may be the first to bring the notions of liberation and theology together in writing, others embark on the same project. To the modern Western interpreter this has often looked like a certain lack of originality (tied to numerous discussions about who "really" came up with the theology of liberation first). Yet originality is not what the new theology is after. It is not concerned with the production of another best-seller on the market of so-called genitive theologies, but with listening to the suffering of the Latin American people. In this sense, theology from the underside signals the end of the theologian as an autonomous, modern self. Theology no longer starts with the genius of its authors. Even the old claim that theology from the underside came into being at a time of euphoria and triumphalism, encouraged by romantic illusions of a few radicals, completely misses the reality of the solidarity with people on the underside of history. Pablo Richard puts it best: "From the viewpoint of the poor and of the exploited classes, there never has been any liberationist, triumphalistic, and euphoric period."[31]

These dynamics give rise to the notion of the preferential option for

---

28. Gustavo Gutiérrez, "The Task of Theology and Ecclesial Experience," in *The People of God Amidst the Poor,* ed. Leonardo Boff and Virgil Elizondo (Edinburgh: T. & T. Clark, 1984), 62.

29. Cf. also Richard, *Death of Christendoms, Birth of the Church,* 147, 148.

30. Gutiérrez, "The Task of Theology," 64.

31. Richard, *Death of Christendoms, Birth of the Church,* 153. Jeffrey Klaiber, S.J., *The Catholic Church in Peru, 1821–1985: A Social History* (Washington, D.C.: Catholic University of America Press, 1992), 300, seems to overlook this issue. Cf. also Gustavo Gutiérrez, "Theology from the Underside of History," PP, 200.

the poor that gives coherence to the document of the Latin American Bishops' Conference in Puebla in 1979.[32] While the way to Puebla was dominated by an interesting alliance of conservatives and modernists over against liberation theology that shows the convergence of the powers of the self and of the text over against the painful presence of the other, Puebla is the proof that the voice of the popular Christian movements and of the related theological challenges cannot easily be defeated. Awareness of oppression keeps growing: The role of women in the church is addressed for the first time (no. 9), and indigenous peoples and Afro-Americans are identified as the poorest of the poor (no. 34). Whereas Medellín, eleven years earlier, had noticed the mute cry for liberation, Puebla notes that "the cry might well have seemed muted back then. Today it is loud and clear, increasing in volume and intensity, and at times full of menace."[33]

The new thing, displayed in the texts of both Medellín and Puebla, is their concrete interest in the poor, accounting for the basic contrast with the traditional church, which often has a "concern for the poor," but only if "it does not raise any questions."[34] Taking into account the viewpoint of the poor leads to a "circle of evangelizing." In Latin America, those who announced the Good News to the poor are now themselves evangelized by the poor.[35]

Interpreting Liberation Praxis

In Latin America people on the underside — Gutiérrez lists "exploited classes, despised ethnic groups, and marginalized cultures"[36] — are gradually becoming involved in theological reflection themselves. At this

---

32. See Puebla (nos. 1134–65), English translation in *Puebla and Beyond: Documentation and Commentary*, ed. John Eagleson and Philip Scharper (Maryknoll, N.Y.: Orbis, 1979). Enrique Dussel, *A History of the Church in Latin America: Colonialism to Liberation*, trans. Alan Neely (Grand Rapids: Wm. B. Eerdmans, 1981), 236, argues that "this text follows most closely the direction begun in Medellín, which actually saved the whole Puebla Conference from irrelevancy." Klaiber, ibid., 315, shows that "the Peruvian delegation in particular helped to make the 'preferential option for the poor' a key point at Puebla." Even though liberation theologians were excluded from the conference, several bishops invited them as private consultants. For an in-depth study of the preferential option for the poor in the context of theology and the church in Latin America see Julio Lois, *Teología de la liberación: opción por los pobres* (San José: DEI, 1988).

33. Medellín no. 2 and Puebla no. 89. In the Puebla document a vivid description of the poverty of the great majority of Latin Americans can be found (cf. nos. 31–40).

34. Gutiérrez, "Liberation and the Poor: The Puebla Perspective," PP, 154.

35. See Gutiérrez, interview in *Theologie der Befreiung im Gespräch*, ed. Peter Eicher (Munich: Kösel Verlag, 1985), 35, 36.

36. Gutiérrez, "Liberation Praxis and Christian Faith," PP, 37. Women are not yet mentioned at this point.

point a deeper understanding of the preferential option for the poor emerges. This option means, according to Gutiérrez's interpretation of the parable of the Good Samaritan, that the neighbor is no longer defined in terms of the self, for "as long as I define my neighbor as the person next door, the one I meet on *my* way ... my world will remain the same."[37] In order to overcome the debilitating blindness of the modern self (which appropriates the other for its own purposes), a social relocation is necessary. The perspective of the underside of history serves as a reminder that orthopraxis or relief actions, as well as reformist, developmentalist, or moralist approaches to theology, based on the powers of the modern self and leaving unchallenged the symbolic order, will no longer do.

In this context the concern for Christian praxis is developed further. Gutiérrez puts strong emphasis on the fact that the reconstruction of both societal and theological concepts "will be authentic only if it is taken on by the oppressed themselves."[38] The use of dependency theory, initially applied only at the political level of liberation (the first level), may illustrate what is at stake. If it is not situated within the framework of the lives of the oppressed, the attention to large-scale structures of dependence between "first world" and "third world" can easily serve as a cover-up of the many details that work together in oppressive situations. In the hands of the people, however, "it helped the popular class to reject the politics of compromise and conformisms" during the decade of the seventies.[39] Another example is the way the encounter with the poor helps reconstruct the second and third level of liberation. Gutiérrez begins to realize that, in regard to the human level of liberation (the second level), references to human dignity that ignore "the in-depth causes of the prevailing social order ... were totally effete and ineffectual."[40] The traditional Christian terminologies that make up

---

37. Ibid., 44. Reference is to Luke 10:36.

38. Ibid., 46.

39. Gutiérrez, "The Historical Power of the Poor," PP, 79. This argument parallels other critiques of dependency theory. Cf. also the later observation of 1988 in "Introduction to the Revised Edition" of TL, xxiv, that the theory of dependency "is now an inadequate tool, because it does not take sufficient account of the internal dynamics of each country or of the vast dimensions of the world of the poor."

40. Gutiérrez, "Liberation Praxis and Christian Faith," PP, 47. For this reason Gutiérrez prefers to speak of the rights of the poor, not of human rights. "This is to say, we do not wish to speak of rights in the liberal, bourgeois, and democratic sense, but in terms more biblical and more conflictual, too." Gustavo Gutiérrez, "The Voice of the Poor in the Church," in *Is Liberation Theology for North America? The Response of First World Churches* (New York: Theology in the Americas, 1978), 29. Furthermore, this perspective reconstructs the individualism of liberal rights language by taking into account

the religious (third) level of liberation need to be reconstructed as well. The Christian notion of peace is an example of how theological terminology can easily become a smoke screen where it hides actual conflicts and neglects the cry for peace of those on the underside in favor of the existing peace on the level of the status quo.[41]

Without immediate encounters with the world of the poor, references to dependency, praxis, and even the theological terminology of liberation can easily be drained of their meaning, or misinterpreted in terms of modern theology's concern for the power and the autonomy of the modern self.[42] The basic mistake is now clear: In the encounter with the poor and oppressed the notion of praxis can no longer refer to the activism of the modern middle-class self, which, in Gutiérrez's words, "does not call anything into question" since "it does not render the 'other' present on the scene but keeps him safely locked away in a closet."[43]

In the encounters with exploited classes, marginalized races and cultures, and, later specifically included, women, the notion of praxis is redefined. Understood this way, praxis is subversive by definition: "In the first place, we are talking about changing history, turning it on its head (*vertir*), and secondly, we are talking about a transforming historical praxis which comes from below (*sub: subvertir*-subversive)." Nevertheless, there is more to this praxis than subversion: "This subversive history is the place for a new experience of the faith, a new 'spirituality,' a new proclamation of the gospel."[44] As Lacan has taught

the communal aspect of the reality of the poor. Cf. Gustavo Gutiérrez, "The Violence of a System," in *Christian Ethics and Economics: The North-South Conflict*, ed. Dietmar Mieth and Jacques Pohier (Edinburgh: T. & T. Clark, 1980), 96.

41. See Gutiérrez, "Liberation Praxis and Christian Faith," PP, 48. "We have to learn to live peace, and think peace, in the midst of conflict."

42. Stanley Hauerwas, *After Christendom? How the Church Is to Behave if Freedom, Justice, and a Christian Nation Are Bad Ideas* (Nashville: Abingdon, 1991), critiques what he sees as liberation theology's alliance with modern theology. For an example in which liberation terminology is drained of its meaning see Paul E. Sigmund, "The Development of Liberation Theology: Continuity or Change?" in *The Politics of Latin American Liberation Theology*, ed. Richard L. Rubenstein and John K. Roth (Washington, D.C.: Washington Institute Press, 1988), 28. Sigmund feels that "for the academic theologian...what was exciting about liberation theology" has somehow to do with a general "rejection of abstract intellectualism." But this can also be found in modern theology.

43. Gustavo Gutiérrez, "Liberation Praxis and Christian Faith," in *Frontiers of Theology in Latin America*, ed. Rosino Gibellini (Maryknoll, N.Y.: Orbis, 1979), 24.

44. Gustavo Gutiérrez, "Statement by Gustavo Gutiérrez," in *Theology in the Americas*, ed. Sergio Torres and John Eagleson (Maryknoll, N.Y.: Orbis, 1976), 310, 311. Juan Luis Segundo has argued that this increasing focus on the praxis of the "other" has now come to occupy "the theological position that the social sciences and their instrumentality for deideologization held in [an earlier stage] of liberation theology." Segundo, "Two

us, in the encounters with the real, two aspects belong together: The real other both functions as an effective critique of the powers that be and, because it can never be completely subdued, is able to envision new horizons.

Poverty Means Death

From the middle of the seventies on the situation grows worse for the poor majority in Latin America. The crisis of the world economy, together with the consolidation of the position of the dominant classes in the newly emerging Latin American "national security" states, is working against the people. By now, the involvement of Christians in the struggles of the poor has led to persecution. In this context the awareness grows that poverty signifies death, "the poor 'die before their time,' from hunger or the bullet." But, as those in power soon find out, the poor cannot be kept down easily; even "their very corpses are subversive."[45] For this reason, corpses are hardly ever released and the true cause of death is always concealed.

The dominant sectors respond with continued spiritualization and idealization of poverty in order to silence the questions raised by the poor. This tendency can be observed even in certain public ecclesial texts like the Preparatory Document for Puebla that, weaving together modernist and traditionalist ideas in defense of Western Christian civilization (see chapter 2), cover up the concrete situation of oppression at a most critical time. As Gutiérrez notes, "Praise for the increased

---

Theologies of Liberation," in *Liberation Theology: A Documentary History,* ed. Alfred T. Hennelly (Maryknoll, N.Y.: Orbis, 1990), 365. Gutiérrez is cited as an example for the later stage of liberation theology that includes the work of Jon Sobrino, Enrique Dussel, and Juan Carlos Scanone. But while Segundo implies that Gutiérrez started out, in the earlier stage, at home in the intellectual world of the universities, Gutiérrez himself does not agree with this interpretation, pointing out that his theology grew out of the solidarity with poor people from the beginning. (Gustavo Gutiérrez, interview, 9/1/1993, in Lima.) Nevertheless, Segundo correctly discerns an important difference between the first two of Gutiérrez's books. If TL is compared to PP, he argues (ibid., 362), the latter is not "of the same intellectual quality," noting that a theologian in such close connection with the people "cannot present serious works, or better, works which would be considered weighty by other intellectuals." Segundo confirms my argument that the disturbing factor of the underside of history (and its praxis) is becoming more and more important in Gutiérrez's work. Another variation of Segundo's critique is Jeffrey Klaiber, "Prophets and Populists: Liberation Theology, 1968–1988," *Americas* 44 (July 1989), 3, who argues that liberation theologians, beginning their work in the early sixties as "thinkers with new and exciting ideas" end up as "populists" by the late eighties. Yet both images do not really fit: Liberation theology was never merely an "original abstract and utopian vision," nor is it now populist in the sense that the work of the intellectual, that is, critical reflection on praxis, drops out.

45. Gutiérrez, "The Historical Power of the Poor," PP, 89.

production rate observed in Latin America is followed by the affirma-tion that *'unfortunately'* we have not yet arrived at a more equitable distribution of income," adding, "we all know that this does not hap-pen 'unfortunately.' "[46] Here Gutiérrez uncovers the typical blind spots of both the powers of the self and of the text: In "making the people believe (and perhaps...themselves) that it is just a bad moment, a nightmare, that will soon pass,"[47] the representatives of the status quo do not have to deal with the seriousness of the situation. Poverty is understood as a problem to be solved sooner or later, and not in terms of a "symptom" (in the meaning that Lacan has given this term) that points to the truth that the powers that be have repressed and that keeps the unjust situation in place. The new perspective grows out of Gutiérrez's insight that "the poor person is the product, or byproduct, of an economic and social system fashioned by a few for their own benefit."[48]

The difference between a theology that listens to the poor and other theological perspectives transcends the level of ideas. Even in modern theology, for all its interest in the world and in history, the debate is often situated on religious terrain, and carried out in terms that address the question of theological authority but not issues of power. The mod-ern self's neglect of the actual conflict between self and other makes this approach possible. Liberal and conservative theology often meet on this level. Theology in touch with the marginalized, on the other hand, can no longer leave out actual power struggles. Gutiérrez put is this way: "Here, right from the start, the rift that separates persons is not a 're-ligious' one at all. Here the rift is between oppressed and oppressors — sharing the same faith, at least superficially. Here the breach is not reli-gious, but economic, social, and political."[49] It is not entirely surprising, therefore, that once people on the underside begin to assert themselves in the Latin American context, liberal and conservative theologies join forces against them.

In this situation "one of the richest and deepest phenomena" in contemporary Latin America arises, the birth of a new spirituality. Deepening its relationship with poor people, theology hits on the fact

---

46. Gutiérrez, "The Preparatory Document for Puebla: A Retreat from Commit-ment," *PP,* 117.

47. Gustavo Gutiérrez, "The Irruption of the Poor in Latin America and the Christian Communities of the Common People," in *The Challenge of Basic Christian Communities,* ed. Sergio Torres and John Eagleson (Maryknoll, N.Y.: Orbis, 1981), 109.

48. Ibid., 111. In this connection it is crucial that the official document of Puebla takes up Medellín's notion of "institutionalized injustice." See Puebla Document no. 1259.

49. Gutiérrez, "The Historical Power of the Poor," *PP,* 93.

that the poor are both oppressed and believing. Lacan has already made us aware of a paradoxical relation between oppression and a potential openness beyond the powers that be, which, in the Latin American context, manifests itself in the faith of the people. Within the context of oppression, spiritual movements arise that combine "a contemplative and mystical dimension — and a dimension of protest and social transformation."[50] Both aspects are mutually interrelated, thus preventing two common reductionisms: On the one hand, there is a spiritual reductionism that can be found not only in certain traditional approaches but in any number of religious populisms as well. Even "popular religion" must be read and reread, therefore, on the background of actual situations of oppression. On the other hand, there is "the reductionism of a political-action approach that ignores the reality of the people's faith (*for this, too, is idealism*)."[51] The two dimensions of a liberating faith and the capacity for revolutionary praxis must be seen together. Here is another indication of how closely authority and power are related.

Conversion to the Other: A Theocentric Event

Gutiérrez reminds us that "the Church is not involved in the question of poverty by the fact that it is present in a poor country. It is involved primarily and fundamentally by the God of the Bible to whom it wants to, and must, be faithful."[52] A central element in theology's encounter with the poor is the witness of the Gospel itself. As we have already seen, the privileged position of the poor in Jesus' message does not have to do with their inherent qualities but with God. "The Beatitudes are less a revelation about the poor than they are a revelation about God. They tell us who God is."[53] This point is extremely important for a new approach to theology and recalls a lesson that Lacan has taught us. At the point where the oppressed are idealized, the real is either lost or becomes incorporated into the "reality" of the powers that be. Idealizing the poor does a disservice not only to poor people but also to theological reflection. The place of the real itself must remain open.

Two things are implied here: a reexamination of the structures of the church in which "vested securities" need to be given up in light of the presence of God, and the development of an authentic praxis that relies on the "strength of the gospel, rather than on the powers

---

50. Ibid., 94. Cf. also ibid., 96ff.

51. Ibid., 98. Emphasis mine.

52. Gutiérrez, "The Poor in the Church," in *The Poor and the Church*, ed. Norbert Greinacher and Alois Müller (New York: Seabury, 1977), 11.

53. Gutiérrez, "The Historical Power of the Poor," PP, 95.

of this world."[54] These insights, formulated at the end of the seventies and early eighties, mark a progress in theology's encounter with the poor. Nevertheless, at this point it has also become more apparent that "today we are still strangers to the universe of the poor."[55]

In these encounters the church must enter a constant process of conversion, an insight that is not far from the Protestant concern for ongoing reform in the church, *ecclesia semper reformanda*. According to Gutiérrez, "this leads us to profound breaches and reorientations in today's church. But these breaches and reorientations will bear no fruit if they express only one's own personal anxiety, identity crisis, emotional reactions, and impatience" — in other words, the pulsations of the modern self. These changes "must be radical — that is, they must go to the root of the problem."[56] The root, in this case, is related to even deeper encounters between the self and the oppressed other, creating new openness to God's Otherness.

An important factor in this process of conversion is the recognition of the dialectic of oppressor and oppressed that modern theology, handicapped by its constant misrecognition of the other, is unable to see. The goal of this conversion, however, is not a simple reversal of the power struggle between self and others, where the oppressed would now establish themselves in the place of the modern self. As Enrique Dussel observes, in the process of liberation "the oppressor is not annihilated by the oppressed, but rather is humanized by the destruction of oppression itself." In this process, "the 'new historical person' is not a slave who has become a master, rather the slave and the master become *brothers*."[57]

By the same token, the "preferential option for the poor," formulated as a result of a continuing conversion of the church to the other, does not signify exclusivity. Gutiérrez talks about "the dialectic of a universality that moves from and through the particular."[58] He learns from the Peruvian writer José María Arguedas that true universality is not rooted in abstract concepts or in the innermost essences of selves, but is tied to the oppressed.[59] Only if the needs of the most needy are addressed will it be possible to proclaim the Gospel to everybody. In Lacanian terms: Where symbolic texts and imaginary selves are confronted with their

---

54. Gutiérrez, "Liberation and the Poor: The Puebla Perspective," PP, 157, 158.
55. Gutiérrez, "The Irruption of the Poor in Latin America," 110.
56. Gutiérrez, "Liberation Praxis and Christian Faith," PP, 70.
57. Dussel, *A History of the Church in Latin America: Colonialism to Liberation*, 241.
58. Gutiérrez, "Liberation and the Poor: The Puebla Perspective," PP, 128.
59. See Gustavo Gutiérrez, *Entre las calandrias: Un ensayo sobre José María Arguedas* (Lima: CEP, 1990), 52.

repressed truth, transformation becomes possible that is relevant across the board. In this process the special interests of the power of the text and of the self can be transcended and integrated into a larger whole.

Beyond Christendom and Modernism

Another Tradition of Liberation

In light of the history of the poor in Latin America and their particular struggles it becomes clear that "the movement of liberation that proceeds from 'the underside of history' is not purely and simply a continuation of the movement for modern freedoms."[60] In fact, the encounter of theology with the poor turns the modern mind-set on its head, initiating another tradition of liberation: "While the movement for the modern freedoms displayed aspects of distance from God and from the poor, the process of liberation that is now going on in Latin America is pregnant with new forms of closeness to the God of life and to the poor in their situation of death."[61] In Latin America the people, emerging as a collective subject, have found ways to combine their spirituality with their participation in the liberation process. While in Europe the working classes formed in the context of a secularized society, in Latin America, according to the Peruvian sociologist Catalina Romero, "the evangelical work of the Church and its choices in doctrine and practice have turned the Christian community and faith into an element of identity which contributes spiritual strength to the people's process of liberation and an opening to transcendency."[62] At the end of the eighties, Romero comments that even the Roman Catholic Church of Peru, once considered one of Latin America's most conservative churches, has become part of this process, as "one of society's main protagonists, a dynamizing factor in social change and element in the nation's cultural identity."[63]

Connected with the underside of history in their own ways, two twentieth-century Peruvian thinkers, José Carlos Mariátegui and José María Arguedas, lend support and credibility to a theology in touch

---

60. Gustavo Gutiérrez, "The Truth Shall Make You Free," in Gustavo Gutiérrez, *The Truth Shall Make You Free: Confrontations,* trans. Matthew J. O'Connell (Maryknoll, N.Y.: Orbis, 1986), 113 (abbreviated: TF).

61. Ibid., 116.

62. Catalina Romero, "The Peruvian Church: Change and Continuity," in *The Progressive Church of Latin* America, ed. Scott Mainwaring and Alexander Wilde (Notre Dame: University of Notre Dame Press, 1989), 264.

63. Ibid., 253. "The core of the change is the Church's option for the poor, and its novelty is to conceive of the poor as subjects in our continent's history." Ibid., 261.

with the poor. Through their own involvement in the suffering and hopes of the Peruvian people, both have come to understand the importance of the "religious factor" (Mariátegui's term) in the struggle for liberation. The crucial insight, formulated by Arguedas, is that the God of the masters and the God of the people are not necessarily the same.[64]

An increasing awareness of the potential of the poor, therefore, does not have to signal the end of theology but can lead to new theological sensitivities. Gutiérrez notes that to opt not to listen to the poor out of fear that the history of modernity may repeat itself "would be to display too mean-spirited an analysis of the situation and a lack of hope in the God who makes all things new."[65] The liberation of the Latin American poor no longer needs to be understood as an extension of the history of the modern self. Theology from the underside of history is part of the production of another tradition of liberation.

In 1990 Gutiérrez points out that his most important discovery in the past ten to twelve years has been of the "complexity of the world of the poor."[66] He has learned by now that "to be poor is also a way of feeling, knowing, reasoning, making friends, loving, believing, suffering, celebrating, and praying." Solidarity with the poor means "entering into their universe (in some cases remaining in it but now with a clearer awareness) and living in it. It means regarding it no longer as a place of work but as a place of residence."[67] Those pushed into the position of the real not only experience oppression, they also share a vision that is

---

64. Cf., e.g., Arguedas's novel *Todas las Sangres,* quoted in Gutiérrez, *Entre las calandrias,* 79. The shift from the "Dios inquisidor" of the powerful to the "Dios liberador" of the poor is the basic theme of Arguedas's book, a shift that is also taking place in Gutiérrez's theology. Cf. ibid., 7, 83. For Mariátegui's position on religion see José Carlos Mariátegui, *Seven Interpretive Essays on Peruvian Reality,* introduction by Jorge Basadre, trans. Marjory Urquidi (Austin: University of Texas Press, 1971), 124–52. Cf. also Gutiérrez, *Entre las calandrias,* 66–67, comparing Mariátegui and Arguedas. From Mariátegui, Gutiérrez learned, as Frei Betto has pointed out, "that technique of cultural cannibalism required to Latin Americanize all the theoretical baggage of his years of study." Frei Betto, "Gustavo Gutiérrez — A Friendly Profile," in *The Future of Liberation Theology: Essays in Honor of Gustavo Gutiérrez,* ed. Marc H. Ellis and Otto Maduro (Maryknoll, N.Y.: Orbis, 1989), 36, 37. Gutiérrez's personal friendship with Arguedas played an important role in his reimmersion in Peruvian culture after his years in Europe, where he studied at the Catholic University in Louvain, Belgium, from 1951 to 1955, graduating with a master's degree in philosophy and psychology. From 1955 to 1959, he was a student at the University of Lyons, France, graduating with a master's degree in theology, and from 1959 to 1960, he studied at the Gregorian University in Rome.

65. Gutiérrez, "The Truth Shall Make You Free," TF, 116.

66. Gustavo Gutiérrez, "Church of the Poor," in *Born of the Poor: The Latin American Church since Medellín,* ed. Edward L. Cleary, O.P. (Notre Dame: University of Notre Dame Press, 1990), 18.

67. Gutiérrez, TF, 10.

not available to those confined to the powers of the text or self. Only through close and personal encounters with people on the underside does theology finally become aware of this.

Even though the eighties and nineties have been decades of in-creased tensions in many Latin American economies, including state corruption, mismanagement, and growth of violence,[68] the people have not ceased to play a crucial role in the struggle for change. The follow-ing statement by Gutiérrez only makes sense in the context of what I have called "approaches to the real": "I can say, without using paradox, that I am now *more* optimistic . . . than I was twenty years ago. . . . What is new in Latin America in the last years is a different historical, social, and political consciousness among the poor . . . the grassroots organiza-tion of people . . . Christian base communities . . . efforts of many people to be committed to the truly poor . . . martyrdom."[69]

We can now lay to rest an old misunderstanding tied to the interpre-tation of the theological encounter with the poor in terms of the history of the modern self. It has often been argued that liberation theology in a first phase up to 1980 emphasized the political aspects of liberation whereas, from 1980 to the present, its concerns have shifted toward spirituality and the church.[70] This overlooks some of the most impor-tant lessons of the theological encounter with the poor, namely, the interrelation of spirituality and life, the interrelation of praxis and theo-logical reflection, and the interrelation of prophetic and contemplative elements.

In response to the question whether his ideas have evolved over time, Gutiérrez maintains that he still identifies with the basic issues of liberation theology "plainly and simply because they were and con-tinue to be less my own than those of the Latin American church and its basic ecclesial communities."[71] While some development is, as Gutiérrez knows, "quite unoriginal" because this happens to every theo-logian, I have shown how the specific form of this development has

---

68. Cf., e.g., the account in Jo-Marie Burt and Aldo Panfichi, *Peru: Caught in the Crossfire* (Jefferson City, Mo.: Peru Peace Network USA, 1992), 15ff. See also Americas Watch, *Peru under Fire: Human Rights since the Return to Democracy* (New Haven: Yale University Press, 1992).

69. Gutiérrez, "Church of the Poor," 21. This basic attitude has not changed even at the end of the nineties. Cf. Gutiérrez, "Liberation Theology and the Future of the Poor," in *Liberating the Future: God, Mammon, and Theology,* ed. Joerg Rieger (Minneapolis: Fortress Press, 1998).

70. This is repeated once more by Arthur Joseph McDonald, "The Practice and The-ory of Liberation Theology in Peru" (Ph.D. diss., University of Pittsburgh, 1993), iii, and serves as the basic thesis of his dissertation.

71. Gutiérrez, TF, 41.

been determined by ever closer encounters with the poor. Here a constant reorientation takes place whose theme, constantly reconstructing the tradition of the church, is a basic openness to the work of the Holy Spirit in historical manifestations on the underside (the "real" side) of history. It is precisely in this dynamic that new maps for the future of theology are generated.

The God of Life

Theology encountering the poor is not about putting prefabricated theological principles into praxis, nor is it simply about receiving an existential cry of help from those who have been neglected. The encounter with the poor leads to new theological impulses, starting with a new understanding of God in relation to the Christian life.[72]

The ongoing quest is how theology can be done while the suffering of the Latin American people endures: "From the unjust suffering of the poor emerges the question: Where is the God who is love? And that question continues to be the source of all that is being asked about God in our part of the world."[73] Out of her agony, a character in one of Arguedas's novels raises another crucial question: Who is God? Gutiérrez comments that "any other aspect of religion (doctrines, institutions, persons) is secondary."[74]

Who is God? Gutiérrez takes up James Cone's dictum that to raise this question is to ask what God is doing, adding that this does not mean that God's distance and transcendence would have to be played down. God is both the one who is close, establishing a covenant with the people, and the wholly Other. Theology from the underside needs to keep both aspects in balance.[75] Describing God's work from the

---

72. This question is worked out in two of Gutiérrez's more recent works. One is his book *On Job.* In the midst of the shattering of rigid doctrinal systems, of theology as a "dialogue of the deaf," Job meets God: "I once knew you only by hearsay, now my eyes have seen you." Cf. Gustavo Gutiérrez, *On Job: God-Talk and the Suffering of the Innocent,* trans. Matthew J. O'Connell (Maryknoll, N.Y.: Orbis, 1987), 21–23, 82ff. (abbreviated: *Job*). This encounter with God goes against a theology that becomes a substitute for reality and, ultimately, for God. Cf. ibid., 29. Gutiérrez's other book on this subject is titled *The God of Life.* The historical and social setting of this reflection on God in Trinitarian terms has to do, as Gutiérrez explains, with "the faith experience of the poor and oppressed that bursts into our lives and our theology." Gutiérrez, GL, xiii. The notion of the God of life goes against the dissociation of God from life and history, a problem of large parts of Latin American Christianity. See Gutiérrez, "The Irruption of the Poor in Latin America," 122.

73. Gustavo Gutiérrez, "How Can God Be Discussed from the Perspective of Ayacucho?" in *On the Threshold of the New Millennium,* special issue of *Concilium* (London: SCM Press, and Philadelphia: Trinity Press International, 1990), 104.

74. Gutiérrez, *Entre las calandrias,* 66, 67.

75. James Cone, *A Black Theology of Liberation,* referred to in Gutiérrez, GL, 2. Cf.

perspective of the Latin American poor, Gutiérrez comes up with an understanding of God as love, as father and mother, and as the source of our joy and commitment.[76]

Another closely related question is, *Where is God?* The purpose of this question, when raised on the underside of history, is not the construction of a metaphysical map but the desire to be near God. Here we learn that encounters with God's presence presuppose a search, for God is not necessarily where we want God to be. The claim that God is everywhere is a false universal, especially if it is assumed that God is everywhere as supporter and sustainer.[77] In the light of ongoing suffering and oppression it becomes ever clearer that the question "Where is God?" cannot be answered without answering the question "Where is your brother?"[78]

Obviously, these questions are not the questions of the modern self and its difficulty in believing in some authority outside of itself. The modern self's question is: "Is there a God at all?" Neither is this new search for God a simple rehash of the old theodicy question of classical doctrinal discourse. The encounter with the underside of history turns around the traditional theodicy question: The main focus is no longer on the question whether the existence of evil challenges the existence of God. The question now is how the existence of God challenges evil.

The oppression and injustice imposed on poor people are, therefore, no longer just matters to be dealt with in social or ethical frameworks. These issues touch on the center of the Christian faith, raising deeply theological questions and pointing to a new understanding of God. This is one of the fundamental differences between theology in touch with the poor and any theology that merely adds to its agenda certain social concerns.[79]

Theological reflection takes place, at this point, no longer on the basis of the identity of the self produced in the misrecognition of the other, as in much of modern theology, or by blind submission to some more or less absolute law, as in certain traditional theological alternatives. Theology grows out of a communal process in which

also Gutiérrez, GL, 27. This dialectic between God as judge and God as friend is also one of the themes of the book of Job. See Gutiérrez, *Job,* 65.

76. See Gutiérrez, GL, 1ff., 188.

77. This is explained in the context of a discussion of Arguedas's work. Gutiérrez, *Entre las calandrias,* 81. Cf. also Gutiérrez, GL, 80, and Gutiérrez, *Job,* 65.

78. Cf. Gen. 4:9. Gutiérrez, "How Can God Be Discussed from the Perspective of Ayacucho?" 112. Cf. also GL, 118.

79. Cf. Gustavo Gutiérrez, "Por el camino de la pobreza," *Páginas* 8:58 (December 1983), 12, 13, and 15 n. 64.

the relationship of self and other is reconstructed on the grounds of God's grace. This new identity has implications for the reconstruction of power as well. In Gutiérrez's words: "To the extent that the ecclesial community begets new persons thanks to a different kind of interrelationship — this is, to the real participation of all and to the respect of the life and freedom of the weakest that it promotes in its own midst — it creates a new style of human community marked by radically different ways of experiencing and understanding human power."[80]

Reconstructing Theological Method from the Underside

New theological impulses emerge where the issue of theological authority is reconsidered in the encounter with the other. New ways of approaching theological method evolve exactly at the point at which the powers of the text and of the self that have governed theology for so long are reconstructed in solidarity with the other.

Two elements help structure this section: According to Gutiérrez, the encounter with the poor introduces a "*freshness* or newness" into the theological process, marking an encounter with God. At the same time, however, he observes that the significance of the encounter with poor people is rooted in "the *continuity* that leads it to sink its roots deep in scripture, tradition, and the magisterium.'"[81]

Three Levels of Liberation

In the theological encounter with the poor, Gutiérrez distinguishes three levels. Unlike modern theology in the distinction of planes model, however, theology from the underside promotes also a strong sense of the unity and interrelation of the three levels, modeled according to the "unity without confusion" of the two natures of Christ.[82]

---

80. Gutiérrez, GL, 107.

81. Gutiérrez, "Introduction to the Revised Edition," TL, xliv. Emphasis in original.

82. Cf. the allusion to the Council of Chalcedon in Gutiérrez, "The Truth Shall Make You Free," TF, 122, 125. Gutiérrez, on 121, points out that, on the basis of this interrelation, liberation theology was the first to speak of "total and integral liberation." Many critics of liberation theology forget, of course, that Gutiérrez does indeed make a distinction. Cf., e.g., Karl Lehmann's and Yves Congar's point that in liberation theology this distinction of different levels is de facto no longer existent. See Karl Lehmann, "Methodisch-hermeneutische Probleme der 'Theologie der Befreiung,'" in *Theologie der Befreiung,* ed. Karl Lehmann (Einsiedeln: Johannes Verlag, 1977), 17–18. Gutiérrez's paradigm of the three levels has also found its way into the Puebla document. Cf. nos. 321–29 and no. 485. For a summary of the three levels of liberation see Gutiérrez, "The Truth Shall Make You Free," TF, 128–35.

The first level, combining political, social, economic, and cultural dimensions, is the subject of the social sciences. On this level the reality of social conflict leads to the struggle for a qualitatively different society. The second level is related to human liberation in terms of interpersonal relationships. On this level are constructed utopias, plans for a new society, and a new human being. The third level of liberation is the level of faith. While the second level is about the construction of a new human being, the third level refers to the new human being according to the Gospel. Here sin is uncovered and addressed in its deepest meaning as the breaking of friendship with God and others.

From this *third level* theological definitions must work their way back to the second and first levels in order to figure out their concrete and historical shape. Without constantly working through all three levels, traditional Christian terminology has little to say to those on the underside: "Liberation from sin does not matter without those [other] two modes of liberation." The poor, experiencing the power of sin first hand as a force that radically distorts their lives, push theology to the insight that "sin in the abstract does not exist, neither does charity in the abstract."[83]

Searching for relationships between the three levels, the *second level* is of special importance as a link between the first and the third: "Faith and political action will not enter into a correct and fruitful relationship except through the effort to create a new type of person in a different society, that is, except through utopia."[84] Gutiérrez argues that without this second level the other levels will either fall apart or will be confused and, either way, will end up in political or religious dogmatism. Lacan has helped us make sense of what encounters with the poor teach us in this regard: Without attention to the level of the self in relation to the other, oppressor and oppressed (Gutiérrez's second level), both social sciences (first level) and theological dogmatics (third level) tend to fall back into the free-floating construction of their own symbolic-order worlds.

Gutiérrez quotes Pope Paul VI in support of his position. The pope, endorsing the concept of the three levels, defines the second level as "a conception of human nature, an anthropology" on which libera-

---

83. Gutiérrez, "Marxismo y Cristianismo," in *Cristianos Latinoamericanos y Socialismo* (Bogotá: CEDIAL, 1972), 24. Gutiérrez cautions that this text, delivered as a speech and published from the notes of a listener, contains a number of mistakes. Gutiérrez did not have the opportunity to revise the text before publication. (Conversation of 4/21/97.)

84. Gutiérrez, TL, 138.

tion "is based."[85] At this crucial point, however, an approach from the underside differs much more strongly than Gutiérrez seems to admit. In the encounter with the underside of history, anthropological reflections are reshaped, no longer deriving primarily from a general anthropology of the modern self, but from the encounter of the self and the other. This is precisely the point of Gutiérrez's earlier comment that "the new human being... is that which emerges time and again in difficult situations."[86] Here modern theological anthropology, which defines the human being at the peak of its powers without much attention to how the other co-constitutes the self, is turned on its head.

Ultimately, the second level is practical at heart: "There is utopia from the moment at which there is a human being that is acting."[87] This level of praxis/utopia is the place where social science and theology, the first and the third level, enter into an encounter that replaces various older attempts at purely conceptual dialogues. Obviously, Marxian analysis (a socioscientific model that resonated strongly with the early struggles of the poor in Latin America) and Christianity do not produce exactly the same utopias. In this sense, their encounter is "an encounter of conflicts, of tensions," but also "of mutual enrichments."[88] Science and theology interact and modify each other on the basis of practical engagement for a new human being and a new society, where parallels as well as differences are discovered. Identification on the conceptual level, developing a common utopia, a common view of the human being (e.g., a Christian humanism or Christian socialism), is not necessary. In fact, such an identification could easily fall back into the production of yet another free-floating text, once more doing away with the dynamic of the relation of the self and other to which the encounter with the poor has opened our eyes.

The practical solidarity with human suffering where utopia takes shape simultaneously reflects and reconstructs scientific and theological insights. This is one of the crucial insights of theology from the underside of history in Latin America. In this connection of all three levels at the "second level," established at the very point at which the oppressed struggle for liberation, the system itself, supported by both the powers of the self and the powers of the text, is questioned.[89] The interrelation

---

85. Pope Paul VI, *Evangelii Nuntiandi*, quoted in Gutiérrez, "Introduction to the Revised Edition," TL, xl.
86. Gutiérrez, "Marxismo y Cristianismo," 25.
87. Ibid., 32.
88. Ibid., 30.
89. Despite its importance, this particular way of uniting the three levels is still little

of the first and the third level must always be worked out in concrete situations, on the underside of history. This is the approach taken in the interdisciplinary research in progress at the Instituto Bartolomé de Las Casas, founded by Gutiérrez in the mid-seventies.[90]

Idolatry and Death

What difference does the relation of the second and the third levels of liberation make for a new theological paradigm tied to the underside of history? While the distinction of the levels underscores once more that the encounter with the other need not be confused with the encounter with God, the relation of the levels serves as a reminder that in every encounter of self and other, oppressor and oppressed, on the second level an encounter with God takes place. Two things grow out of a new awareness of the relation of the second and the third levels, of humanity and God, which now includes the oppressed: the struggle for a new humanity and a new theological paradigm. The third level, faith, can therefore no longer be interpreted as strictly confined to an absolute, ideal realm.

In the encounter with the Latin American poor Gutiérrez learns that "the modern, bourgeois mentality is not overcome in ideological dialogue, but in a dialectical opposition to the social contradictions."[91]

understood. Robert McAfee Brown, *Gustavo Gutiérrez: An Introduction to Liberation Theology* (Maryknoll, N.Y.: Orbis, 1990), 104–6, for instance, simply gives a summary of the three levels and does not consider their interrelationship or their location within Latin American and Roman Catholic theology. Curt Cadorette, *From the Heart of the People: The Theology of Gustavo Gutiérrez* (Oak Park, Ill.: Meyer-Stone, 1988), 125, without even mentioning the three levels, leaves it at the following explanation: "The church, in a manner of speaking, is 'above' but not 'out' of politics." The most extensive discussion, which does, however, not do much more than summarize Gutiérrez's writings, can be found in Miguel Manzanera, *Teología y salvación-liberación en la obra de Gustavo Gutiérrez: Exposición analítica, situación teórico-práctica y valoración crítica* (Bilbao: Universidad de Deusto, 1978).

90. In an interview in Lima, 8/21/1993, Catalina Romero, a sociologist and coworker at the Instituto, explains that the interdisciplinary work at the institute is not based on one agreed-upon methodology but on a "revisión de hechos de vida," a reflection on what is going on. The fact that this reflection is based on a common praxis allows an interaction between different points of view that does not get stuck in simply adding up different perspectives, but leads to interrelations. The following summary contains all the elements of my argument in this section: "More than anything else, it is the system itself that is being called into question by the exploited, and it is impossible to live the faith outside the framework of this questioning. This is why the popular movement is also the locus of encounter of the social sciences and Marxist analysis with theology — an encounter, to be sure, involving criticism of theology, and an encounter undertaken within the dynamics of a concrete, historical movement that transcends individuality, dogmatisms, and transitory enthusiasms. Hence any and all intellectual terrorist tactics simply miss the mark." Gutiérrez, "Theology from the Underside of History," 192.

91. Gustavo Gutiérrez, "The Limitations of Modern Theology: On a Letter of Diet-

The "second level" of liberation is indispensable. Theology done on the third level alone, in terms of the opposition of believer and nonbeliever as in modern theology, "where the religious element creates a division among persons sharing the same quality of life and the same social world," is inadequate. In a North American context this "distinction of planes," implicitly assumed by modern "first world" societies, can easily be used to replace real-life conflicts with religious ones. It is quite telling that the religious culture wars of our time are fought almost exclusively on the third level. In Latin America, on the other hand, where "the oppressors and the oppressed share, superficially at any rate, the same faith," while "what differentiates them is precisely their economic, social, and political levels,"[92] splitting off the third level is even more dangerous since it reinforces the illusions of a false peace.

The question of theological authority gains new significance, therefore, where the relationship of the two levels is realized. It is precisely the encounter with those on the underside that reminds theology in North and South that authority and power are related. Christians who live in solidarity with nonpersons are, as Gutiérrez observes, "keenly aware of the conformist ideological role which the ruling classes assign Christianity." Here theology becomes more important than ever before. Yet the basic theological problem now is no longer atheism but idolatry, defined as "placing one's trust in something or someone that is not God, or playing on the ambiguity of asserting God with one's lips while actually seeking other securities and motivations."[93]

The encounter with the poor makes us aware that theology is a matter of life and death. In the sixteenth century Bartolomé de Las Casas realized that idolatry could lead to the deaths of thousands of Indians. The contemporary break of traditional and progressive theologies with the theology of liberation is, thus, not simply a theological break at the level of authority. There is also a break at the level of power. The reconstruction of authority in the struggle against the ideological distortions of the text and of the self goes hand in hand with a reconstruction of power. At the same time we must not forget that we can never achieve a complete reconstruction of power, since the place of ultimate authority remains open, in the hands of God.[94]

rich Bonhoeffer," PP, 232. Gutiérrez credits both Barth and Bonhoeffer with discerning "a glimmer of a dialectic in the history of the Christian faith."

92. Gutiérrez, "Theology from the Underside of History," PP, 193.

93. Gustavo Gutiérrez, *Las Casas: In Search of the Poor of Jesus Christ*, trans. Robert R. Barr (Maryknoll, N.Y.: Orbis, 1993), 440 (abbreviated: IS). Here the biblical critique of idolatry put forth by the prophets of the Old Testament assumes new life.

94. In Gutiérrez's words: "The gospel message is a message that can never be iden-

Whose Text? *The Church and the Reconstruction of Authority*

At the beginning of this chapter two elements were put in relation: change and continuity. The concern for continuity leads theology to sink its roots deep into Scripture, tradition, and the magisterium. Realizing not only that we read the Bible, but that the Bible reads us in turn, Gutiérrez reminds us "that the word of God issues its challenges. The scriptures are not a passive store of answers to our questions.... In many instances, our very questions will be reformulated."[95] Here is a strong contrast to modern theology, exemplified, for instance, by Paul Tillich, who argues that the existential questions that initiate the theological enterprise need to be formulated as if, for all practical purposes, the theological answers were not known.[96]

Many theologians in North America and Europe have been puzzled by Gutiérrez's close relationship to the Roman Catholic Church and its tradition, a puzzlement that is largely due to the false assumption that a radical theology in modern times must be opposed to tradition in principle.[97] Those who are under the impression that an encounter with the underside of history must lead to a complete rejection of any theological continuity tend to understand this as a conservative remnant in Gutiérrez's work.[98]

Even as Gutiérrez moves deeper into the world of the poor, close reflections on official writings of the church continue. In this way he often supports and further develops basic themes of liberation theology — for instance, the notion of the "preferential option for the poor," endorsed by the Puebla Conference in 1979 and confirmed by the Latin American Bishops' Conference in Santo Domingo in 1992. But even the two Instructions of the Roman Congregation for the Doctrine of the Faith

---

tified with any concrete social formula. The word of the Lord is a challenge to its every historical incarnation and places that incarnation in the broad perspective of the radical and total liberation of Christ the Lord of history." Gutiérrez, "Liberation Praxis and Christian Faith," PP, 69.

95. Gustavo Gutiérrez, *We Drink from Our Own Wells: The Spiritual Journey of a People*, foreword by Henri Nouwen, trans. Matthew J. O'Connell (Maryknoll, N.Y.: Orbis, and Melbourne: Dove, 1984), 34 (abbreviated: WD); cf. also Gutiérrez, *Job*, xvii–xviii.

96. See chapter 1.

97. As the French theologian Christian Duquoc, "Liberación y 'Progresismo occidental,'" in *Teología y liberación. Perspectivas y desafíos: Ensayos en torno a la obra de Gustavo Gutiérrez* (Lima: Instituto Bartolomé de Las Casas and CEP, 1989), 302f., points out, for European theology the critique of church and tradition by Latin American liberation theology appears too weak.

98. Cf., for instance, Alistair Kee, *Marx and the Failure of Liberation Theology* (London: SCM Press, and Philadelphia: Trinity Press International, 1990), who, reading liberation theology in classical "first world" Marxian terms, interprets Gutiérrez's interest in issues of religion and the traditional church as an inconsistency within liberation theology itself.

of 1984 and 1986, which offer a critique of "certain aspects of the theology of liberation," are appropriated by Gutiérrez as clarifications that contribute to the development of liberation theology.[99] This attitude, which is difficult to understand for North American readers socialized into the "ego's era," seems closely related to Gutiérrez's hope that a theology from the underside need not fall into the stardom of intellectuals and the oppositions of schools that ignore the people.[100] Theological discourse is always responsible to a communal reality and its texts.

The importance that Gutiérrez attributes to the textual reality of the church can be seen, for instance, in his critique of the assumption that the spirit of the councils of the church is more important than its texts. He is worried that by "avoiding the letter which kills," theology will give in to a false spiritualism. Arguing that "the spirit of the council is embodied in its texts," where "its bite for the present" is located, Gutiérrez envisions a reconfiguration of theology that transcends both the mood swings of the modern self and the ecclesiocentric tendencies of the text.[101]

Yet while Gutiérrez maintains the "primacy of the word,"[102] especially of the biblical word, he does not imply that the word is static. The encounter with the underside of history throws new light on the word and the texts: The role of the Bible in the communities of the poor is a case in point. Until the second half of the twentieth century the Bible was not even accessible for most Latin Americans, but now it is read especially by the poor. Here a crucial shift in the construction of authority takes place: The Bible is no longer the exclusive property of church officials, or of seemingly neutral specialists (as in much of Western university theology). The Bible is now read in the context of the communities of the oppressed, where its "bite for the present" is uncovered.[103] The decentering of the church implies a decentering of its texts in relation to a new center, God's work in Christ and the Holy Spirit in the life of those who suffer the most. The Bible must be read quite literally in the streets.

---

99. The 1984 Instruction considers the expression "liberation theology" to be valid and useful. Gustavo Gutiérrez, "Criticism Will Deepen, Clarify Liberation Theology," 1984 interview, published in *Liberation Theology: A Documentary History*, ed. Alfred T. Hennelly (Maryknoll, N.Y.: Orbis, 1990), 423.

100. See Gutiérrez, "The Truth Shall Make You Free," TF, 87 and 176 n. 9.

101. Gustavo Gutiérrez, *Vaticano II y la Iglesia Latinoamericana* (Santiago, Chile: Educación y Comunicaciones, 1985), 18 n. 38.

102. Gutiérrez, "The Truth Shall Make You Free," TF, 94.

103. See Gustavo Gutiérrez, *Revelación y anuncio de Dios en la historia* (Lima: Servicio de documentación del MIEC-JECI, 1977).

In this process, the biblical texts are wrenched from those who have often made their authority innocuous. But what is at stake here is not a simple replacement of the authority of modern selves (or of self-centered traditions) by the authority of the people. The point, as Gutiérrez clarifies, is a "rereading of the gospel message from within the praxis of liberation,"[104] where the Gospel is not only reread but also rereads those involved in liberation praxis. The central place of the Bible in all of Gutiérrez's writings[105] confirms the point that biblical texts unfold their authority on the underside of history where, in the critique of the false authority of selves produced on the back of others or of texts in the service of the powers that be, and without "facile direct applications," God's word may be heard. In the encounter of Job with his theologian friends this problematic is central: "His friends prefer to repeat ideas they learned in the past, instead of turning to the concrete lives of living persons, asking questions, and in this way opening themselves to a better understanding of God and God's word."[106]

The recovery of both Scripture and tradition is thus a crucial factor in reshaping theological reflection from the underside. In this context the traditional texts are important because they sustain those at the margins in ways in which the freewheeling pulsations of the self cannot. Conversely, however, the texts are also reconfigured by them, enlivening the tradition of the church. Gutiérrez knows that "the creative capacity shown by a poor, believing people, its spontaneous generosity, its facility for creating symbols and for demonstrating its feelings . . . are usually their only means of self-expression."[107] The texts of the church approved by the magisterium, especially Medellín and those of the Latin American church, are crucial: "I know very well that things are not limited to texts, but I also know that the texts express

---

104. Gutiérrez, "Liberation Praxis and Christian Faith," PP, 6.

105. Most notably in *Job*, which is the struggle with a book of the Bible in the context of human suffering, but WD and GL are centered on biblical reflection as well. Cf., in addition, TL and its impressive index of biblical quotations. This commitment to the interpretation of biblical texts is crucial in the later writings of Gutiérrez as well: From 1985 on, he has written numerous biblical reflections for the journal *Páginas*. See also Gustavo Gutiérrez, *Sharing the Word through the Liturgical Year*, trans. Colette Joly Dees (Maryknoll, N.Y.: Orbis, 1997), a collection of reflections on all three cycles of the Sunday lectionary readings.

106. Gutiérrez, *Job*, 27.

107. Gustavo Gutiérrez, "Speaking about God," in *Different Theologies, Common Responsibility: Babel or Pentecost?* ed. Claude Geffré, Gustavo Gutiérrez, and Virgil Elizondo, Concilium Series no. 171 (Edinburgh: T. & T. Clark, 1984), 31 n. 1.

experiences and provoke other [experiences]. And they also provoke resistance."[108]

The Poor and Theological Method

In the encounter with the poor, reflection on theological method comes at the end. At this point we need to take a systematic look at the methodological impulses born in those theological encounters with the underside. The reader of Gutiérrez's work soon gets tangled up in how to see together, for instance, such different elements as the three levels of liberation, the question of theory and praxis, discussions of different forms of rationality and of different modes of theology, and various sketches of hermeneutical circles. While it is not possible to solve all that within the confines of this section, I will take a look at the broad lines of the picture.

In the encounter with the underside, a new appreciation for praxis emerges. This concern does not set aside theoretical issues but integrates them into a new perspective. Thoughts arise in praxis settings, are formulated as hypotheses, and in this form are further tested in praxis. This interrelationship of praxis and theory as first and second act is one of the earliest and most genuine issues in the methodological development of the theological encounter with the other. Reconstructing theological authority in relation to the challenges of the praxis of those on the underside of history, Gutiérrez announces pointedly that "the poor person, the other, becomes the revealer of the Utterly Other."[109]

The Lacanian notion of the real can help us to understand better the implications of this crucial issue. It should be clear by now that Gutiérrez does not imply that the other would become the focus of ultimate authority, substituting for the function of the texts in orthodoxy or the function of the self in modernity. The basic achievement of the marginalized other is to create an awareness for the way in which authority is usurped by those in power and to initiate a new theological appropriation of the ecclesial texts and the modern self, leading to new attention to the word of God. Building solidarity with those on

---

108. Gustavo Gutiérrez, "Emancipación e identidad," in *Nuestra América frente al V Centenario: Emancipación e identidad de América Latina: 1492–1992* (Mexico City: Joaquín Mortiz, Planeta, 1989), 112. The critical power of the symbolic order can also be glimpsed in the case of the Indians' resistance, "which in spite of everything managed to preserve cultural traditions and keep alive our languages, which nourish the present and are a vital element in our identity." Gustavo Gutiérrez, "Towards the Fifth Centenary," in *1492–1992: The Voice of the Victims*, ed. Leonardo Boff and Virgil Elizondo (London: SCM Press, and Philadelphia: Trinity Press International, 1990), 3.

109. Gutiérrez, "Liberation Praxis and Christian Faith," PP, 52.

the underside of history, theological reasoning is liberated from certain "forms of idealisms that beset it."[110]

Here a language emerges in which contemplative and prophetic elements complement each other. Gutiérrez puts it this way: "Without prophecy, the language of contemplation runs the risk of detachment from the history in which God is acting and in which we encounter God." Encountering God's presence with the poor, theology can no longer afford to withdraw from the conflicts of everyday life. On the other hand, "without the mystical dimension, the language of prophecy can narrow its vision and weaken its perception of that which makes all things new."[111] Prophetic critique of the causes of suffering and destruction, tied to the relation of rich and poor, can only be worked out in light of the full range of God's promises.

As a result, theology must be a second step, following what Gutiérrez often calls "commitment" and "contemplation." Parallel to Frederick Herzog's vision, the two steps are tied together not in a hierarchical sense, as primary and secondary in terms of a temporal succession, but rather in a logical relationship in which mutual critique becomes possible. The justification of positions already taken is not the job of theology. While theology is enriched by praxis, it also feeds back into it and gives it new direction. Rethinking the relationship of praxis and theory in light of the underside of history is not just an abstract methodological issue, it turns out to be a matter of life and death: "What brought Jesus to his death, and is bringing his present-day followers to their death, is precisely the coherence of message and commitment."[112]

Gutiérrez is well aware that he is "not speaking of syntheses that are fully successful and without defects, but rather of a process whereby one achieves a diversified presence that is open to a variety of experiences and that progresses only amid setbacks."[113] In other words, theological method, as seen from the underside, is not the place for the construction of a new system in which some fundamental element could serve as the warrant for its universal truthfulness. The poor do not take up the place of the modern self as yet another Archimedean point. Lacan has made us aware that at the end of the self and of the normalcies of the text a neat system is no longer possible. The real does not emerge as synthesis of the imaginary and symbolic orders. It emerges rather at

---

110. Ibid., 60.
111. Gutiérrez, TL, 17. Cf. also Gutiérrez, "Speaking about God," 31. This is also an important issue in *Job*.
112. Gutiérrez, "Introduction to the Revised Edition," TL, xliii.
113. Ibid., xxxii.

the point of intersection of these different vectors, not in evolutionary fashion but in a revolutionary breakthrough, amid setbacks, gushing up through the cracks of (imaginary and symbolic) repressions.

Theology in touch with the poor develops a new vision of the relation of God and humanity. Like modern theology, it emphasizes that we cannot understand God in Godself. God can only be understood in relation to humanity. But Gutiérrez no longer talks in general about the relationship between God and the human being. He talks specifically about the relationship between God and the poor, as the location God freely chooses, inviting humanity as a whole to join those who hurt the most. In this connection, the constant tug-of-war between modern humanity and God in terms of authority and power is no longer at the center. In solidarity with the poor, humanity finds itself in a new position of listening.

The hermeneutical rupture that accompanies the theological encounters with the poor is, therefore, based on a new insight into the relationship between God and human being, a relationship that becomes most dense in Christology. In Christ's person, God and humanity come together. But Christ does not take on humanity in the abstract. Christ's own humanity, born in a stable and always in solidarity with those at the margins, must now be seen less in terms of the modern self and more in terms of suffering humanity.

Nevertheless, this hermeneutical rupture is relevant not only to those who are poor and suffer, but also to those who are rich and successful. As the French theologian Christian Duquoc notes, the viewpoint of the poor "brings to light," as well as reflects, "the rupture hidden in the success of a society like the European."[114] Here, the implications for mainline North American theology become clearer as well. The encounter with the poor, the oppressed, initiates a process of conversion for those who benefit from perpetuating and not noticing the subterranean ruptures of our societies.

Last but not least, theology in touch with the poor has to learn that it must not overestimate its reach. Gutiérrez rejects the question that would ask what the "concrete, actual impact of liberation theology" is at present. The two questions that need to be raised are, "What is the impact of the liberation process in Latin America today?" And, "What is the impact of the Gospel in Latin America today?"[115]

---

114. Christian Duquoc, in a discussion of Gutiérrez's work, published in Gutiérrez, TF, 19.

115. Gutiérrez, "The Voice of the Poor in the Church," 30.

Conclusion

The fundamental place of the preferential option for the poor in the faith of the church has been reaffirmed by the Latin American Bishops' Conference in Santo Domingo in 1992 over against the preparatory document which included a number of other "preferential options" — for family, laypeople, the evangelization of modern culture, and so on. Even though many forces now seek to restrict further theological encounters with the poor, their voice can no longer be ignored: "The cry of the poor which Medellín has noted and which Puebla has called 'clear, growing, forceful and, occasionally, threatening'... has today become deafening."[116]

Theology can no longer be a self-serving endeavor when it encounters the poor. In Gutiérrez's work, listening to the point of view of the poor leads back to a new concern for evangelization, the announcement of the Gospel. The concern for evangelization, often either played down or integrated into the status quo by theologies that have grown comfortable with the way things are, points to the hope that God will make a difference with regard to the powers that be, both in church and world.

In listening to the poor, the individualistic deception of the modern self, pretending to be independent from the other, is exposed. Already in the Old Testament, Job discovers an alternative path when, according to Gutiérrez, he "sees that commitment to the poor puts everything on a solid basis, a basis located outside his individual world, in the needs of others who cannot be ignored."[117] At the same time, the false realisms of the text are exposed as well: "We want to do theology from the 'other,' from a point outside of ourselves, that is to say, to recognize that until now Christianity has been linked with a culture, a race, and a certain way of production and, therefore, in great measure with a particular class."[118] In both cases, theology is profoundly reconstructed from the point of view of those at the margins.

Ultimately, the poor and oppressed themselves are the ones who announce the Gospel to the rest of the world. This is where Gutiérrez notes the greatest resistance of theology and the church, even among those who enjoy talking about social concern. What is at stake can be seen, for instance, in his discussion of the place of women: "The woman

---

116. Gustavo Gutiérrez, "Una agenda: La IV Conferencia de Santo Domingo," *Páginas* 18:119 (February 1993), 15.

117. Gutiérrez, *Job*, 48.

118. Gutiérrez, "Statement by Gustavo Gutiérrez," 311.

is praised in the abstract, but she is underestimated in the concrete."[119] This is a mechanism to which Lacan has called our attention as well. Since the powers that be cannot allow for an actual relation to the oppressed, they create the myth of such a relation and, idealizing those on the underside, make them a part of the system. As soon as those who are repressed make their presence felt, however, the powers that be react with further acts of repression.

This is precisely the situation of poor Latin American women who find themselves at the intersection of a number of different repressive structures, determined by differences of class, race, culture, and gender. At the same time, however, their role in the base communities is of increasing importance. Gutiérrez realizes "their sensitivity to the sufferings of others, their stubbornness in keeping commitments, their realism in approaching situations," as well as their greater creativity, energy, and courage,[120] traits that have nothing to do with their femininity as such, but with the fact that women are among the most oppressed.

These characteristics bear close resemblance to those of the Lacanian real other who functions as the stand-in for the real. Poor Latin American women, reclaiming their part in the construction of theological authority, impose real limits on the mystification of established authority and power structures, making sure that suffering and repression will not be simply explained away or covered up. In this, they contribute to a reconstruction of both modern and traditional theologies. Creating new relationships between the self and the other, they initiate a transformation of the modern self. Addressing and reworking the repressions of the text, they open the way for a re-formation of tradition. Nevertheless, these developments do not happen automatically. "The poor" or "the Latin American woman" in general, as both Gutiérrez and Lacan know, do not exist in and of themselves: Gutiérrez insists with good reason that "even the poor must make the option for the poor (I know many poor persons making the option to be rich)."[121] Poor people must learn to understand the peculiarity of their own position and how to make constructive use of it.

In this perspective an often criticized notion like "class struggle" is still of certain importance, not as a metaphysical concept or as an ideal,

---

119. Gustavo Gutiérrez, "La Mujer: Lo último de lo último," *Mujer y Sociedad* 11:44 (August 1991), 14. For comments on the difference between social sensitivity and acceptance of the poor as actors, cf. Gutiérrez, "Church of the Poor," 22.

120. Gutiérrez, GL, 166. Gutiérrez alludes to the creativity, energy, and courage of Peruvian women in an interview in *Somos* 537 (March 22, 1997), 15.

121. Gutiérrez, "Church of the Poor," 16.

of course, but as a description of the actual situation from the point of view of people on the underside of history. In light of theological systems that are unable to see the conflictual character of contemporary reality, owing either to the blindness of the self to the other, or to the mystifying tendencies of the text, the perspective of those on the underside is all the more important. What is lacking in much of mainline theology is not good intentions but an analysis of what is actually going on.[122] Those who are afraid that such an awareness of conflict would lead to hatred and to a simple reversal of the power struggle between the self and the other must be reminded that we are confronted with a structural problem that will only become worse when actual conflicts are played down.

In the encounter with the poor, a profound reconstruction of what it means to do theology has taken place. Gutiérrez summarizes: "What we care about is not a matter of having 'our own theology,' the way the petit bourgeois used to dream of having 'their own house some day.'" He knows full well that "such a dream does haunt the intellectual world."[123] Due to the fact that liberation theology is done primarily by history's nameless ones, it makes little difference whose name appears on articles and books. The modern self seeking to affirm itself has, therefore, little place in the production of theology from the underside.

Theology in touch with the poor raises questions that are often neglected by others in the field. Is it "possible and useful" to do theology in the midst of suffering and oppression? Realizing the power of theological reflection in Latin America, the question is answered in the affirmative. In this reflection people on the underside confirm their existence, initiating an ongoing process of rewriting theology. Gutiérrez notices the impact of closer encounters with the poor: "There is a difference, too, between our autocriticism today and that of yesterday. Today, we ask our questions with greater realism."[124]

Ultimately we need to be aware that, as Gutiérrez puts it, conversion to the other can only "follow an asymptotic curve: a constantly closer approach that can, however, never reach the point of real identification

---

122. For the notion of class struggle see Gutiérrez, TL, first English edition (Maryknoll, N.Y.: Orbis, 1973), 272ff., section titled "Christian Brotherhood and Class Struggle," rewritten in the 15th revised edition as "Faith and Social Conflict."

123. Gutiérrez, "The Historical Power of the Poor," PP, 91. Those of us at work in the fast-paced academic market of the United States don't need much explanation of this statement.

124. Ibid., 100. A reference to the "others" confirming their existence in reflection can be found on 102. For the notion of the power of reflection see Gutiérrez, "The Voice of the Poor in the Church," 29.

with the life of the poor."[125] In this sense, the relation to the poor is a continuing challenge for theology even when it affirms its concerns for the underside. At the end of the eighties, Gutiérrez concludes that the role being played by the poor themselves "will certainly be one of the richest veins to be mined by liberation theology in years ahead."[126] The challenge continues, tempered by the ever more pressing question at the end of the twentieth century of where the poor will sleep in the next.[127]

---

125. Gutiérrez, WD, 126.
126. Gutiérrez, "Introduction to the Revised Edition," TL, xxiii.
127. This is one of the major themes of one of Gutiérrez's latest essays, "Liberation Theology and the Future of the Poor," in *Liberating the Future: God, Mammon, and Theology*, ed. Joerg Rieger (Minneapolis: Fortress Press, 1998).

Part III

A PARADIGM SHIFT
IN THEOLOGY

I N THIS PART I will draw together the most important elements and terms of the theological paradigm shift introduced by the encounters with people on the underside of history. This part includes a theological reflection on history from the underside (chapter 6). North and South finally meet face-to-face in a chapter on power and authority in the Protestant North and the Roman Catholic South (chapter 7). The question of the relation of the eruption of the marginalized and the irruption of God develops the central themes for a new theological vision in a transcultural and transdenominational perspective (chapter 8). Chapter 9 deals with the overall shape of the new theology and the related transformation of those who produce theological reflection.

Chapter 6

A Theological Look at History
from the Underside

A Different View of History

ONCE THEOLOGY encounters the marginalized it can no longer be done in ahistorical fashion. Yet not just any theological reference to history as such will do. In certain ways the major approaches to history mirror the two major theological camps in North America and Latin America. Modern historical thought, by and large, tends to understand itself as presenting an objective picture of the past, the way it "really was." The dilemma of this position becomes clear in light of a growing sense of the limits of the modern self as historian. Since the social location of this self — its position in relation to the other — is reflected only to a very limited degree or not at all, the modern view of history is easily universalized and promoted as absolute truth. In recent years, postmodern perspectives have suggested alternatives. These perspectives do not necessarily claim to reconstruct what really happened. Here, past forms and events are added together less systematically in the construction of narratives, stories, and other textual realities, a process that resembles premodern approaches to history insofar as they are less concerned about objectivity and representation.[1]

Neither of those positions is of much help for a theology in touch with the underside of history. While marginalized people are not easily fooled by universal historical claims — they know full well that their histories differ from those written from the perspective of those in power — their histories do not need to fade away into the free-floating construction of reality of postmodern narratives either. Jacques Lacan's

---

1. Fredric Jameson, "The Cultural Logic of Late Capitalism," in Fredric Jameson, *Postmodernism; or, The Cultural Logic of Late Capitalism* (Durham: Duke University, 1991), 18, talks about postmodern historicism as "the random cannibalization of all the styles of the past." Cf. also the discussion of Sepúlveda's premodern approach to history in chapter 2 above.

notion of the real helps us to account for yet another way of dealing
with historical data. History, in this model, aims at a reconstruction of
the past in relation to the present in terms of the reappropriation of the
repressed parts of history.[2] History is no longer the recollection of past
events in general, as in modern historical thought, but the reconstruction of those events that have been covered up, thus opening the way
into the future.

In the encounter with the underside of history, repressed persons and
their stories of the past and the present, an alternative account to mainline histories is developed, which — whether modern or postmodern —
often tell only the stories of those who succeed. Historical study that
pays attention to what has been repressed will not only change the view
of the past but will also contribute to the transformation of the present.

The new historical perspective differs from mainline history as well
as from certain forms of contemporary postmodern historicism. As
Fredric Jameson has pointed out, "history is not so much a text," any
text, as the postmodernists claim, as "a text-to-be-(re-)constructed."[3]
The postmodern "turn to language," today even supported by many who
would like to go back to premodern modes of history, is not sufficient.
In reconstructing mainline historicism, theology does not have to fall
into the other extreme, adopting the view that any story that weaves
together elements of the past would be history. History, written in the
encounter with the underside (the "real"), is never completely subjected
to the power of the text or the self and thus may help to initiate the
transformation of both. This is the point of Jameson's aphorism that
"history is what hurts."[4]

To sum up: The newly emerging historical consciousness on the
underside adds an important impulse for rethinking theology because

---

2. In regard to the past "we teach the subject to recognize as his unconscious . . . his
history — that is to say, we help [the subject] to perfect the present historization of the
facts that have already determined a certain number of the historical 'turning-points'
in his existence." Jacques Lacan, "The Function and Field of Speech and Language in
Psychoanalysis," in Jacques Lacan, *Écrits: A Selection,* trans. Alan Sheridan (New York:
W. W. Norton, 1977), 52.

3. Fredric Jameson, "Imaginary and Symbolic in Lacan," in Fredric Jameson, *The Ideologies of Theory: Essays 1971–1986* (Minneapolis: University of Minnesota Press, 1988),
vol. 1, 107. A similar contrast exists in psychoanalysis between those who make "reference to the supposedly organic stages of individual development" and those who actually
undertake "research into the particular events of a subject's history." Lacan, ibid., 51.

4. Fredric Jameson, *The Political Unconscious: Narrative as a Socially Symbolic Act*
(Ithaca: Cornell University Press, 1981), 102. Jameson goes on: "This is indeed the ultimate sense in which History as ground and untranscendable horizon needs no particular
theoretical justification: we may be sure that its alienating necessities will not forget us,
however much we might prefer to ignore them."

it differs, on the one hand, from modern historicism, which, in its de-
scriptivist tradition, lacks a critique of the self of the historian as well
as a deeper understanding of the power of the text and of the power of
stories. History is, after all, part of an ongoing story that must be rewritten time and again. But, on the other hand, a look at history from the
underside differs also from a more "postmodern" historicism, which, owing to its antidescriptivist sentiment, fails to take seriously that which
has been pushed outside of the flow of given texts.

One caveat: If the modern self or the texts are no longer the ultimate arbiters of history, there is no end to the task of theology. If
history is understood as the reconstruction of repressed history, it can
only approach the real asymptotically and never be identical with it.
Marginalized people often know better than anybody else that the path
to truth is not mapped out in advance but must be built in the process.

Two Concepts of History

In modern North American theology there has been no lack of theologies interested in historical issues. Usually, these approaches see
themselves as alternatives to more philosophical and conceptual ways
of doing theology. The perspective from the underside, however, introduces a new aspect. In the encounter with the African American other,
Frederick Herzog begins to understand that we need to reflect more
specifically on how the historical task is to be approached. New questions emerge: "At whose bidding is the science of history done? What
if the science of history were largely a tool of the affluent, partly aiding
their conquest and control of the world?"[5]

Historical theology is in danger of falling into the traps of ideology when it lacks real-life context, Herzog tells us. The problem is, of
course, not really that the study of history would ever be completely
removed from real life but that its context is not subject to reflection.
If matters of context are not reflected, they tend to return through the
back door. At the same time, a greater awareness of context must not
be misunderstood to mean that any context is equally valid, as various postmodernists seem to conclude. Theological reflection on history
needs to pay attention to God's own context. Herzog puts it this way:
"History is not primarily a matter of recollection in turning to the past
in faith, or of turning to the future in hope, but of God's liberation

---

5. Frederick Herzog, "Liberation Hermeneutic as Ideology Critique?" *Interpretation*
28:4 (October 1974), 391.

breaking into the present through the coming of Jesus Christ."[6] History is created in God's acts of transformation.

In the Latin American context, the problem is less with historical theology turned ideological than with theology that is unhistorical to begin with. Yet merely historicizing the perspectives of traditional theology, as modern theology has done, is not enough. In his own encounters with the Peruvian poor, Gustavo Gutiérrez becomes aware of the contrast of two very different concepts of history, one of which is the modern evolutionary view of history according to which history is the celebration of the triumph of the modern self. A second type of history starts from the point of view of the other, the victims.[7]

The goal of theological attention to history that would be sensitive to the underside cannot be, therefore, merely to perpetuate from a different perspective the history of the victors who make it into the history books. History, as the history of God's liberation of the oppressed, aims at a reconstruction of the past in relation to the present in terms of the reappropriation of what has so far been repressed in the history of the victors. In this process, the course of mainline history is neither copied by those on the underside nor dissolved into pluralism and abandoned. It is rewritten.

A New Awareness of the Present

Although some theologies have stressed the aspect of hope that often arises most forcefully in hopeless situations, a theological rereading of history that deals with the reality of suffering must be equally emphatic about the present. While historical thinking from the underside is no longer geared to the past, as in modern historicism, sheer leaps into the future do not help. Historical thinking needs to be retooled to engage the present. At the same time, the present that is promoted from the underside of history has not much to do with the synchronic world of postmodernism, where the multiple realities of the present blot out the repressed aspects of history and conflict is domesticated as pluralistic diversity.

Theologically, the present is important first of all as it relates to

6. Frederick Herzog, *Liberation Theology: Liberation in the Light of the Fourth Gospel* (New York: Seabury, 1972), 257 (abbreviated: LT).

7. See Gustavo Gutiérrez, "Emancipación e identidad," in *Nuestra América frente al V Centenario: Emancipación e identidad de América Latina: 1492–1992* (Mexico City: Joaquín Mortiz, Planeta, 1989), 105. Cf. also Gustavo Gutiérrez, "Towards the Fifth Centenary," in *1492–1992: The Voice of the Victims,* ed. Leonardo Boff and Virgil Elizondo (London: SCM Press, and Philadelphia: Trinity Press International, 1990), 1.

specific manifestations of God's own presence in unexpected places.[8] Herzog reminds us that "it is useless to shift around on the spatial and chronological scales of our mind unless we face the question of the otherness of God."[9] While God may indeed be everywhere, the traditions of Israel and the church also know of a special concern for those on the underside. God's presence with the outcasts in Jesus sets the tone for everything else that follows. Stronger than the critics of liberal theology, Herzog understands that there can be no respect for God's Otherness without respect for the human other, manifest in a fundamental solidarity with the poor and the oppressed. In the encounter with this presence, the power of the modern self is restricted, creating new openings for the other. Herzog explains that "the Jesus of the road is key today because he teaches us limits of human control within which alone the engine of historical change can move history on constructively."[10] The initial solidarity with the other that grows out of God's own solidarity contributes to an alternative historical vision "from below," turning history on its head and leading to a new search for what motivates human life.

In the Latin American context Gutiérrez has learned that "the present acquires density and substance when it is nourished by the memory of a journey, when the courage is found to identify unsolved problems and wounds not yet healed."[11] Here the concern for the present is very closely related to unresolved suffering. Even the strongest concern for the present is meaningless without awareness of the oppressive moments that are a part of it.

Gutiérrez reminds us of what the poor already know, namely, that history has been written by a "white hand," by those in charge. Reconstructing history from a different point of view is not an easy task, however, since the memory of the poor is not readily available in the

---

8. Herzog formulates the challenge in this way: "Before I answer the question whether God is acting in history I first need to ask: Which action are we talking about?" Frederick Herzog, *Justice Church: The New Function of the Church in North American Christianity* (Maryknoll, N.Y.: Orbis, 1980), 35 (abbreviated: JC).

9. Frederick Herzog, "Towards the Waiting God," in *The Future of Hope: Theology as Eschatology,* ed. Frederick Herzog (New York: Herder and Herder, 1970), 65, referring to Günther Bornkamm's observation that Jesus' contemporaries were either captivated by the traditions of the past or fascinated by the future without having much sense of the present.

10. Frederick Herzog, *God-Walk: Liberation Shaping Dogmatics* (Maryknoll, N.Y.: Orbis, 1988), xiii (abbreviated: GW).

11. Gustavo Gutiérrez, *Las Casas: In Search of the Poor of Jesus Christ,* trans. Robert R. Barr (Maryknoll, N.Y.: Orbis, 1993), 457 (abbreviated: IS). The notion of density is taken up again in the title of Gutiérrez's latest collection of essays: *Densidad del presente: Selección de artículos* (Lima: Instituto Bartolomé de Las Casas, CEP, 1996).

present: "great efforts have been made to blot out the memory of the oppressed." Nevertheless a new process is under way, for "today the humiliated nations are trying to understand their past in order to build their present on solid bases."[12] The discovery of the point of view of the other marks the ground on which a different kind of awareness of the present is built.

History, still written by those in power, is now rewritten by the oppressed themselves whose authoritative position is inspired by, without having to claim identity with, God's presence. The poor and oppressed, those who have no effective power, are open to what God is doing in history in new ways: "God's presence, God's dwelling, among us enables us to say with Mary and the entire Bible that history is in the hands of the poor."[13] Rewriting the theological vision of history in light of those on the underside, Gutiérrez goes beyond modern theology's more general allusions to the relation of theology and history that have been so influential on the early stages of his work. God is at work in history not first of all in a general way but in God's own way, with those who, throughout the Bible, are closest to God's heart.

The Past

In the encounter with the other, theological accounts of history gradually move from the rehearsal of historical data to a reconstruction of the past. Lacan's reconstruction of history in light of the real (as the moment at which repressed identifications of the past are reworked in the present) has offered a model for better understanding this process. This points to the importance of new ways of listening in the process of examining historical truth.

Herzog takes up a suggestion of the German theologian Georg Eichholz that, contrary to common opinion, continuity with the past is not necessarily maintained where the flow of tradition that feeds into the present is preserved, but rather where it is ruptured. This argument can be exemplified by the fact that the dominant traditions have neglected the initial variety of social locations of the people whom Jesus met. Where today women, people from the "third world," and other marginalized persons rupture the monism of the dominant traditions, hidden

12. Gustavo Gutiérrez, "The Poor in the Church," in *The Poor and the Church,* ed. Norbert Greinacher and Alois Müller (New York: Seabury, 1977), 13. In Gustavo Gutiérrez and Richard Shaull, *Liberation and Change* (Atlanta: John Knox Press, 1977), 198 n. 55 (abbreviated: LC), Gutiérrez identifies Leonardo Boff as the one who coined the expression of history written with a white hand.

13. Gustavo Gutiérrez, *The God of Life,* trans. Matthew J. O'Connell (Maryknoll, N.Y.: Orbis, 1991), 188 (abbreviated: GL).

layers of the tradition are uncovered that remind us of the significance of these different locations.[14] In the context of their own encounters with God, the marginalized bring to life again the critical force of the Christian tradition. In short, the tradition of the church always needs to be reconstructed in light of what it has repressed.

From the Latin American perspective, Gutiérrez reminds us that any encounter with the poor must be very careful not to contribute to the "historical amnesia" with which the powerful seek to sedate the people. Poor people's memory of the past is crucial, he argues, because "memory of past battles is not a matter of reassuring nostalgia and pleasant reveries. It is a subversive memory."[15] Where it is understood that history is what hurts — the encounter with those unhealed wounds of the past — historical conflicts that extend into the present can be addressed, conflicts that have often escaped modern historians as a result of their failure to see the struggle between the self and the other.

The fundamental problem, in Gutiérrez's words, is that as Christians we are "not used to thinking in conflictual and historical terms. We prefer peaceful conciliation to antagonism and an evasive eternity to a provisional arrangement." This is true, of course, and not only in Latin America. Both the theologies based on the power of the self and the theologies based on the power of the text are not much help in this regard. The autonomous self is unable to realize its assimilation of the other, and in the world of the text conflict often tends to be relegated to the symbolic realm where it is easily domesticated, especially if the suffering of those at the margins is left out. Here theology can learn from a new historical vision that does not cover up conflict and repression. This is not to say, of course, that conflict needs to have the final word. Gutiérrez suggests that theology needs to learn "to live and think of peace in conflict and of what is definitive in what is historical."[16]

Within these parameters the heritage of the Christian faith can be reinterpreted. Nostalgia is not part of the picture, for "to remember does not mean being fixed in the past. It is important to remember yesterday, but this is because it helps us to risk the morrow, to move ahead,

---

14. See Frederick Herzog, review of Georg Eichholz, *Das Rätsel des historischen Jesus und die Gegenwart Jesu Christi,* in *Deutsches Pfarrerblatt* 86 (January 1986), 40.

15. Gustavo Gutiérrez, "The Historical Power of the Poor," in Gustavo Gutiérrez, *The Power of the Poor in History,* trans. Robert R. Barr (Maryknoll, N.Y.: Orbis, 1983), 80 (abbreviated: PP).

16. Gustavo Gutiérrez, *A Theology of Liberation: History, Politics, and Salvation,* Revised 15th Anniversary Edition, trans. Sister Caridad Inda and John Eagleson (Maryknoll, N.Y.: Orbis, 1988), 75 (abbreviated: TL).

to travel by unknown ways."[17] The study of the past, therefore, no longer serves the conservation of the status quo and its mystifications but becomes a means of transformation. In this sense, "memory...has the function of conditioning a creative liberty," oriented toward the future.[18]

The Future and Eschatology

The strong emphasis on the present, the "here and now" that grows out of the underside of history, has implications for a new perspective on the future and eschatology. This is a major difference between those modern liberal theologies oriented toward the present and a perspective developed in touch with poor and marginalized people. While the modern self can afford to locate its main interests in the present, poor people cannot. They live by a hope that, although it is deeply rooted in the present, cannot easily be grasped by those in power.

Realizing that future and present are closely related in the words and deeds of Jesus Christ, Herzog suggests a move away from the classic idea of imitation of Christ to that of "innovation of Christ." The term *innovation* expresses a strong openness toward the future without neglecting past and present. Such an innovation involves several elements. One is the moment of planning as mapping out new paths into the future that will reduce the suffering and pain of the present. This process of drawing a map on grounds of experiences of oppression and repression is related to what, in Lacanian terms, can be described as the reconstruction of the symbolic order in relation to the repressed real and, ultimately, leads to the theological reinterpretation of the symbolic texture of the whole of Christian tradition. Past and present, no longer either glorified or repressed, get a new hearing.

On the other hand, planning also leads to new closures and repressions. For this reason, Herzog explains, God "invites us ever anew to break through our best planning and to see the neighbor as the person he is."[19] Eschatology from the perspective of those who are cut off from power and influence only makes sense if it is connected to people's lives. This moment of rupturing the map in the encounter with the neighbor

---

17. Gutiérrez, GL, 35.

18. This process can also be observed in the writings of the Old Testament, for "the faith of Israel moves in this dialectic of memory and liberty. This is what is celebrated in its *worship*." Gutiérrez, "God's Revelation and Proclamation in History," PP, 12. Emphasis in original.

19. Herzog, "Towards the Waiting God," 71. For Herzog's discussion of the innovation of Christ see ibid., 63, as well as LT, 173, and GW, 154.

is the other element in the innovation of Christ and, not unlike the Lacanian real, leads us to the crucial place of the other that throws light
on the repressions of the symbolic constructs of our maps and, thus,
initiates their constant reconstruction.

The strong connection of present and future is also one of the main
topics in the Latin American encounters with the poor. Eschatology
in its biblical meaning, according to a widely accepted definition, signifies an event that is already present but has not yet attained its full
form. At the same time, eschatology cannot be merely the infinite extension of the present. The poor understand better than anybody else
the limits of the present system.[20] Theology in touch with the underside
begins to understand what the modern self, despite a vague and general
awareness of its own finitude, was never quite able to see.

Eschatological hope provides an image of the future that, when tied
to the suffering of the present, moves history. In this way, eschatology
is no longer opium for the people but becomes the "engine of human
history,"[21] motivating a new type of human action that no longer needs
to see itself as absolute. An example of an interpretation of eschatology that does not pay enough attention to the present — and in this
evaluation Gutiérrez and Herzog are very close — are the European
theologies of hope to which theology in touch with the underside is
often compared. Those who cannot afford to wait remind us that "the
hope which overcomes death must be rooted in the heart of historical
praxis," otherwise it is a "futuristic illusion."[22] In touch with the poor,
theology begins to understand what most theological reflections on eschatology do not realize, namely, that our concepts "limp after reality."
Gutiérrez goes on to explain that "theology does not initiate this future
which exists in the present. It does not create the vital attitude of hope
out of nothing."[23]

---

20. In Gutiérrez's words, TL, 97, "we are also led to a permanent detachment."

21. Gustavo Gutiérrez, *Líneas pastorales de la Iglesia en América Latina* (Lima: CEP,
1970), 62. Cf. also Gustavo Gutiérrez, "Una tierra nueva," *Páginas* 13:94 (December
1988), 11.

22. Gutiérrez, TL, 124. (Gutiérrez acknowledges, however, that, for instance, in Moltmann's later works the future is tied more closely to the present.) In this connection it
could be misleading to follow Curt Cadorette, "Peru and the Mystery of Liberation: The
Nexus and Logic of Gustavo Gutiérrez's Theology," in *The Future of Liberation Theology: Essays in Honor of Gustavo Gutiérrez,* ed. Marc H. Ellis and Otto Maduro (Maryknoll,
N.Y.: Orbis, 1989), 57 n. 2, in his conclusion that the "concept of futurity" is fundamental
to Gutiérrez's theology.

23. "Moltmann says that theological concepts 'do not limp after reality.... They illuminate reality by displaying its future.' In our approach, to reflect critically on the praxis
of liberation is to 'limp after' reality." Gutiérrez, TL, 11.

Eschatological hope, therefore, grows out of the present of those who are both oppressed and believers, as Gutiérrez describes the Latin American poor. It does not need to be produced by theology, but it must be analyzed and reflected by it. Christian base communities tend to understand that hope is ultimately rooted in God's presence, the Other who validates their own otherness, but is never usurped by it. Hope is rooted in the presence that constantly breaks up historical fixations and opens up the future.

Realpresence and Utopia

This brings us to the place of the "real itself," which Lacan left open. While there is no need to identify that place with God in a theological or philosophical equation, theology might learn from the acute awareness of a definite limit not only emphasized by Lacan but understood by many people on the underside of history as well. The experience of God's presence with those who are suffering differs significantly from one of the key principles of modernity, identified by the French thinker Jacques Derrida as "metaphysics of presence,"[24] referring to a sense that God, truth, and reality itself are ultimately available to humanity. The various manifestations of the metaphysics of presence seek to establish a center as the place where God's presence can be guaranteed, but the underside of history teaches us that God's presence can only be glimpsed in the rupture of such centers, in the encounters with the Otherness of the Word and the otherness of the oppressed neighbor. God's presence is not something that can be taken for granted like the presence of the modern self.

While both the Otherness of the Word of God and the otherness of the neighbor are taken up in the work of Herzog, ever closer encounters with the world of the oppressed lead to a shift in his theology from an emphasis on "wordpresence" to a more inclusive emphasis on "realpresence." Earlier Herzog, making use of the power of the text, has argued that "God's Word clearly taught disenthralls us from our captivity to national chauvinism or private preoccupations"; later the presence of Christ becomes more central. The teaching of God's Word is important insofar as "it opens our eyes to the eucharistic presence of Jesus, the radical immersion of God in history" at the places of suffering and oppression.[25] At this point, Christ's presence is no longer

24. Cf. Jacques Derrida, "Structure, Sign and Play," in *Critical Theory since 1965*, ed. Hazard Adams and Leroy Searle (Tallahassee: University Presses of Florida, 1986), 84.

25. Frederick Herzog, "What Does Full Communion Mean?" *EKU/UCC Newsletter* 1:4 (November 1980), 5. The latter statement can be found in Herzog, GW, 150.

just "a presence in words,"[26] even though that aspect is still part of the picture, but a specific way of being present with the oppressed. This presence on the underside, aware of its limits, defies the easy identifications of the metaphysics of presence. Whether "wordpresence" or "realpresence," the basic issue is the same: God's presence cannot easily be captured in terms of what counts as "reality" at any given time. In Herzog's words, "God's Word is a power that pries open reality and questions the philosophies that seek to interpret it."[27]

While "first world" modernity has pushed a metaphysics of presence, many people in "third world" contexts have tended to put more trust in the past. One of the basic problems in Latin America is, according to Gutiérrez, that "large numbers of Latin Americans suffer from a fixation which leads them to overvalue the past." Like the famous educator Paulo Freire, he sees this as sign of a precritical consciousness that has not taken hold of its own destiny. Gutiérrez confirms that this problem is actually reversed in the rich countries, where people are attached "not to the past, but rather to an affluent present which they are prepared to uphold and defend under any circumstances."[28]

Here the notion of utopia suggests itself. Utopia, contrary to its popular usage, does not mean fiction. Utopia is a map for a different society, working toward the transformation of the status quo. In other words, utopia is geared not just to the future but to the present of the church of the poor. "None of this would mean anything to us," Gutiérrez points out, "were it not for the fact that a rough draft — unpretentious and tentative — of this Christian community of tomorrow is already spread out before our eyes, all over Latin America."[29] In a North American context where the presence of the real is taken for granted, notions like wordpresence and realpresence are needed to rupture the modern self's security and to create room for those on the underside. In the Latin American context, however, where many people do not dare to step out of the past, theology's job is to identify the glimpses of utopia developing here and now in the lives of the poor.

The utopian perspective changes the understanding of what history is all about. In Gutiérrez's words, "Historical reality . . . ceases to be the field for the application of abstract truths and idealistic interpretations; instead it becomes the privileged locale from which the process of

---

26. Herzog envisions this "presence in words" in LT, 18.
27. Ibid.
28. Gutiérrez, TL, 122.
29. Gutiérrez, "Liberation Praxis and Christian Faith," PP, 71.

knowledge starts and to which it eventually returns."[30] In other words, rather than determining the essence of history once and for all and locking God into this construct, history needs to be kept open so that it can be rewritten in walking with God where the pain is. History is what hurts.

Reconstructing History

While modern perspectives on history are clear about the importance of ongoing historical research, they make few provisions for fundamental shifts in their accounts of history. Established historical metanarratives are not easily changed. Modern historians know that future research will add further detail to their studies; nonetheless, they would not go along with the postmodern trend to admit the validity of numerous and even contradicting accounts of history.

Yet, in the midst of the tension between historical micronarratives and metanarratives,[31] another perspective emerges on the underside. At a time when it has become clearer that the metanarratives of modernity are unable to address the needs of the people, the breakdown of history into micronarratives is not the only option. Instead of pluralistic fragmentation where each group follows its own agenda and tells its own story, people on the underside will not let us get away without addressing the repressions of the dominant perspectives. For this reason Herzog suggests a reconstruction of history that involves repentance, defined as "creative mind-change with no attendant guilt feelings or morose self-pity,"[32] which frees us for a new relationship to the other and renewed participation in God's work. History, as we are beginning to understand with the help of those at the margins, is not something to be celebrated or despised, not something to be proud of or to feel guilty about, but a reconstruction of the past in relation to the present in terms of the reappropriation of repressed history.

In the context of Herzog's own denomination, the United Church

---

30. Gustavo Gutiérrez, earlier version of "Liberation Praxis and Christian Faith," in *Frontiers of Theology in Latin America*, ed. Rosino Gibellini (Maryknoll, N.Y.: Orbis, 1979), 19. Cf. also the newer versions of this material in Gutiérrez, PP, 59, and Gutiérrez and Shaull, LC.

31. For the terms *metanarrative* and *micronarrative* or *grand narrative* and *little narrative*, see Jean-François Lyotard, *The Postmodern Condition*, trans. Geoff Bennington and Brian Massumi (Minneapolis: University of Minnesota Press, 1984).

32. Frederick Herzog, "Pre-Bicentennial U.S.A. in the Liberation Process," in *Theology in the Americas*, ed. Sergio Torres and John Eagleson (Maryknoll, N.Y.: Orbis, 1976), 144.

of Christ, he finds that "the great thing we are doing right now is that we are examining what Barbara Brown Zikmund calls our Hidden Histories," adding that "at the same time we cannot turn away from the contemporary moment of this process."[33] Hidden histories are uncovered and repressed history is reappropriated in the participation in God's work with the oppressed. In theological discourse, attention to historical points of friction ultimately leads to the new development of Christian doctrine at the symbolic-order level as well.[34]

Theology encountering the underside does not promote another closed system, based on abstract ideals, but seeks to identify the difference that God makes in the midst of the tensions of history. Absolute reason based on the self, in its rationalistic or idealistic sense, must give way to a form of historical reason in tune with God's reconstruction of our histories: "Reason can conceive of God. But it always limps after the self-realization of God."[35]

According to Gutiérrez, the encounter with the underside teaches that historicism, "a fixation upon former painful and traumatic occurrences" that never gets beyond the narcissism of a self constantly circling around its repressions and guilt, changes nothing. Gutiérrez agrees with Bartolomé de Las Casas that "history is the teacher of all things," provided that we do not "remain fixed in the past."[36] Yet while the metanarratives of the modern self are crumbling, postmodern nostalgia, perpetuating in the present random styles of the past, does not help produce a liberating vision either. Looking at the underside of actual history, a more constructive encounter with history as a whole opens up.

History, therefore, is not so much a text that is given but, according to Fredric Jameson's interpretation of Lacan, a text-to-be-reconstructed. Historical study on grounds of the dominant text, be it a meta- or a micronarrative, is in danger of being merely an addendum to the status quo in all its metamorphoses; here Christendom theology and certain modes of modern and postmodern theology are not all that different.

---

33. Frederick Herzog, "Liberation and Process Theologies in the Church," *Prism* 5:2 (Fall 1990), 65, included in *Theology from the Belly of the Whale: A Frederick Herzog Reader*, ed. Rieger. The reference is to Barbara Brown Zikmund, *Hidden Histories in the United Church of Christ*, 2 vols. (New York: United Church Press, 1984, 1987).
34. Cf. Frederick Herzog, "Dogmatik IV," in *Theologische Realenzyklopädie*, vol. 9, ed. Gerhard Krause and Gerhard Müller (Berlin: Walter de Gruyter, 1982), 112; a translation is included in *Theology from the Belly of the Whale: A Frederick Herzog Reader*, ed. Rieger.
35. Ibid., 114.
36. Gutiérrez, "Towards the Fifth Centenary," 4.

While certain helpful elements of the past might be recovered in this way, the past of the victims is invariably overwritten.

Confronted with the powers that be, the task is to reconstruct history in terms of the reappropriation of repressed history and thus, in Gutiérrez's words, to "regain the memory of the 'beaten Christs of the Indies.'"[37] The history produced out of this encounter goes back as far as the history of the resistance of the Indians against the conquest. This initial resistance has helped establish structures that are still effective, such as cultural traditions and languages that, as Gutiérrez points out, "nourish the present and are a vital element in our identity."[38]

Reconstructed history does not immediately have to turn into another metanarrative, a text of nearly absolute power. Recovering the repressed memory of the people on the underside leads beyond a black-and-white vision of history, to a more honest account of history that is aware of shades of gray, helping us to overcome those structures of mystification so typical of the metanarratives of the status quo.

Conclusion

In the encounter with the underside of history it is becoming ever more clear that theology is inextricably tied to historical processes. The study of history is no longer a question of preference or choice. Theology needs to face its own involvement in history, a factor that has often been neglected. Yet historicism will no longer do. A tension emerges between theological accommodation to history and God's involvement in history. This tension is mirrored, according to Herzog, "in the contradiction between a historicist relationship to Jesus and a living relationship to God's work in Christ in present history." The problem is that "religion can leave Messiah Jesus in the past and do its own thing with God in the present."[39] In this situation, theological references to history become irrelevant at best or smoke screens at worst. History needs to be rewritten in encounters with Christ on the underside of history.

In the Latin American context, theology in touch with the poor develops new insights into the role the poor play in the reconstruction of history. Gutiérrez develops "a dynamic and historical conception of

---

37. In the sixteenth century Bartolomé de Las Casas talked about the "beaten Christs of the Indies." Gustavo Gutiérrez, "Statement by Gustavo Gutiérrez," in *Theology in the Americas,* ed. Sergio Torres and John Eagleson (Maryknoll, N.Y.: Orbis, 1976), 310.

38. Gutiérrez, "Towards the Fifth Centenary," 3.

39. Herzog, JC, 24.

the human person, oriented definitively and creatively toward the future, acting in the present for the sake of tomorrow."[40] When read in a North American context, this may sound like putting too much emphasis on the agency of the self. But the Latin American reality of the poor reminds us that, even at a time when we begin to understand the limits of the modern self, we must not give up the concern for the self altogether. The newly emerging self of the future must learn from the mistakes of modern selfhood, most important, its narcissistic and aggressive conquest of the other. A new self, challenged and reshaped by actual encounters with the other, will play an important part in shaping new theological accounts of history and in transforming its course.

Oppressed people in both North and South know that ultimately there is only one history in which all share. Dominant histories and the history of the oppressed always overlap and are tied together. Likewise, God's own history cannot be separated from the history of the world. In contrast to all sorts of attempts to play off against each other — church and world, inside and outside, rich and poor, real humanity and ideal humanity — Gutiérrez reminds us that "we do not have two histories, one by which we become children of God and the other by which we become each other's brothers."[41]

At the same time, the difference between various histories must not be forgotten. People on the underside know better than anybody else that, while history is one, there are different stories. Herzog reminds us of the need to realize the different histories in North America, especially at the point at which God's history and the history of the powerful have been equated, for instance, in the history of Manifest Destiny.[42] The affirmation of the unity of history can easily be misused. History from the underside will not let us get away without an account of existing differences. Theology from the underside can, therefore, not be a theology of history in general. It is rather an approach to God's history, a history that starts to shine through where past, present, and future are reconstructed in a self-critical encounter with their repressions.

---

40. Gutiérrez, TL, 21.
41. Gutiérrez and Shaull, LC, 86.
42. Frederick Herzog, "Introduction: On Liberating Liberation Theology," in Hugo Assmann, *Theology for a Nomad Church* (Maryknoll, N.Y.: Orbis, 1976), 5, included in *Theology from the Belly of the Whale: A Frederick Herzog Reader*, ed. Rieger. A similar problem can be seen in Nazi Germany's "self-deification on grounds of the history-as-*Heilsgeschichte* thesis." Ibid., 6. It is for this reason that a distinction needs to be made between God's history and human history. Cf. also Frederick Herzog, "Dual Citizens," in *Theology from the Belly of the Whale: A Frederick Herzog Reader*, ed. Rieger.

Chapter 7

Toward a New Understanding of the Other in North and South

N A WORLD that is becoming ever more interdependent, few things are more important than a new understanding of the challenge of the other, not only at home but also in different locations around the world. In this context, we need to explore the challenge of the encounters with the underside of history for a new global outlook on theology. On a global level, the encounter with marginalized groups introduces two challenges. First, the experience of suffering and oppression transcends national or geographic boundaries and creates more wide-ranging bonds of solidarity. Second, however, the fact that the marginalized have different stories in different parts of the world calls for new models of global solidarity, pushing for a broader horizon without falling into the modern trap of neglecting differences. As Jacques Lacan has taught us, all generalizations of marginalized people imposed from the outside fail: *The* woman for instance, as categorized by those in power, does not exist. Only where those false universals are exposed is the way open for new models of solidarity.

Modern perspectives, despite their concern for universality, were never completely able to escape the narcissism of the modern self. Since others are always seen in terms of the self, it is no accident that modern theology has often led to false universals, unable to pay much attention to difference. The view from the underside will help to develop universal perspectives that respect the differences of others and deal with their challenges.

The modern impasse has manifested itself in different ways. North American encounters with Latin America may serve as an example. The North has often dealt with the South in terms of development, not only economically but also politically and culturally, based on the idea that those who are "other" need a chance to become like us.

The other side of this relationship can be seen in the praxis of importing ideas developed at the periphery without much account of the difference in social location, not unlike cultural artifacts and styles. It is not surprising, therefore, that Latin American versions of liberation theology, for example, have initially found easy entrance into North American liberal theology, especially where its ideas seemed to reinforce familiar theological paradigms. This phenomenon has resulted in the common misperception (among others) that liberation theology is all about orthopraxis or right action and the moral improvement of the modern self, a view that leaves the self's authority and power intact. If the challenge of the other is recognized at all, she is often romanticized. Even at present both supporters and critics often still interpret theological perspectives developed in Latin America and elsewhere through the lens of the Euro-American history of ideas with little consideration for the differences.[1]

Despite recent concerns for otherness and difference, introduced by postmodern tendencies, it appears that on the upper levels of society differences play another role and ultimately matter less than on the underside. While, for instance, a lower-class woman in the United States whose native language is Spanish is painfully reminded of difference on a daily basis, many well-to-do postmodern minds have found the entertainment value of difference. The phenomenon of the tourist exemplifies my point. Today's tourists are increasingly attracted by the differences and curiosities of other cultures, but those differences are never allowed to provide much of a challenge in return.[2] Even such widely practiced forms of expressing concern for the other as volunteer services do not necessarily introduce a big advantage over the modern misrecognition of the other if the position of the self is left unchal-

---

1. For an example of the ethical interpretation of liberation theology see Craig Nessan, *Orthopraxis or Heresy: The North American Theological Response to Latin American Liberation Theology* (Atlanta: Scholars Press, 1989), 409. The Euro-American view is presupposed by Stanley Hauerwas, *After Christendom?* (Nashville: Abingdon Press, 1991), 50–55, who suspects that Immanuel Kant is responsible for Gutiérrez's notion of the "new man," rejecting the concept on those terms. From a Latin American point of view, Jeffrey Klaiber, arguing that liberation theology has served, and therefore can serve, as "an ecumenical bridge between social-minded Catholics and liberal Protestants in both the First and Third Worlds," perpetuates the misperception of a natural affinity of liberal and liberation theologies. Jeffrey Klaiber, "Prophets and Populists: Liberation Theology, 1968–1988," *Americas* 44 (July 1989), 14.

2. For alternatives to the tourism approach, cf. *Beyond Tourism: Mentoring as a Grass Roots Approach to Theological Education*, ed. Susan B. Thistlethwaite and George F. Cairns (Maryknoll, N.Y.: Orbis, 1994).

lenged.[3] In this context it is imperative to understand what impact the challenge of the other might have on theological reflection at home.[4]

In order to get some sense of the challenge that global contexts of oppression and marginalization pose for theology, we must explore another level of dialogue. Searching for a more constructive encounter with the Latin American other in North America, two things need to be combined: an understanding of the difference of other contexts and an initial understanding of the challenge of marginalized people at home as an interpretive framework.

In this framework, a theological approach that takes difference seriously does not necessarily have to give in to radical pluralism. Although many postmodern thinkers promote unrestricted pluralism as a remedy for the modern self's monism, theology in touch with the underside understands the limits of pluralism. The awareness of difference is complemented by a desire for connecting with other perspectives of suffering and oppression. The solidarity of those who suffer helps us deal with difference in new ways. Theology in North and South finally comes together, not in another synthesis that smooths over the rough edges of difference, but in light of its encounters with the underside of history.

Distributing Power

Both the theological turn to the self and the turn to the text have rarely addressed the relation of theology and power, but those without power have made us aware that the question of power is a genuine issue for theology. Theology can no longer be done without paying attention to the distribution of power in society.

---

3. In the United States eighty million people, 45 percent of the adult public, do volunteer work. See Robert Wuthnow, *Acts of Compassion: Caring for Others and Helping Ourselves* (Princeton: Princeton University Press, 1991), 5–6. For new ways of thinking about Christian praxis in relation to the other see Joerg Rieger, "The Means of Grace, John Wesley, and the Theological Dilemma of the Church Today," *Quarterly Review* (Winter 1997–98), 377–93.

4. We need to develop new ways of interacting theologically across national and cultural boundaries. Even sympathetic receptions of Latin American liberation theology in the North, for instance, like Arthur F. McGovern, *Liberation Theology and Its Critics: Toward an Assessment* (Maryknoll, N.Y.: Orbis, 1989), still lack the mutuality that is required. In this work, liberation theology seems to be "assessed" and defended as long as it fits the more general presuppositions of theology in North America. Self-critique in light of the other does not appear to be a major part of the project. John C. Meagher, e.g., "Liberation (?) Theology (?) for North America (?)," in *Liberation Theology: North American Style,* ed. Deane William Ferm (New York: International Religious Foundation, 1987), is more responsive to the differences, but there is still no constructive reflection on what really can be learned from Latin American theology in the North.

Parallels and Differences

The North American church historian Sydney Ahlstrom points out a connection that helps us to sketch an initial understanding of the relationship of power and theology in North and South. "The impulses which led Luther to the Wittenberg church door," he argues, "were integrally related to those which sent Spanish caravels out across the Western Sea."[5] Ahlstrom's point is that there were forces at work that were greater than the reformers, the pope, or the emperor, forces that produced relations between Europe and America out of which would grow the history of America and the American church. These powers are centered in imperial structures that arise in Europe in conjunction with the conquest of America.[6]

Ahlstrom points out what for those without power is often not terribly difficult to see: There are de facto interconnections between theological authority and the dominant powers, often structured by economic developments. As this history develops, the actual relations of power and authority assume different shapes. When North America enters the equation, the Reformation and Roman Catholicism are joined by the growing authority of Puritanism, Enlightenment thought, and revivalism.

Whereas in Latin America the connections of power and theological authority in the conquest may be more openly visible, the constitutional separation of church and state in the United States has often made an investigation of their connection seem less necessary. Nevertheless, in both cases the implications of the alliance of theological authority and power are least recognized by those who benefit from it. Only a reading from the underside will lead to a more self-critical perspective in both Americas. It is no accident that both Gutiérrez and Herzog understand that the most pressing problem of modern theology is not that it has become relegated to the private sphere of the modern self,

---

5. Sydney E. Ahlstrom, *A Religious History of the American People* (New Haven: Yale University Press, 1972), 25. Herzog refers to this passage first in "Am Ende der Nachreformation," *Evangelische Kommentare* 12:9 (September 1979), 503.

6. See Ahlstrom, ibid., 17, 25, 27. Additional support for this observation comes from Phillip Berryman, who describes this initial parallel between Europe and Latin America thus: "The overall pattern was that of a single 'Christian' society where civil and religious authority were closely connected. This model arrived in Latin America just as it was beginning to unravel in Europe, starting with the Protestant Reformation." Phillip Berryman, *Liberation Theology: The Essential Facts about the Revolutionary Movement in Latin America and Beyond* (New York: Pantheon Books, 1987), 10.

an often repeated criticism, but that theology has become politicized without being aware of it.[7]

In the wake of a globalizing economy North and South have been pulled together more closely, and religion has at times become a prime battleground in an intensifying struggle for hegemony and power. In the eighties the Reagan administration identified Latin American liberation theology as a dangerous element[8] while, at the same time, neoconservative forces in the United States started a broad campaign at the level of the churches and civil society that, in the nineties, has led to ever stronger alliances of the Religious Right and the Republican Party. In addition, well-funded organizations like the Washington, D.C.–based Institute for Religion and Democracy have entered the fray. Founded in 1981 by Richard John Neuhaus and Michael Novak in order to take on Latin American liberation theology, this group now focuses on what it perceives as the threat of liberal Protestantism and monitors all major denominations closely.

In this situation the powerless force theology to take a self-critical look at its relation to power structures. A reflection on the relation of authority and power from their perspective offers two things: a better understanding of the impact of power structures on theology, especially where those structures go unrecognized (see part I), and an awareness for the need of a transformation of those structures of power from a theological perspective (see part II). Yet no transformation can take place on the level of theological ideas alone. The all-pervasiveness of the powers of the self and the powers of the text can easily undermine even the best theological intentions. Theologies in touch with the underside of history in both North and South continue to remind us that theology needs to be reconstructed in light of actual accounts of our own social location and a new awareness of the actual conflicts of our society.

So far, the burning issues have often looked different in North and South. Early North American encounters with the African American other have, as Herzog's work exemplifies, led to a deeper understanding of racism and the political tensions involved. In a context where

---

7. See, for instance, Gustavo Gutiérrez, *A Theology of Liberation: History, Politics, and Salvation*, Revised 15th Anniversary Edition, trans. Sister Caridad Inda and John Eagleson (Maryknoll, N.Y.: Orbis, 1988), 129–30 (abbreviated: TL), and Herzog, *Justice Church: The New Function of the Church in North American Christianity* (Maryknoll, N.Y.: Orbis, 1980), 106 (abbreviated: JC).

8. The conclusion has been drawn that "U.S. policy must begin to counter (not react against) liberation theology as it is utilized in Latin America by the 'liberation theology' clergy." Committee of Santa Fe, 1980. Quoted in Berryman, *Liberation Theology*, 3.

African Americans did not have a voice in society, one of the central problems is identified as the disparity of power in political terms. In Latin America, on the other hand, the question of poverty is primary for obvious reasons. In a world where the majority of the population is without work and poverty levels are extremely high, economic inequalities shape the agenda.[9]

Nevertheless, as closer and more personal encounters with the world of the poor have developed in Latin America, other factors have gained in importance. Gutiérrez explains that the encounters with the poor have led to more sensitivity for the complexity of their world: "For myself, this has been the most important (and even crushing) experience of these past years. The world of the poor is a universe in which the socio-economic aspect is basic but not all-inclusive."[10] An interrelation of various perspectives is necessary. The economic dimension and a point of view that pays attention to cultural and political differences, for instance, need to inform each other. Gutiérrez reminds us that "there is no question of choosing among the tools to be used; poverty is a complex human condition, and its causes must also be complex."[11]

The encounters with marginalized groups in North America on the other hand cumulate in an increasing awareness that economic structures are involved in various forms of oppression, ranging from the position of women and children to the struggle of the races. One of the first theologians to take note of this development was Frederick Herzog. The close connections which he developed to Latin America from the mid-eighties on might have been of help here. His latest work was focused more and more on economic issues. Summarizing forty years of struggle against "anonymous powers," Herzog argues that the nineties need to be seen in light of the challenge of the global power of money.[12]

---

9. No wonder Karl Marx's economic analyses have made sense in this context. To Herzog's question of why he uses aspects of Marxian thought, Gutiérrez responds, "Because the people use him." Reported in Frederick Herzog, "Birth Pangs: Liberation Theology in North America," *Christian Century* 93:41 (December 15, 1976), 1123.

10. Gutiérrez, "Introduction to the Revised Edition," TL, xxi.

11. Ibid., xxv.

12. Cf. Frederick Herzog, "Kirchengemeinschaft und Eucharistie," *Berliner Theologische Zeitschrift* 8:1 (1991), 118, English translation in *Theology from the Belly of the Whale: A Frederick Herzog Reader*, ed. Rieger. In the civil rights struggle of the sixties, the problem was racism, during the Vietnam War in the sixties and seventies it was neocolonialism, and in the eighties the debate concerned nuclear arms. For his more recent work see Frederick Herzog, "Tradición Común Shaping Christian Theology: Mutualization in Theological Education," Working Paper Series 12, Duke-UNC Program in Latin American Studies (April 1994), 20, also included in *Theology from the Belly of the Whale: A Frederick Herzog Reader*.

Despite the differences of North and South, a certain consensus is emerging in the wake of the pressures of a globalizing economy. Theologians all over the globe begin to realize that after the so-called victory of capitalism, power is more and more defined by economic arrangements.[13] Future exchanges between North and South will need to tackle this issue in new ways.

North and South: North American Lessons

"As medieval Catholicism blessed the feudal order, so Protestantism came to bless the bourgeois order, likewise without a serious sustained effort to judge or transform it."[14] This programmatic statement sets the stage for the challenge that the underside of history poses to North American theology. This challenge is twofold. On the one hand, the existence of the underside raises new questions for theology in touch with the status quo. Theology needs to find out in what ways it has indeed given its blessings to the middle class. On the other hand, theology in touch with the underside must take care not to fall back into the old mode of blessing those aspirations to omnipotence that are so characteristic of the modern self.

On the grounds of this constant temptation in the "ego's era," North American theology needs to take a different path than theology in Latin America. One of the basic lessons taught by the encounter with the poor in Latin America was, against the backdrop of Christendom theology, a new awareness of the context of theology. In North America, on the other hand, liberal theology has dealt with matters of context for a long time. Here the challenge is not so much to become aware of the context. The question rather is to which context theology needs to be attentive. Modern theology, whose context is determined by wherever the modern self finds itself, has never seriously raised this question.

One of the fundamental problems for theology in the United States is an underlying confidence in the reasoning capacity of the modern self, which, unlike its European counterpart, never had to face any serious critique.[15] Small wonder that the modern self has become the starting

---

13. See the essays by Gutiérrez and Herzog and other essays from Europe and the United States in *Liberating the Future: God, Mammon, and Theology,* ed. Joerg Rieger (Minneapolis: Fortress Press, 1998).

14. Herbert J. Muller, *Religion and Freedom in the Modern World,* quoted in Herzog, JC, 69 n. 11.

15. See Frederick Herzog, "Dogmatik IV," in *Theologische Realenzyklopädie,* vol. 9, ed. Gerhard Krause and Gerhard Müller (Berlin: Walter de Gruyter, 1982), 108; a translation is included in *Theology from the Belly of the Whale: A Frederick Herzog Reader,* ed. Rieger. European critics of modernity and of the concept of reason, like Friedrich Schelling,

point by default, "authorizing" the theological enterprise. Power and the production of theological authority meet here.

In this connection, the power of the text has had a different, more subordinate, function in the north than in the south. In Herzog's words: "North America . . . has never experienced the universal claim of dogma in medieval Roman Catholicism. It also never experienced the attempt . . . to recover the universal claim of dogma for the churches of the Reformation."[16] In the beginning of much of North American theology is not the text but the self. Even in the later tug-of-war of liberalism and neoorthodoxy, liberalism wins out; the modern self continues to set the stage for North American theology. And while neoorthodoxy has not been abandoned, it has been co-opted and prevented from developing an effective critique of the power of the self. Whether the postmodern challenge will be more effective remains to be seen. As I have shown earlier, the turn to the text does not always take care of the power of the self, and even the increasing concern for otherness and difference can be found catering to the self. Without an encounter with the other and the question, "Who put (and keeps) the other in place?" the self cannot be reconstructed.

At the apex of the ego's era, the symbolic texts of the church can transform the self only in connection with the position of the repressed. At this point, the various elements of my argument come together: The turn to the (symbolic-order) biblical and traditional texts help reconstruct the (imaginary-order) self repressing its other, as long as the interpretations of those texts are tied to a new awareness of God's presence with those on the underside of history (the real).

This reconstruction of theology is no longer based on the authority of yet another set of modern selves. Its energy is not primarily identified with the names of a few great theologians, but is growing out of basic Christian communities and churches in touch with the underside. It may take a while to take hold, since it emerged first on the underside of history and no powerful church boards are likely to make it an institution. Yet at a time when much of the polarization within theology and our churches seems to have become self-serving,[17] our theological

---

Arthur Schopenhauer, Friedrich Nietzsche, and Martin Heidegger, have been lacking in North America. See also Frederick Herzog, "Vernunft der Weisheit: Amerikanische Aufklärung im Licht kritischer Spiritualität," *Evangelische Kommentare* 18:10 (October 1985), 552.

16. Herzog, "Dogmatik IV," 104.

17. The sociologist Rhys H. Williams reminds us, for instance, that the culture-wars idea (which has of course shaped the theological landscape as well) "is not the only game in town." Rhys H. Williams, "Is America in a Culture War? Yes – No – Sort of," *Christian*

future will depend on listening to the many voices on the underside of history, that part of contemporary reality that refuses to go away despite the rise of postmodern pluralism and the related political, economic, and theological shifts. Looking for signs of this transformation in North America, we will not necessarily find large events, but theology must learn to pay attention to the small things, those "glimpses of the real" that normally go unnoticed.

South and North: Latin American Lessons

While much of theology in the North is related to the power of the self, the genesis of Latin American theology is deeply related to what we have called the powers of the text. Already in the sixteenth century King Ferdinand of Spain used those structures for a justification of his actions. The *Requerimiento* (1517), a theological text that, on the basis of medieval notions of papal supremacy, argues that the power of the church over the Indian heathens has been delegated to the king of Spain by the pope, becomes the basis of the king's power in the Indies.[18] In the theology of Christendom a symbiosis of worldly and religious power is achieved, kept in place by the power of the text, since worldly power is considered to be at the service of religious power.

Here the modernist impulse, restricting the power of the text through closer attention to the authority of the modern self and its world, serves an important function. The questions of the modern world introduce a new perspective that helps to break open the structures of power maintained by Christendom. For this reason alone the Second Vatican Council has been a watershed moment in the history of the church. Nevertheless, the turn to the self is not sufficient to overcome oppression, as those on the underside of Latin American society know full well. Modernity has produced its own oppressive structures. The poor experience in their lives what Gutiérrez has formulated in this way: "The movement for modern freedoms, democracy, and the universal and rational thought in Europe and the United States, meant for Latin America a new type of oppression and more cruel forms of despoilment of the poor classes." Any benefits of the dynamics of modernity for the Latin American poor are therefore always tempered by "a traumatic ex-

---

Century 114:32 (November 12, 1997), 1043. It not only neglects other differences such as class (and we must add race and gender), it also fails to pay attention to other forms in which people become involved in the life in society.

18. Cf. Gustavo Gutiérrez, *Las Casas: In Search of the Poor of Jesus Christ,* trans. Robert R. Barr (Maryknoll, N.Y.: Orbis, 1993), 112 (abbreviated: IS).

perience which cannot be forgotten when one speaks of freedom and democracy in the continent."[19]

While their analyses of modernity and modern theology may not be as refined as those in the North, Latin Americans, as a result of their experience of the most disruptive aspects of the modern world, be it through the influence of the global market or through efforts at development that often fail, might teach us much about the powers of the modern self and the ambiguity of our North American fascination with postmodernity. Gutiérrez reminds us early on that there is no easy way out of the dilemma, for "to proclaim a 'postmodern era' while the representatives of the social class — the bourgeoisie — who sustain the modern ideology are still in charge, is to entertain illusions."[20] We need to understand that the powers of modernity are not easily overcome. Yet a simple return to the powers of the text works even less well in Latin America.

The religious populisms, for instance, which lately have been used to boost the Christendom model and new theological turns to the text, do not automatically offer a reconstruction of the modern self, a self that is now entertained by all kinds of differences, and loves to collect artifacts and local stories. The Preparatory Document for the Bishops' Conference at Puebla, for instance, has no trouble interpreting popular religiosity as "a bulwark of the traditional values"[21] that helps to preserve the values of Western civilization. At a time in which the turn to the text has become fashionable once more, we must not forget the dangers and false promises of the Lacanian symbolic order.

In the tension of Christendom and modernity, the poor are still overlooked. Only actual encounters with the world of the poor to which the majority of people belong will help to break out of the vicious circle which helps to retain established structures of power. Nevertheless, this

---

19. Gustavo Gutiérrez and Richard Shaull, *Liberation and Change* (Atlanta: John Knox Press, 1977), 71. During the 1990 elections in Peru, those hit hardest by the continuing process of economic modernization, the poor, the provinces, and the Indians, voted against neoliberal politics and for Alberto Fujimori (who, nevertheless, almost immediately after his election also imposed neoliberal economic structures). Cf. Jo-Marie Burt Aldo Panfichi, *Peru: Caught in the Crossfire* (Jefferson City, Mo.: Peru Peace Network USA, 1992), 19.

20. Gustavo Gutiérrez, "The Preparatory Document for Puebla: A Retreat from Commitment," in Gustavo Gutiérrez, *The Power of the Poor in History*, trans. Robert R. Barr (Maryknoll, N.Y.: Orbis, 1983), 113 (abbreviated: PP). For Gutiérrez's latest reflections on postmodernity see his "Liberation Theology and the Future of the Poor," in *Liberating the Future: God, Mammon, and Theology,* ed. Rieger.

21. Gustavo Gutiérrez, "The Preparatory Document for Puebla: A Retreat from Commitment," PP, 123.

break can happen without abandoning the more helpful aspects of both camps. The concern for popular religiosity, for instance, picks up a new vitality where it is no longer made to serve the interests of the powers that be but is seen in relation to its own genuine location, the underside of history. When related to the underside of history, the turn to the self can help theology to think about God in relation to the world in more specific terms.

As I have argued, the Latin American perspective cannot be understood without the tension of center and periphery. Even at a time when dependency theory has become less useful as an analytic tool, dependence is still a major factor of life at the periphery, including the church. We have seen how the powers both of the self and of the text are always in danger of serving the center in their own ways. People on the underside of history remind us that in every attempt to see theology in North and South together, the asymmetry of power between center and periphery must be taken into account.

It is clear now that liberation theology in North America cannot be a copy of its more famous Latin American counterpart. History has shown that the Latin American struggle with the power of the text, a matter of life and death, can easily be co-opted by North American liberalism. Herzog warned early on that "the more the fixation on Latin American theology as problem-solver of our North American dilemmas grows, the more shackled to capitalism we will become."[22]

Building Bridges

While it is clear that the historical context of the North is, from its very beginnings, that of modernity and a capitalist economy, this question is more complicated in the South. Some have argued that capitalism was already part of the conquest, but others have stressed the feudal structures of Latin American society, some of which are still in place even today.[23] Without having to decide this question here, we must realize the simultaneous presence of different structures in Latin America, which now include late capitalism and the neoliberalism of the nineties.

---

22. Frederick Herzog, "Introduction: On Liberating Liberation Theology," in Hugo Assmann, *Theology for a Nomad Church* (Maryknoll, N.Y.: Orbis, 1976), 19, included in *Theology from the Belly of the Whale: A Frederick Herzog Reader*, ed. Rieger.

23. José Carlos Mariátegui, *Seven Interpretive Essays on Peruvian Reality*, introduction by Jorge Basadre, trans. Marjory Urquidi (Austin: University of Texas Press, 1971), shows the coexistence of both feudal and capitalist structures, while Pablo Richard, *Death of Christendoms, Birth of the Church: Historical Analysis and Theological Interpretation of the Church in Latin America*, trans. Phillip Berryman (Maryknoll, N.Y.: Orbis, 1987), 27, considers the feudal traits of colonial Christendom to be a "secondary contradiction."

These differing structures have left their mark on the theological land-scape as well. At the time of the early theological encounters with the poor, there coexist "a traditional theology (a reflection of the classes tied to agriculture), a theology of development (of the bourgeois and petit-bourgeois classes), and the theology of liberation (which expresses the faith of the emerging classes: workers, peasants, the marginalized, and radicalized sectors of the middle)."[24] Nevertheless, as we have already seen, the classes in power have a tendency to draw closer together in times of crisis. The theology of development is now often allied with the more traditional outlook. Theology in touch with the underside, on the other hand, always stands on its own.

In North America, two civil religions that by now fiercely oppose each other in the "culture wars" have emerged out of a more unified economic situation. Yet both camps have more in common than they tend to realize. Encounters with the underside of history have helped us to see the obvious: In both camps the modern middle class is in control. For this reason, the liberal camp, lacking in the "vertical" dimension of faith, cannot immediately transform the conservative camp, crippled in the "horizontal" dimension, or vice versa.

Ultimately, theology in both the United States and in Latin America shows in different ways how the "self" and the "text" have forged alliances in the production of theological authority. At a time when the "first world" middle-class self is at the peak of its powers, even the existing orthodoxies tend to fit in because their critiques of the self never mention one of the most basic features of the power of the self: its self-promotion on the back of the other. In other words, if the modern self's inability to acknowledge the existence of the other is not addressed, it makes little sense to introduce the claims of the Other (be it doctrine, the Bible, or Godself). Without respect for the other, respect for the Other is in trouble.

In this connection, the view from the underside of history has deep-ened theological analysis and helped to uncover the interrelation of authority and power. But this must not lead to another "realism." As we have seen, that which takes up the position of the real in any given setting cannot assume the ultimate position of authority or power. Gutiérrez expresses it best: "We are not so sure about the possibility

---

24. Enrique Dussel, "Sobre la historia de la teología en América Latina," in *Liberación y cautiverio: Debates en torno al método de la teología en América Latina*, ed. Enrique Ruiz Maldonado (Mexico City: Comité Organizador, 1976), 50.

of another, really different society. But we are convinced about the non-necessity of the present society."[25]

Contrary to the suspicion of its critics, theology listening to the underside does not end up confusing theology and politics. Theology in touch with the Latin American poor, for instance, having experienced the results of Christendom's confusion of authority and power in their own bodies, is well aware of this problem. Theology in relation with marginalized people in North America, beginning to understand that the culture wars and the related culture-Protestantisms are serving only the interests of a certain group of people, might teach us to be equally cautious.

Rather than politicizing theology, theology encountering the underside exposes the way everything is already politicized. Theology from the underside can, therefore, no longer take place in the sphere of ideas alone. At different points, both Gutiérrez and Herzog wonder whether, in order to change prevailing structures of power, it might be necessary to place the means of production in the hands of the people.[26] Ultimately, we may find that this statement applies to the production of theology as well.

Relocating Authority

Leonardo Boff has argued that a reconstruction of authority can only emerge in a certain vacuum of power that he finds in Latin America: "Given the power structure at the center, the periphery is the only place where true creativity and freedom is possible."[27] My observations so far, however, suggest that it is exactly the other way around, for the periphery, like any other place on the underside of history, is the point where power and its consequences are experienced as most pressing, threatening, and deadly. It is precisely in this situation that an insight into the dangers of such power, which extends to the debates of theological authority, emerges. As we have seen throughout these chapters, when confronted by oppressive power, the question of authority becomes more important than ever. Authority is reconstructed from the

---

25. Gustavo Gutiérrez, "The Voice of the Poor in the Church," in *Is Liberation Theology for North America? The Response of First World Churches* (New York: Theology in the Americas, 1978), 33.

26. See, for instance, Frederick Herzog, *God-Walk: Liberation Shaping Dogmatics* (Maryknoll, N.Y.: Orbis, 1988), 44 (abbreviated: GW).

27. Leonardo Boff, *Church: Charism and Power: Liberation Theology and the Institutional Church*, trans. John W. Diercksmeier (New York: Crossroad, 1985), 62.

underside of history, where the excesses of power are most obvious and most damaging.[28]

Realizing the Differences

In both Americas theology plays an important role because the churches have a fairly significant place in society. In Latin America theology is more important than in most other places of the "third world" since Christians are in the majority. North Americans are often surprised to learn that in the United States theology is still more influential than in most other places of the "first world," which, like Europe, are highly secularized. Given this fundamental importance of theology, theological discourse in North and South needs to focus on different issues. An initial comparison may start with Herzog's sense of this difference: "In Latin America generally, our sisters and brothers are struggling with the subjective component, faith, or an anthropological starting point. In North America the issue is basically the character of God and christology as both relate to history."[29]

What is at stake can be explained in relation to two well-known critiques of religion. The North American situation is closer to a problem addressed by Karl Barth, in which religion is the means by which the human being tries to control God. The Latin American situation corresponds more to Dietrich Bonhoeffer's analysis of the problem of religion, in which God ends up suppressing the human person. Gutiérrez assumes that Bonhoeffer's critique of religion, unlike Barth's, corresponds to a phenomenon of Western history.[30] But, as I have shown, Barth's critique of the modern self is de facto related to a historical phenomenon as well and may be more pertinent for the "first world's" love affair with the self than Bonhoeffer's.

In Latin America, the major problem is that it is God, more precisely the texts of the church, which in the theology of Christendom tend to stand in for God, that subjugate all of life. In this context, the Latin American encounter with the poor, throwing light on the conflictual

---

28. In the encounter with the underside, theology has learned that the notions of center and periphery, initially used to describe the relation of North and South, also point to realities that exist within these settings. Both North and South have learned their specific lessons: Having started out with the broader picture of global dependency in the Latin American context, Gutiérrez is becoming more and more aware of the microcosm of power within Latin America and Peru. In the North American context, on the other hand, the awareness of the macrocosm is growing, as exemplified by Herzog's work, which was initially rooted within the specific setting of the southern United States.

29. Herzog, GW, 238 n. 14.

30. See Gutiérrez, "The Limitations of Modern Theology: On a Letter of Dietrich Bonhoeffer," PP, 230.

relation of the self and the other, raises new theological questions that introduce a different dimension into a theology shaped by the symbolic-order forces of the text. This dynamic does not necessarily lead to the reduction of the authority of the symbolic texts to the authority of the self, as often happened in modern theology in the North, because the newly found relationship to the other opens up the self for new encounters with the texts of the church as well. In the encounter with the other, the self learns to give up its desire for control. Why should the Latin American poor, especially where they preserve their sensitivity for the plight of the other, assume the controlling character of the modern self?

In the North American context, on the other hand, theology must come to grips with the central position of the self in the ego's era. The major problem of mainline Protestant theology is that the human being, more precisely the modern self — typically white, male, and middle class — which now controls much of the planet, has extended its reach to God's own place. Here, the encounter with the underside provides a different challenge. In Herzog's words, "Liberation theology, as created for us by the poor, makes us accountable to the Bible."[31] Aware of the neoorthodox emphasis on the texts of the church, which leaves the modern self untouched, we need to develop new readings of the Bible that listen more closely to the concerns of those who have been victims of the power of the modern self. Here the encounter with the underside leads to a major relocation of authority, taking more seriously the texts of the church, which was not possible where the modern self ruled supreme.

Lessons from the Underside

North and South can learn from each other on a number of different levels. We now see more clearly that many attempts to overcome the problems of the predominant theologies in each hemisphere are insufficient: The power of the modern self in the North, for instance, is not effectively overcome by the powers of the text alone. In some cases the self is even reinforced and protected by the text. On the other hand, we have seen that the powers of the text in the South (which still serve the center) cannot be effectively overcome by substituting the pulsations of the modern self, which shuts out its connection to the other. In both

---

31. Frederick Herzog, "From Good Friday to Labor Day," *Journal of Religious Thought* 34:2 (Fall–Winter 1977/78), 18.

cases only something else, a look from the perspective of the underside of history (the position of the Lacanian "real"), will make a difference.

In North America, theology needs to find its bearings in relation to the power of the (biblical) text that knows its limits in the encounter with those on the underside of history. In Latin America, theological change is geared to the power of a new self that finally gets to know its other in the context of a reconstruction of the traditional texts. In both instances, people on the underside of history move closer to the center of theological reflection without usurping ultimate authority. The encounters with the ("real") other help to break open the rigid structures of the (imaginary-order) self in the North and the (symbolic-order) text in the South, reminding us that neither the self nor the text must occupy the place of God. In this way both self and text are set free from their captivity to entrenched structures of power, ready for more constructive participation in the formation of theological authority.

The common theological theme that emerges here is a deeper aware-ness of the nature of the relation of God and humanity. A common misunderstanding goes like this: As theology from the underside of his-tory, liberation theology is "admittedly 'horizontal' in its approach. The primary focus is on man and his environment, not on God and eternity. The 'nasty now and now' takes precedence over the 'sweet bye and bye.'"[32] While it is hardly necessary to spend much time on comments like this, another observation along these lines is worth closer attention. As I have argued from the outset, theology from the underside of his-tory shares in the awareness of theology in modern times that we can only talk about God in relation to the human being, and it is for this reason that the horizontal-vertical dichotomy breaks down. At a time when the debate over how much authority is to be attributed to either side is still in full swing, a new option is created: Theology no longer needs to follow either modern theology's emphasis on the human being or the orthodox tendency to emphasize the role of God. The terms of the debate shift when theology talks about God in God's relation to the suffering and oppressed human being. Here the tug-of-war for authority between humanity and God is no longer the primary issue; at stake is a new relation of God and humanity at the point where the human being is no longer in a position to usurp ultimate power.

Here a new vision of the human being emerges in conjunction with a new understanding of God and Christ. In the Latin American con-

---

32. John Ronald Blue, "Origins of Gustavo Gutiérrez's *A Theology of Liberation*" (Ph.D. diss., University of Texas at Arlington, 1989), 44.

text, Gutiérrez understands that in the encounter with the other, the self is transformed and opened for God at the same time: "If it is true . . . that one must go through humankind to reach God, it is equally certain that the 'passing through' to that gratuitous God strips me, leaves me naked." Christology is where it all comes together: "In Christ humankind gives God a human countenance and God gives it a divine countenance."[33] From the North American perspective, Herzog is more specific yet. Christ does not become human in general, Christ becomes human in a specific setting, time, and place: "As the divine person enters human deprivation in the 'nonperson,' the deprived 'nonperson,' Jesus, also constitutes God. So God as person is constituted also by the homeless, the faceless."[34] In the encounter with the other, God can be more fully respected as Other. In other words, those on the underside remind us that without embracing the human other we are not able to embrace the Otherness of God. And, vice versa, without embracing the divine Other no real encounter with the human other is possible.

Emerging Dialogue

Theologies dealing with the underside of history in various parts of the Americas had their first organized meeting at the 1975 "Theology in the Americas" conference in Detroit. The *National Catholic Reporter* commented that this meeting "brought together for the first time the (Latin American) fathers of liberation theology and their North American disciples."[35] This common misunderstanding, which sees theology from the underside of history as a Latin American phenomenon, fails to understand that in North America encounters with the underside have developed in their own right. If North American theology simply followed the still somewhat fashionable flights into the "third world," dialogue between North and South would be impossible.

Only on the grounds of our own encounters with marginalized people in the North can a meaningful relation to the struggles of the South be established. Liberation theology language without such encounters will end up keeping the real conflicts of our times concealed and get stuck in the theological mainline. What ultimately keeps theologians apart and prevents dialogue is not only the difference in

---

33. Gutiérrez, TL, 119.

34. Frederick Herzog, "A New Spirituality: Shaping Doctrine at the Grass Roots," *Christian Century* (July 30–August 6, 1986), 681. In GW, xv, Herzog argues that Christology today can no longer do without a "focus on Jesus as refuge and refugee, person and non-person, for Jesus' person embraces also all who have been rejected as persons, the marginals and the poor."

35. September 5, 1975.

geographical or cultural location. Gutiérrez finds "the dividing line between two experiences — two eras, two worlds, two languages,"[36] in real
encounters with people struggling on the underside of history. Theological dialogue of the future will in no small part depend on the
participation in the experiences of those on the underside of history.

Most instrumental in such a dialogue are Christian communities at
the grass roots since, according to Gutiérrez, "the practice of these
communities continually leads them beyond themselves,"[37] opening up
the closed ranks of the church, building networks of solidarity, and
thus becoming truly evangelistic. In this respect the North can learn
a great deal from the South. At a time when "the church framework
for liberation theology in North America is practically nonexistent,"[38]
Herzog's active participation in the rebuilding of grassroots communities is tied to his perception that a new dynamic is emerging on the
underside. His own work with small groups of divinity school students
amounts to nothing less than a protest "against our whole Western conquest tradition" because "all our European roots are at stake at the
same time."[39] There are numerous parallels between the Latin American base communities and the direction certain emerging grassroots
communities take in North America. These communities share four
basic concerns, as listed by Herzog: "(a) Reading the bible afresh (from
below). (b) Celebrating the eucharist more frequently. (c) Strong lay
leadership. (d) Social analysis in full awareness of social location."[40]

It is in these groups, where the Bible is read and poor and oppressed
people take on leadership and develop networks of support, that the
modern self is transformed into a communal self that learns to relate
to the other. This is no easy task and Herzog reports difficulties. Even
in the nineties the gap between white and black is still wide at Duke

---

36. Gutiérrez, "Liberation Praxis and Christian Faith," PP, 70.

37. Gustavo Gutiérrez, "The Irruption of the Poor in Latin America and the Christian
Communities of the Common People," in *The Challenge of Basic Christian Communities*, ed.
Sergio Torres and John Eagleson (Maryknoll, N.Y.: Orbis, 1981), 118.

38. Herzog, GW, 19.

39. Frederick Herzog, "Full Communion Training," *Covenant Discipleship Quarterly* 5:5
(May 1990), 13, included in *Theology from the Belly of the Whale: A Frederick Herzog
Reader*, ed. Rieger. Cf. also Herzog's report on the covenant discipleship groups at Duke
in "Laying the Groundwork at Duke Divinity School," *Covenant Discipleship Quarterly* 1:3
(April 1986), 4.

40. Herzog, "Full Communion Training," 11. See also Herzog GW, 51–52. Herzog
is especially interested in the revival of the traditional Methodist class meetings in the
so-called covenant discipleship groups. Cf. also David Lowes Watson, *Covenant Discipleship: Christian Formation through Mutual Accountability* (Nashville: Discipleship Resources,
1991).

and elsewhere.[41] To speak of theology in touch with the underside of history in the North in terms of "an 'irruption of the poor,'" as Gustavo Gutiérrez does in regard to the liberation struggle of the poor in Latin America, would be inaccurate," Herzog explains. He recalls that "there were slums in Durham, North Carolina, it is true. But there was not the vast poverty of the *asentamientos humanos,* the shanty towns, of Peru or any other 'Two-Thirds World' country." At the same time, however, even in North Carolina "a change took place. The voiceless found a voice and the nonpersons discovered themselves as persons."[42]

The importance of Christian base communities among the poor in the Latin American context is undisputed.[43] But there are also North American strands developing that bear close resemblance to Gutiérrez's summary of their importance as "places for reflection within a church born of the faith of the people," where lives are transformed, hope is kept alive, and bread is shared. In such communities poor people read the Bible in the context of their lives, an experience that brings those who participate closer to each other and to God.[44] Any future dialogue between North and South will do well to make use of this basis as the place where the self, the other, and the texts of the church are tied together in condensed forms, thus opening new theological vistas. Dialogues that take place solely on the levels of the texts of the church or the modern self miss an important aspect.

Toward a "Common Tradition"

Parallel to the emerging dialogue of North and South, theological encounters with the underside turn the established self-understanding of the ecumenical process back from its head to its feet. From the sixties on, a new ecumenical movement has been on the rise that bases itself in the life of grassroots Christian communities. Ecumenical disputes about doctrinal issues remain significant, but ecumenical relations can no longer take place at the level of the ecclesial texts alone. Like the dialogue of North and South, ecumenical relations need to be tied back to the praxis of the church in specific settings.

41. Cf. Herzog, "Full Communion Training," 14.
42. Frederick Herzog, "Liberation and Process Theologies in the Church," *Prism* 5:2 (Fall 1990), 61, included in *Theology from the Belly of the Whale: A Frederick Herzog Reader,* ed. Rieger.
43. For an in-depth study of their dynamics see, for instance, Daniel H. Levine, *Popular Voices in Latin American Catholicism,* Studies in Church and State (Princeton: Princeton University Press, 1992).
44. Gutiérrez, "The Irruption of the Poor in Latin America," 118.

In this context, the scope of both transdenominational and transnational theological dialogues is changing. Gutiérrez finds the deeper significance of such dialogues not on the theological level alone but in the bridges that are built between Christian communities, including their specific contexts.[45] In the midst of a growing awareness of global interdependencies, the awareness grows at the grassroots that, as Herzog puts it, God "makes us respond *together* to the global pressures of the liberation process."[46] Here different theologies can join forces across denominational and national boundaries in new ways. On the basis of a common commitment to those at the margins, a reconstruction of the symbolic-order discourse of the church becomes possible in which all sides can learn from each other without prescribing a unilinear theological outcome.

In joining God's involvement with people on the underside, something like a "common tradition" develops.[47] This tradition is no longer primarily rooted in an exchange of ideas at the level of theological systems and formal appeals from the top down. Herzog explores another ground for the restructuring of ecumenical relationships, from the bottom up: "If we come to understand God in the Catholic community of which poor Christians are a part, do we not through them and with them have 'a common history of oppression and common struggles for liberation'?"[48] Theology needs to become aware of the links that are already in place.

The common tradition that unites the Americas is first of all a common tradition of violence that produced the death of 100 million Indians from Hispaniola to Wounded Knee.[49] On the basis of the dominance of the human being defined in economic terms in both North and South all the way back to Christopher Columbus, Herzog points out

---

45. See Gutiérrez, "Introduction to the Revised Edition," TL, xxxvi.

46. Frederick Herzog, "Pre-Bicentennial U.S.A. in the Liberation Process," in *Theology in the Americas*, ed. Sergio Torres and John Eagleson (Maryknoll, N.Y.: Orbis, 1976), 162. See also Frederick Herzog, "Wenn Supermacht zum Götzen wird," *Evangelische Kommentare* 8:8 (August 1975), 459.

47. In the context of the relation of North and Latin America Herzog has coined a Spanish term for it: *tradición común*. See Herzog, "Tradición Común Shaping Christian Theology: Mutualization in Theological Education."

48. Frederick Herzog, "Athens, Berlin, and Lima," *Theology Today* 51:2 (July 1994), 272–73. Almost nine years earlier Herzog, "Pre-Bicentennial U.S.A. in the Liberation Process," 165, had put it like this: "Under the global pressures, the tough historical realities override the 'religious' differences of the past. We have a *common* task in a world of need. The power of the *one* history of God propels us towards oneness as Christians."

49. According to the estimate of historians. Cf. Frederick Herzog, "New Birth of Conscience," *Theology Today* 53:4 (January 1997), 479. This essay is also included in *Liberating the Future: God, Mammon, and Theology*, ed. Rieger.

that "the vast masses of the poor and the destruction of the environment on both continents have become an all-encompassing challenge
for our interpretation of the Bible, of the whole Christian tradition,
and of our modern human selfhood."[50] What ties North and South
together is not first of all a common essence, common tastes, or a common history of ideas, but the reality of massive suffering at the hands of
Europeans that has never been fully accounted for. The common tradition grows out of an account of the suffering of humanity and of all
of creation that often goes unnoticed. Today, oppressive structures, particularly the growing pressures of a global economy, are bringing those
who are left out closer together.

Such an understanding of a common tradition does not impose uni-
formity. Shaped in an awareness of the underside of history, it will allow
for listening to diverse voices of pain. Practical solidarity in suffering
leads to new relationships so that to the common history of oppression
corresponds a common history of liberation. Out of this process grow
new models for transnational and transdenominational relationships
among Christians.[51] Not even in the church can a common tradition be
built from the top down anymore. A common tradition emerges where
relationships are built at the grass roots, where people join in God's
work in specific settings.

The perspective of the underside of history keeps us aware that a
common tradition must not do away with different identities. Early on
in the civil rights struggle Herzog learned that the idea of the "melt-
ing pot" is an illusion. He promotes a different model: "The goal is to
weave the separate histories into one history in which the single strands
do not lose their original color."[52] The main objective of the search for
a common tradition is not the creation of a single identity in which
everything becomes alike but rather a fresh encounter with the plight
of the other, including a better understanding of common structures of

---

50. Herzog, "Tradición Común Shaping Christian Theology: Mutualization in Theological Education," 6, 7. This paper reports on the preliminary results of this effort to
initiate "research on the shared memories and interests as well as the complicities of
North and South in order to arrive at a 'mutualization' of theological education." (Cf.
abstract.)

51. Gutiérrez, TL, xxxvi, sees the importance of international theological dialogues
"not in the coming together of theologians, but in the communication established among
Christian communities and their respective historical, social, and cultural contexts, for
these communities are the real subjects who are actively engaged in these discourses
of faith." Cf. also Frederick Herzog, "Kirchengemeinschaft im Schmelztiegel — Anfang
einer neuen Ökumene?" in *Kirchengemeinschaft im Schmelztiegel*, ed. Frederick Herzog and
Reinhard Groscurth (Neukirchen-Vluyn: Neukirchener Verlag, 1989).

52. Herzog, "Wenn Supermacht zum Götzen wird," 458.

oppression. In this process the "first world" can finally learn from the "third world," those in power can finally learn from those at the margins, men from women, whites from blacks, the rich from the poor, and so on. In a "first world" setting, the objective must be, first of all, a fresh encounter with the other, the realization of the blindness out of which our identity has been constructed. The encounter with our mission history south of the border, for instance, can, according to Herzog, "be a very creative moment when all of us begin to work together, those who still in their flesh bear the marks of formation and deformation through this mission . . . , and those who are the heirs of the missionary sending agency."[53]

Nevertheless, the reconstruction of the common tradition of the Americas is a most sensitive issue because any hope for dialogue will need to keep in mind the existing asymmetries between North and South as well as between those at the margins and those in control. All attempts initiated by the North and by those in control that seek to "liberate" the South and to help the poor, rather than to examine one's own role in the mirror image of the other, are therefore highly problematic. In order to develop the dialogue between North and South, new relationships need to be built in which control is given up and power is shared. Who would be better suited to remind us of this than those forced to live on the underside of history?

---

53. Herzog, "Tradición Común Shaping Christian Theology: Mutualization in Theological Education," 14, 15.

Chapter 8

Eruption or Irruption?

THEOLOGY ENCOUNTERING the underside of history combines a concern for the human other with a concern for the divine Other. We have already seen that here a new relationship between God and humanity develops that reshapes modern theology's tug-of-war between the authority of the self and the authority of God. In this chapter I will take a look at how this relationship is developed.

In this process, a fresh discernment of God's work and the power of the Holy Spirit becomes possible, tying together an account of how God's work manifests itself in history and an awareness (which is often in jeopardy in those theologies that focus on the self or on the texts alone) that the real can never be reached or contained. Thus, a theology is born that raises concrete historical questions in locating God's presence but is at the same time aware of the ongoing need for questioning and self-critique. The goal is not determined in advance and the way is established as we go.

Liberation Spirituality

The encounter with the poor and oppressed has initiated a closer connection of theology and spirituality, deeply rooted in the reality of basic Christian communities in both Americas. As Pablo Richard has pointed out, this focus on the community and the spirituality aspect that goes with it are no luxuries: "Above all, it is the poor who need a community to survive."[1]

This new emphasis on spirituality promotes the insight that the theological enterprise is a second (although not a secondary) step, a critical reflection on praxis. The significance of this new outlook can only be understood against the background of the dominant theological models in North and South: In Latin America, and particularly in Peru,

---

1. Pablo Richard, "The Church of the Poor in the Decade of the '90s," *LADOC* 21 (November/December 1990), 19.

Roman Catholic Christendom and New Christendom have grounded themselves immediately in the texts and dogmas of the tradition, often limiting spirituality to the repetition of theological truths. In this approach, spirituality, doctrine, and theology are confused. In the United States, various theological attempts to focus on the texts of the church have promoted a similar tendency. Yet here we must also keep in mind the general emphasis of liberal theology on the autonomy of the modern self, an emphasis that tends to identify spirituality and orthopraxis. In this latter instance, theology is often still a first step whose subsequent application to praxis is more or less a matter of "technique."

These processes, which have led to a narrowing of spirituality, are reversed in the encounter with the underside of history. Spirituality becomes once more a holistic enterprise, a way of life in which the text, the self, and the other are all tied together in the formation of new community. In this sense, it is just another term for the traditional "following of Christ." The apostle Paul defines it as "walking according to the Spirit," an interaction with God's Spirit that encompasses the whole of life.[2] In following Christ a spirituality emerges in which both the mechanistic focus on the text and the self-centeredness of the modern self are transformed.[3]

At this point, however, a significant difference in the approach to spirituality emerges. In Latin America, responding to the traditional stress on orthodoxy in Christendom and a related neglect of the praxis of the poor, theology develops a new vision of a creative relation of orthodoxy and orthopraxis, right belief and right praxis.[4] Here the encounter with the underside leads to an "eruption." Poor people, pushed into positions of repression, finally make their presence felt in the life of the church. Coming to terms with its repressed underside, theology picks up new energy. In North America, on the other hand, the notion of orthopraxis often tends to reinforce the power of the modern self, and marginalized people can easily be sucked into a "just do it" mode that does not work for the powerless. Here the encounter with the under-

---

2. Cf. Gustavo Gutiérrez, "¿Qué es espiritualidad?" *Diakonia* 9:33 (January–March 1985), 2, 6, and Gustavo Gutiérrez, *We Drink from Our Own Wells: The Spiritual Journey of a People,* foreword by Henri Nouwen, trans. Matthew J. O'Connell (Maryknoll, N.Y.: Orbis, and Melbourne: Dove, 1984), 3 (abbreviated: WD).

3. Cf. Frederick Herzog, "Kritische Spiritualität," *Evangelische Kommentare* 17:10 (October 1984), 543.

4. Cf., e.g., Gustavo Gutiérrez, "Introduction to the Revised Edition," in Gustavo Gutiérrez, *A Theology of Liberation: History, Politics, and Salvation,* Revised 15th Anniversary Edition, trans. Sister Caridad Inda and John Eagleson (Maryknoll, N.Y.: Orbis, 1988), xxxiv (abbreviated: TL).

side leads to what I call an "irruption." In the encounter with God's own praxis, which interrupts and challenges the structures of dominant orthopraxis and thus creates new space, alternative forms of spirituality and praxis emerge. Theology can no longer be business as usual.

Eruption

In the Latin American encounters with the underside, theology is re-shaped in the eruption of the church of the poor in history. This is tied closely to the spirituality of the people as the nodal point where both praxis and theological reflection come together. Two things must be considered. First, we must keep in mind the development of the base communities in Latin America, creating a church that is not just *for* the poor, but *of* the poor. Second, the reflection on the praxis of the church as "eruption in history" is tied to a theological reinterpretation of the classic Roman Catholic emphasis on the role of the church.

The work of Gustavo Gutiérrez is one of the best examples of how these impulses are drawn together theologically. In the eruption of the church of the poor in history, the Holy Spirit assumes a central role; it is the Spirit who establishes the connection of the church and Christ. In this context, practical spirituality means that *the church appropriates Christ in the power of the Holy Spirit.* Without an account of the dynamic of this interrelationship of ecclesiology, Christology, and pneumatology, the challenge of the underside of history to theology can hardly be understood. All these elements are related most closely at the Eucharist.

Gutiérrez discusses the Eucharist under the (traditional) heading of the church, which, according to Roman Catholic understanding, is the primary sacrament. The definition of the Second Vatican Council of the church as "sacrament of history" sets the stage for a critique of the ecclesiocentrism and self-referentiality of traditional Christendom. The council begins to understand that the starting point for theological reflection is the presence and activity of the church in the world.[5]

In this perspective Gutiérrez interprets the Eucharist as "a memorial of Christ which presupposes an ever-renewed acceptance of the meaning of his life" and a "thanksgiving for the love of God which is revealed in these events." He goes on to explain that "in the Eucharist we celebrate the cross and the resurrection of Christ, his Passover from death to life, and our passing from sin to grace."[6] This interpretation puts a strong emphasis on the praxis of the church in the acts of remembering

---

5. Gutiérrez, TL, 7. Gutiérrez refers to *Gaudium et Spes*, no. 1.
6. Ibid., 148, 149.

and gratefully accepting the meaning of the life of Christ. That grace, which is generated by Christ, needs to be made real now by the church.[7]

Yet Gutiérrez, and this is crucial, does not end his reflections with this focus on the church. He argues that the center of liberation, and thus the foundation of all theological reasoning, is God's love manifest in Christ.[8] In this he sides again with the spirit of Vatican II against the ecclesiocentric positions that have enjoyed a resurgence lately in Peru and elsewhere in Latin America. The church of the poor cannot be imagined without a strong Christological center.[9]

The importance of the Christ event is that it sets in motion a dynamic vision of history. Nevertheless, the kingdom of God does not emerge without our acceptance of this dynamic in the Eucharistic "dialectic" of "thanksgiving to God and in deeds done for our brothers and sisters."[10] In this account Christian praxis is emphasized at least as strongly as Christ's concrete presence. Our hope, according to Gutiérrez, is that — this quotation is quite telling — Christ "will understand us, because even today, as he sits at the Father's right hand, some of Galilee's dust must still be on his feet."[11] This does not mean that Christ is absent, but his presence is strongly related to the poor of today: "By identifying himself with the poor of the world, the Lord to some extent hides his face and activity behind them, thereby telling us that the casting out of the poor is a denial of the kingdom and causes his absence." The church is called to identify and proclaim God's hidden presence with the poor.[12]

The focal point of the argument is the church's *imitatio Christi*, its imitation and appropriation of Christ in the power of the Holy Spirit. It is the role of the church to make Christ's victory present in history. At the Eucharist, "we express our wish and intent to make our own the meaning Jesus Christ gave to his life, and to receive the Spirit, the gift of loving as he loved."[13] In this way Christ is the norm of our theol-

---

7. "The followers of Jesus are those who translate the grace they have received... into works done for the neighbor and especially the poor." Gustavo Gutiérrez, *The God of Life*, trans. Matthew J. O'Connell (Maryknoll, N.Y.: Orbis, 1991), 132 (abbreviated: GL).

8. Gutiérrez, TL, 187 n. 55.

9. See, for instance, Gustavo Gutiérrez, "The Truth Shall Make You Free," in Gustavo Gutiérrez, *The Truth Shall Make You Free: Confrontations*, trans. Matthew J. O'Connell (Maryknoll, N.Y.: Orbis, 1990), 170 (abbreviated: TF).

10. Gutiérrez, GL, 102.

11. Ibid., 100.

12. Gutiérrez, "The Truth Shall Make You Free," TF, 157.

13. Gustavo Gutiérrez, "Liberation Praxis and Christian Faith," in Gustavo Gutiérrez, *The Power of the Poor in History*, trans. Robert R. Barr (Maryknoll, N.Y.: Orbis, 1983), 52 (abbreviated: PP). Cf. also GL, 98.

ogy and life. Christian praxis will make a difference according to the "messianic inversion,"[14] which leads to a new understanding of power, now reinterpreted as service, and God's self-identification with the poor. Christ's appropriation by the church of the poor has two aspects that belong together: Christ is appropriated in following the way of Christ in service with the poor and in the encounter with his presence in people on the underside of history. "In our dealings with the poor we encounter the Lord (see Matt. 25:31–46), but this encounter in turn makes our solidarity with the poor more radical and more authentic"[15] — in other words, more Christ-like.

All of this leads to the conclusion that the specific emphasis on presence characteristic of liberation spirituality (cf. chapter 6) is centered in the praxis of the church of the poor, the underside of history erupting into dominant history, motivated by the Holy Spirit. This is "the process whereby God dwells in history."[16] Put in terms of the theological encounter with the underside of history, "True liberation will be the work of the oppressed themselves; in them, the Lord saves history."[17] Here the Roman Catholic tradition is reread in a constructive fashion: In addition to a new focus on the praxis of the church, the Christological impulse of Vatican II is taken up. This is then interpreted, with the Latin American Bishops' Conferences in Medellín, Puebla, and Santo Domingo, in light of the underside of history. Following Christ in Latin America now grows out of an encounter with the poor.

Irruption

In the context of North American mainline theology, in which the modern self is fully aware of its historical powers, theology developing in relation to the underside hinges on the irruption of Christ into concrete historical settings. This irruption aims at the enlistment of the church's praxis in solidarity with the oppressed. In the North American encounter with the underside of history two elements must be considered. Touched by the liberation struggle of the African American community early on, Frederick Herzog has become aware of the liberating role of Christ. Christ joins with the nonpersons, to the point of becoming a nonperson himself, giving new identity to people on the underside and calling to account those on top who consider themselves persons without being aware that they deprive the other of his or her

---

14. Gutiérrez, GL, 88.
15. Gutiérrez, TF, 3.
16. Gutiérrez, GL, 86.
17. Gutiérrez, TL, 120.

personhood. The second element, closely related to the first, has to do with a reinterpretation of the typical Protestant focus on Christ.

In Herzog's development of these issues, similar to Gutiérrez's approach, the Holy Spirit occupies a pivotal position. In the process of Christ's irruption into history, the Spirit establishes the connection to the church. In this context, the formula describing the Latin American dynamic can be inverted: *Christ is appropriating the church through the Holy Spirit.* Again, we need an account of the interrelation of Christology, ecclesiology, and pneumatology. The Eucharist is once more the central place where we can best observe all aspects at work.

The central position of Christ in this process can perhaps best be demonstrated by the fact that Herzog locates the discussion of the Eucharist under the heading of Christology. Although this move takes up the traditional Protestant emphasis on Christ as the primary sacrament, it is a novum in the structuring of dogmatics and implies a certain critique of the church.

"What happened in Jesus," according to Herzog, "was that a hermeneutic of Christology was turned into a hermeneutic of Christopraxis." Theology needs to understand that "in this praxis God entered history, so that thought finally could rise from praxis and we too could act our way into thinking."[18] With this approach to Christology, theology is put on a new basis that differs significantly from both liberal approaches "from below" and orthodox approaches "from above." One of the key questions of Herzog's later work is "What is Jesus doing now?"[19] Jesus' praxis creates a new corporate reality that specifically rehabilitates the nonpersons and exposes the individualistic character of modern societies.

The parallel between North and South is clear. In both settings, the Holy Spirit takes up a central role. But in the North, liberal and Protestant, more emphasis needs to be put on the presence of Christ. The Spirit does not merely present to humanity what Christ did once and for all in cross and resurrection. In North American liberation spirituality, Herzog explains, we have to move "from Jesus sitting at the right hand of God . . . to the Jesus struggling as the right hand of God in history."[20] Here a twofold notion of praxis is developed, distinguishing between God's own praxis in Christ and human praxis. After Auschwitz, one

---

18. Frederick Herzog, *Justice Church: The New Foundation of the Church in North American Christianity* (Maryknoll, N.Y.: Orbis, 1980), 50 (abbreviated: JC).

19. See, for instance, Frederick Herzog, *God-Walk: Liberation Shaping Dogmatics* (Maryknoll, N.Y.: Orbis, 1988), xxiii (abbreviated: GW).

20. Ibid., 116.

of those moments in modern history when the limits of the modern self have become most clear, Christology can no longer be based on orthopraxis but has to grow out of God's own praxis.[21]

Only at this point does the church enter the picture. Its existence is rooted in Christ's realpresence at the Eucharistic event. The mystery of the realpresence at the Eucharist is embodied in the actual sharing of food, in judgment and forgiveness, as well as in the corporate implications that include "the healing of the race, sex, and class divisions, the divisions between generations, and the healing of the nations."[22] The character of Christ's own praxis implies that Christians need to "find the outcast and join God there. Otherwise we won't find the church."[23]

The Eucharist, as the place where Christopraxis and the praxis of the church come together, is not primarily about the imitation of Christ. Herzog coins a new expression when he talks about *innovatio Christi*. In this innovation, the church is "gripped by a new reality."[24] This is crucial since Herzog is convinced that "the problem with white Christianity is not that it does not do enough . . . , but that it does not have power enough to do effectively whatever it does."[25]

The point of all this is not primarily to build a stronger church. Exactly the opposite. Herzog knows that the church must not become the thing itself: "The liberation church is not a matter of being realized here and there in beautifully visible groups. As soon as we begin to point to the holy few . . . we have surrendered our theological integrity." We need to learn to focus beyond ourselves, "to the place where we can see God doing his thing, quiet, unobtrusive, inconspicuous — where we least expect it."[26] The church is not expected to provide all the answers or to construct another system of power. In fact, part of the disturbing experience of the early theological encounters with the underside in North America is that "we no longer know what church is."[27]

---

21. While Herzog is zeroing in on the suffering of the innocent in an international context that includes his own "backyard" in the southern United States, he assumes that "Auschwitz stands out all by itself. German people as Christianized people callously denied their intimate link to the people of God." Herzog, GW, xxvii. Given Herzog's own involvement with Germany and its culture, this is not just a statement about others.

22. Ibid., 140.

23. Frederick Herzog, *Liberation Theology: Liberation in the Light of the Fourth Gospel* (New York: Seabury, 1972), 196 (abbreviated: LT). Later Herzog clarifies that "if we do not begin with the very real presence of Messiah Jesus, no research as such will produce the reality of what the church is rooted in." GW, 91.

24. Herzog, GW, 92. The term *innovatio Christi* is referred to on 154.

25. Herzog, LT, ix.

26. Ibid., 222.

27. Ibid., 194.

In sum, North American liberation spirituality's emphasis on real-presence needs, according to Herzog, to be tied first of all to Christ's irruption into history and his presence with those who have been excluded from being human. "Jesus' suffering continues as inroad on history," he explains. "It is present reality, not mere memory."[28] Here two moments that have often been played off against each other in the two camps of mainline Protestant theology are related: In the Eucharist there is Christ *together* with the community, and there is Christ *as* community.[29] If either of these moments is missing, we might end up with the power of the text in orthodox or postliberal theologies where often the implications of Christ's presence (drawing even the nonpersons into the community) are underrepresented, or with the power of the self in liberal theology where the body of the church has a tendency to lack its head.

Central Issues in the Reconstruction of Theology

It is clear now that, contrary to widespread opinion, the theological encounter with people on the underside of history is not first of all about political theories or economic strategies, even though those aspects can no longer be separated from theological reflection. Its central concerns cannot be grasped in a linear succession of ideas either, be they theological, philosophical, or part of the social sciences. The new theology grows out of an attempt to rethink Christian spirituality in relation to the praxis of both God and the church at the underside of history. Three main themes are emerging that connect the new theological impulses developed in North and South.

Holy Spirit

Ultimately, the similarities of both approaches are more crucial than their differences. In both cases the Holy Spirit is central in the practical appropriation of both Christ and the church in distinct historical settings on the underside of history. The Holy Spirit is as decisive in Gutiérrez's more traditional notion of *imitatio Christi* as in Herzog's emphasis on *innovatio Christi*. For this reason, the ideal of the imitation of Christ is partly relieved of the mechanistic implications that elsewhere have arisen under this concept. In the encounter with the Latin American poor, the notion of the imitation of Christ in the power of

---

28. Herzog, GW, 165.
29. See ibid., 109.

the Spirit makes sense, since works righteousness and the security of a "just do it" mentality are not the problems of those who fight for survival. In North American encounters with people at the margins, reference to the innovation of Christ is helpful, since it does not refer to a freewheeling spirituality that would innovate theology without an often painful awareness of its limits.

Only insofar as the basic parallels are clear can we discuss the implication of the differences. It is now easy to see how, from the perspective of North American Protestant mainline theology, especially if this emphasis on the Holy Spirit is neglected, Latin American theology with the poor could be interpreted in terms of liberal theology, where Jesus is seen as a mere prototype and model. By the same token, if the specific role of the Spirit and practical spirituality on the underside of history is left out, Herzog's North American model could easily be accused of not getting beyond the basic dogmatic assertions and a spiritualizing relationship to Christ.

In the context of Roman Catholicism in Latin America, the Holy Spirit and the church form the decisive unity that, in its eruption in history, makes Christ and Christ's victory present in the world. It is most fascinating how on these grounds a new appreciation develops for the different facets of popular religiosity and the struggle of the poor. This sensitivity for faithful Christian praxis on the underside may well challenge not only an ossified Latin American church which has aligned itself with the status quo, but also many mainline North American churches that would be well served to heed the warning that the church's task is not to survive but to serve. The flip side of this, of course, which would certainly not be less problematic in a North American setting, could be a certain theological idealization and overemphasis of the marginalized. The church of the poor, even though it is providing a necessary critique of the prevailing system and large parts of the church, might still find it difficult at times to be self-critical in its high calling to make Christ present in history.

In the North American Protestant perspective we have found that the Spirit and Christ form the all-important unity that brings about creative innovation, irrupting into history. Because the emphasis on the unity of history, which is so important in Latin American theology in response to all kinds of unhistorical theologies, has all too often had the ring of Manifest Destiny and of a predominantly white, male, middle-class civil religion in the history of North America, the twofold notion of praxis comes as a relief. Stressing Christians' enlistment and participation as coworkers with Christ's praxis helps correct the modern self's dreams of power and control. In this context activism based on a set of theological ideals can easily fail, and so grace must no longer be understood in a quasi-substantial way, as an essence that is either deposited in the church or infused into humanity, or owned by the ecclesial text or by the modern self. Grace is now tied to the praxis of a person, Jesus Christ, who identifies with nonpersons everywhere.

Here, the mainline churches are challenged even more radically, but now the church of the poor is included as well. A thoroughgoing self-critique of the church in all its various settings is crucial. The church becomes a "detective,"[30] finding out where and how God is at work, and uncovering human and ecclesial failure. In this model the sensitive issue is, of course, how to keep Christ's sovereign irruption into history and the praxis of the church on the underside of history together, so as not to idealize either of them or play them off against each other.[31]

North and South together remind us that we must not separate the eruption of the people and God's irruption. In a world that is becoming more and more interdependent, the time seems right for the further development of a truly ecumenical and transnational dialogue. The different theological encounters with the underside in the Americas have the potential of interpreting each other and holding each other accountable in regard to God's work in world and church.

Eucharist

A central element that the theologies from the underside in North and South share is the emphasis on the Eucharist. In the case of the Latin American priest Gustavo Gutiérrez, this concern for the Eucharist is hardly surprising: "I belong to a people who have a strong sense of the sacraments, and with that people I live the faith and practice it."[32] While in the Latin American context the significance of the sacrament is generally acknowledged, in the Protestant North this situation is, of course, very different. In addition to less emphasis on the Eucharist in general, in mainstream Protestant churches Christ's presence at the Eucharist is often imagined in more individualistic terms, related to the individual believer.

Encountering the underside of history, the strong Latin American

---

30. The notion of the "church as detective" was coined by Herzog in a lecture at the University of North Carolina at Chapel Hill in the fall of 1991.

31. This seems to be the problem of Ray S. Anderson, *Ministry on the Fireline: A Practical Theology for an Empowered Church* (Downers Grove, Ill.: InterVarsity Press, 1993), who also uses the term *Christopraxis*.

32. Gutiérrez, *TF*, 45.

emphasis on the sacraments is transformed and the North American Protestant view is expanded. Gutiérrez is well aware of the problems. Even a strong traditional emphasis on the Eucharist can become, "for want of the support of an authentic community," an "exercise in make-believe."[33] The sacraments look different from the underside: "Here, on the terrain of real life, among the very poorest, is where the eucharistic celebration takes on its full meaning of a sharing in the death and resurrection of Christ. In 'the breaking of the bread' — that staple lacking to the disinherited of the earth — the life of the resurrected Christ becomes present reality."[34] The power of the Eucharist is experienced in new ways where the conflicts and brokenness of poor people are included. In this context, the Eucharist becomes one of the nodal points where new thought about the redistribution of power and authority begins to germinate.

In the North the trouble is that the Eucharist has more or less dropped out of the theological perspective. Its power to transform human life as a whole is hardly taken into account. In Herzog's words, "We do not participate eucharistically in God's work, but we are called moralistically to human work. When modern people assume that they easily know God's will and act according to it, anthropological hubris is clearly evident."[35] Mainline Protestantism, whether liberal or conservative, needs to develop a new sense of the realpresence of Christ that cannot be controlled. Gathering together at the communion table, sharing the elements and reading the Scriptures together with those on the underside who defy our control, new encounters with Christ occur. Herzog puts it this way: "Two things need particular clarification in our suburban churches — the poor Christ in the Eucharist, and the Word presence of the poor Christ in the Bible. Only thus will we grasp the presence of Christ in the poor."[36]

Theology from the underside realizes that the Eucharist is not the property of the church and that neither are worship and Christian doctrine. Theology must start over in light of a new vision of the Eucharist that is more open to God's work in church and world. The Eucharist helps expand the Christian search for God's presence without falling back into the control mentality: Where the suffering of the other is

---

33. Gutiérrez, TL, 75.
34. Gutiérrez, "The Historical Power of the Poor," PP, 107.
35. Frederick Herzog, "Thesen zum Zusammenführen der Ströme der Reformation," *Evangelische Theologie* 43:6 (November/December 1983), 550.
36. Frederick Herzog, with Gustavo Gutiérrez, "Dealing with the True Problems," *Books and Religion: A Monthly Review* 13 (March 1985), 12.

realized, a new encounter with Christ at the Eucharist takes place, transforming the theological reliance on the self and on the texts from the bottom up.

Drawing together Christ's presence and the presence of the marginalized, the Eucharist becomes a nodal point where different traditions that have been repressed and kept apart can come together. Herzog's vision of the Eucharist includes a new listening to the silenced traditions of the church. As the "traditions of oppressed groups," those traditions reshape theological thinking in unexpected ways.[37] The Eucharist is where a whole range of different building blocks of theological reflection — Scripture, the liturgy and the creed, the elements of bread and wine, prayer, and the community at the table — are joined in actual solidarity with those on the underside of history in North and South. At the Eucharist, a symbolic sharing takes place of that which is often scarce in the life of many people: food and drink. Here God's praxis and human praxis meet in a most intimate way. No wonder the Eucharist is one of the privileged locations from which a global liberation spirituality emerges.

This leads me back to the title of this book. In remembering Christ at the Eucharist ("do this in remembrance of me," 1 Cor. 11:24), the poor are "remembered" as well, a challenging memory for those in the church who tend to forget their presence. This remembering includes a "re-membering" in which the oppressed finally become full members in the body of Christ, and the creation of new forms of solidarity, power, and authority, where nonpersons become persons. Here eruption and irruption are interrelated most closely.[38]

Praxis

The specific mark of the newly emerging spirituality is, as I have argued, that it is worked out in critical reflection on Christian praxis on the underside of history. Christ relates to those at the margins, as the Gospels and many other biblical traditions in both testaments show. The new insight is, in Herzog's words, that "the Gospel cannot be understood from the top down, only from the bottom up."[39] This look at reality from "the underside" implies a radical theological shift. One of the first to start thinking from this perspective was Dietrich Bonhoeffer, whose work has long given support to theological reflection from the

---

37. See Herzog, "Kritische Spiritualität," 542.

38. The suggestion to give more explicit expression to the various layers of "remembering the poor" comes from my research assistant, John Havea.

39. Herzog, JC, 26.

underside in both North and South. His intuition that theology will need to be done "from below" does not mean, as liberal theology assumed, that theology needs to start from the human being in general or with those who enjoy the privileges of the modern self. Theology needs to start anew from the perspective of the oppressed with whom God freely identifies. The move to the underside of history and practical solidarity with the oppressed is, therefore, a theological one that ties the perspectives "from below" and "from above" together because it "seeks to follow God where [God] has already preceded us."[40]

In this context, praxis is no longer the autonomous praxis by which the modern self perpetuates and preserves its power. In modern liberal theology, even in the Social Gospel movement, the modern self and its power is not reconstructed. In Herzog's words, "The liberal premises seemed to be legitimating doing good for others while not changing oneself."[41] But even where the emphasis is on conversion as reorientation within the private self, the result is often not much different from liberal activism, since the person "is not really *in* his action, but somewhere else, i.e., in his private shell."[42] Poor people, on the other hand, are more likely to understand that the praxis of resistance and the reconstruction of power implies the death of the self, which, in Latin America, sometimes takes on literal forms. Gutiérrez identifies the central element of the power of the poor as living "the love of Christ to the point of giving one's life for one's sisters and brothers."[43]

Consequently, when Gutiérrez talks about one of the levels of liberation (the second level) as ethical, ethics is not understood in terms of some type of activism of the autonomous self, as "a moralistic attitude destined for individual consumption," but as "an element of human and cosmic fellowship."[44] Here ethics is closely related to new human beings emerging out of the ruins. Without the new women and men everything stays the same. All of this is becoming more and more clear once the notion of praxis is redefined as the praxis of those on the underside of history. This is no longer the self-propelled and self-serving praxis of the autonomous modern self.

---

40. This is Eberhard Bethge's interpretation of Bonhoeffer, quoted in Gutiérrez, "The Limitations of Modern Theology: On a Letter of Dietrich Bonhoeffer," PP, 229.

41. Herzog, JC, 137 n. 9.

42. Frederick Herzog, "United Methodism in Agony," *Perkins Journal* 28:1 (Fall 1974), 5. This essay is also included in *Doctrine and Theology in the United Methodist Church*, ed. Thomas A. Langford (Nashville: Kingswood Books, 1991).

43. Gutiérrez, "Liberation and the Poor: The Puebla Perspective," PP, 148.

44. Gustavo Gutiérrez, *Entre las calandrias: Un ensayo sobre José María Arguedas* (Lima: Instituto Bartolomé de Las Casas and CEP, 1992), 37.

In the larger perspective, one of the most central theological concepts, the notion of grace, is reshaped. Grace is not a foundationalist lifesaver or an anthropological constant, something that humanity owns, no matter what. Grace is not a power at the disposal of the self. Grace is what puts people on the way to solidarity with the neighbor, under the guidance of Christ, empowered by the Holy Spirit. This is one of the common threads that runs throughout the work of Gutiérrez as it takes shape in encounters with the underside of history. He sees this as the easily overlooked central message of the book of Job: "Historically . . . commitments lacking this perspective have quickly suffered exhaustion."[45]

At this point "orthopraxis" is no longer social activism in which the modern self affirms itself. In the interplay of grace and demand a space is carved out in which new selves and a community of resistance are created in the encounter with the other. Herzog has learned a similar lesson when he points out that "the core of ethics is participation in God's character in history."[46] Christian praxis must not be confused with a self-centered ethic. Christian praxis on the underside of history is a witness to God's grace, which is most powerful in weakness (2 Cor. 12:9). This kind of praxis leads to a discovery of who God is and to a participation in what God does. Dogmatics and ethics are tied together in God's involvement on the underside.

Nevertheless, theology in touch with the underside is misunderstood if it is seen as the identification of orthopraxis and orthodoxy. This misunderstanding is particularly tragic in the liberal North. One interpreter, for example, argues that Herzog and Latin American liberation theology "fully agree . . . that it is praxis on behalf of the world's poor which is the final measure of church and theology."[47] No doubt, this thesis does not even work for the use of the notion of orthopraxis in Latin America. Gutiérrez, for instance, insists that "the challenge is to be able to preserve the circular relationship between orthodoxy

---

45. Gustavo Gutiérrez, *On Job: God-Talk and the Suffering of the Innocent* (Maryknoll, N.Y.: Orbis, 1987), 128 n. 23.

46. Herzog, *GW*, 28.

47. Craig L. Nessan, *Orthopraxis or Heresy: The North American Theological Response to Latin American Liberation Theology* (Atlanta: Scholars Press, 1989), 171. Cf. another interpreter of liberation theology, Arthur F. McGovern, *Liberation Theology and Its Critics: Toward an Assessment* (Maryknoll, N.Y.: Orbis, 1989), 45, who assumes that according to liberation theologians, orthopraxis should receive priority over orthodoxy. Theodore Runyon, "How Can We Do Theology in the South Today?" *Perkins Journal* 29 (Summer 1976), 3, makes a similar claim about Herzog's work.

and orthopraxis and the nourishment of each by the other."[48] Herzog, writing in closer proximity to the center, never even uses the term *orthopraxis*. It is in "Theo-praxis" that right Christian praxis and belief originate and are brought together. Christian praxis is essential but not ultimately authoritative. It is simply the place where we encounter something new, pushing beyond self-centeredness: "Whenever we are walking together with people in a common justice struggle, the 'stranger' is walking with us. Thus: God-walk."[49]

In the emerging dialogue between North and South we must not forget that Herzog's strict emphasis on God's praxis has been met with initial resistance by Latin Americans. At the Theology in the Americas Conference in 1975, Hugo Assmann raised the question whether "your North American theology is God's action in history without going through history."[50] In the Latin American struggle with the authority and powers of the Christendom church, a lot depends on how the action of the church is determined. This concern serves as a reminder that sheer talk about God's liberation without actual commitment can never be enough. Herzog's point, however, may help North American theology develop a more radical way of "going through history." In the encounter with God's own praxis on the underside, the North American enchantment with the self that cuts its own path through history may finally be challenged and going through history together with the other becomes possible.

Only if the historical and theological differences between North and South are neglected could it be assumed that the difference between an emphasis on "eruption" and a focus in "irruption" is merely a symbolic one. The difference of social location must be respected and acknowledged in order to develop new proposals that reshape the theological debate at the beginning of a new century.

Conclusion

In the final account those pushed to the margins remind us that the church cannot be built exclusively from within. We can no longer afford

---

48. Gutiérrez, "The Truth Shall Make You Free," TF, 104.

49. Herzog, GW, xi.

50. As reported by Alfred T. Hennelly, "Who Does Theology In the Americas?" *America* (September 20, 1975), 139, and quoted in Frederick Herzog, "Introduction: On Liberating Liberation Theology," introduction to Hugo Assmann, *Theology for a Nomad Church* (Maryknoll, N.Y.: Orbis, 1976), 16, included in *Theology from the Belly of the Whale: A Frederick Herzog Reader*, ed. Joerg Rieger, forthcoming from Trinity Press International.

to confine God's own praxis to the ecclesial or "supernatural" sphere. Too much is at stake. Often this issue becomes quite literally a matter of life and death. Praxis, as Christopraxis or as the praxis of the church on the underside of history, can no longer exclude the political realm and an analysis of the prevailing economic modes of production. With the Second Vatican Council, the Roman Catholic Church officially opened up to the world. But today we need to be more specific. Gutiérrez sums it up: "We are called to build the church *from below.*"[51]

Theology encountering the underside is led to expose a spirituality in which social or even political concerns may well be central, but nothing is effectively changed or questioned since, in the words of Gutiérrez, "the 'other' of such a system is not made present, and one remains 'within the family.'"[52] In other words, a simple perpetuation of theology based on the power of the self or the power of the text that neglects the "real other," those who are repressed, will no longer suffice, even if it is done in the name of "transformation" and "social concern." Theology must transcend the typical blindness of the modern self and the ecclesial texts by reading between the lines and venturing into that which, from the perspective of selves and texts, exists only in repressed form.

Theology from the margins is, therefore, never completely unrelated to, but also never immediately identified with, the dominant political and economic modes of production of society. Attention to the political and economic realms is not optional because these spheres strongly affect both people's lives and the faith of the church. At the same time, the view from the underside allows for a critical distance from dominant political and economic systems that avoids both the uncritical support of political and economic activities and the silent endorsements of a spiritualistic attitude that closes its eyes to political and economic realities.

In participating in the reality of those who suffer repression, new avenues for theology open up that liberate theology from circling around the self or being caught up in a closed web of selected ecclesial texts. It is along those lines that the methodological implications of Christopraxis and orthopraxis will need to be discussed further. Here authority

---

51. Gutiérrez, "God's Revelation and Proclamation in History," PP, 22. Cf. also Herzog's discussion of why the church cannot exclusively be built from within in Frederick Herzog, "Dual Citizens," in *Theology from the Belly of the Whale: A Frederick Herzog Reader,* ed. Rieger.

52. Gustavo Gutiérrez and Richard Shaull, *Liberation and Change* (Atlanta: John Knox Press, 1977), 86.

and power are reconstructed in ways that break open closed structures without immediately creating another closure. People on the underside in North and South, knowing that they are not in ultimate positions of authority and power, may help all of theology to understand God's own authority and power in new ways.

Chapter 9

Into the Twenty-First Century

The Underside of History

WE ARE NOW ABLE to envision a different solution to the old tension between those who try to respond to the challenge of the underside by elevating the oppressed to a prominent place of authority and control (not unlike the place occupied by the modern self in much of modern theology), and those who make them recipients of charity and well-meaning support. This turns out to be a false dilemma. If the latter model with its implicit disregard for the person of the other and her contribution to theology is no longer viable, the former is not automatically the only alternative. A theology that includes people on the underside of history, as I have argued throughout, does not necessarily have to end up circling around yet another autonomous self constructed in analogy to the modern self. A new theological paradigm is born out of a better perception of the role of oppressed people in the formation of power and theological authority. This new paradigm, while integrating some of the core insights of modern and traditional theologies, goes beyond yet another "synthesis" or search for a middle road.[1]

In the previous chapters I have explored new perspectives. In regard to authority and power nothing would change if those on the underside of history simply emerged once more as those "autonomous subjects" that, in their classic inability to relate to their neighbors, are part of the problem itself. This is the fundamental lesson to be learned in a liberal North American context. By the same token, the construction of another symbolic-order realism, another ecclesial text or structure that functions as one more hegemonic discourse without genuine regard for others outside of one's own group, does not solve anything either, even if it bears the predicate *popular*. While this lesson comes

---

1. The search for ways of synthesizing the liberal and traditional camps has a long history. For a synthesis that tries to relate the dichotomy of liberation *for* the people and liberation *of* the people see Michael R. Candelaria, *Popular Religion and Liberation: The Dilemma of Liberation Theology* (Albany: State University of New York Press, 1990), 103ff.

to us most strongly from the Latin American context, it raises fundamental questions also for those in the North who (hovering at the end
of modernity) promote the now fashionable theological "turn to the
text" in various ways. The work of Gustavo Gutiérrez serves as a reminder that we must not romanticize any text, not even the texts of
the faith and culture of the poor. What pulls Latin American Christians on the underside of history together most strongly is not primarily
their cultural-ethnic unity, their popular cultures, their embeddedness
in local traditions, or a common system of belief, but rather the fact
that they share repression and marginalization.

Without a doubt, there has been a development in understanding
the role of people on the underside in theology over the past fifty years.
Herzog records the basic framework in terms of the challenge of poverty: "The ecumenical concern for the poor . . . moved from an overview
approach to becoming a pivot around which the dogmatic task as a
whole might turn." In this process, as he observes further, "the word
'poor' became less sentimental."[2] While it seems that the time when
the perspective of the underside might reshape theology as a whole is
still to come, there are numerous instances, around the world and at the
margins of our own countries, that are proof that this process is under
way. The emergence of the voices of women within African American and Hispanic theologies in the United States is but one example
that attention to *the* poor, *the* marginalized, *the* oppressed is becoming less sentimental, less abstract, and more constructive in theological
discourse. To paraphrase Jacques Lacan once more, "*The* poor do not
exist."

The major question for theology that takes seriously those dynamics
is, therefore, no longer what the rich can do for the poor, or what the
poor can do by themselves. The main concern is participating in God's
work of liberation already going on in both church and world and thus
creating new forms of solidarity of rich and poor, oppressors and oppressed, and self and other. Here theology is reshaped. The point of this
solidarity is neither to do something for the people nor simply to record
their actions and ideas as absolute truth. In a reconstruction of the
texts and teachings of the church, which is what theology is ultimately
all about, the theologian draws together in the light of the Gospel the

---

2. Frederick Herzog, "Poor," in *Dictionary of the Ecumenical Movement,* ed. Nicholas
Lossky et al. (Geneva and Grand Rapids: WCC Publications, Wm. B. Eerdmans, 1991),
804.

implications of the eruption of the people in the history dominated by the powers that be, and God's irruption into this same history.[3]

If Latin American theologians say, therefore, that the poor are the teachers, this does not mean that they would own the truth in some a priori fashion, like the modern self.[4] That the poor are teachers has to do with the fact that they and others who share the burden of marginalization are open to something else beyond the authority and powers of ecclesial texts and the modern self. As excluded from, and repressed by, both the powers of the self and of the text, marginalized people can help to cultivate a new look at the way things are, thus providing a desperately needed outside perspective on mainline theology. The poor as teachers are able to expose hidden fault lines and to raise new questions that lead us beyond the current impasse.

More important yet, the "preferential option for the poor" — by limiting the authority of the self and of the text and restricting the reach of the powers that be — creates space for the work of the Holy Spirit. This encounter with the Spirit in places where we least expect it makes possible a new listening both on the level of interpersonal relationships and on the level of Scripture and the traditions of the church. Here new selves are born which are better able to relate to God and their neighbors, and the Scriptures and traditions come alive in new ways. Encounters with people on the underside teach us that the Gospel must always be reread in terms of the concrete struggles and repressions of life where God's saving power is at work, struggles often blended out by those who benefit from them. For this reason theological reflections on authority need to include an account of the power factor as well.

The question may be raised whether all this does not still put too much emphasis on people on the underside. Part of the answer is provided by the historical context itself. Gutiérrez reports the reaction of somebody who had just read a critique of the preparatory document for Puebla: "'Wearisome,' he said, 'it's irritating. All you find here is the poor, the poor, the poor!' To which someone else replied, 'Yes, indeed.

---

3. Other encounters with the underside of history outside of theology record similar dynamics. See, for instance, Neil Larsen, "Postmodernism and Imperialism: Theory and Politics in Latin America," *Postmodern Culture* 1 (September 1990), 41, 42, discussing the approach of Miguel Marmol, the legendary Salvadoran revolutionary described in Roque Dalton's classic *Miguel Marmol*: His task is "not that of 'enlightening' the 'backward' masses, nor is it simply to acknowledge 'what the people thought' as sovereign. Rather, it is to collect these isolated concepts, to articulate them, and to draw the logically necessary conclusions."

4. Modern foundationalism, for instance, provides such an a priori. Obviously, access to a priori truth, to an Archimedean point, helps a great deal in the endeavor to prop up the authority and power of the self.

And the worst of it is, that's all you find in the streets too!'"[5] Perhaps the biggest surprise is not that theology is slowly discovering the world of the underside of history but that even at a time when 35,000 children die every day from preventable causes, so much of theology both in North and South is still oblivious to this issue. Herzog responds to a similar concern in this way: "As far as the poor in *our* midst are concerned, I too, perhaps, may have tended to focus my attention too much on them. But then most of the white churches in the south were not paying attention at all to the liberation process."[6] It is time for all theologians to ask ourselves, If our theologies are not with the people suffering on the underside, where are they? Even though most of us mean well, our various theological camps can become so preoccupied with themselves that this question is never raised.

It is becoming more obvious every day that the other will not go away. It is not just that people suffering from poverty and oppression are still with us, their numbers are growing. At the beginning of the twenty-first century, a time when we have all gotten used to the victory of capitalism, poverty levels and other indicators of imbalance and injustice are increasing not only in certain parts of the "third world" but in the "first world" as well.[7] There is still much left to be done (and to be undone). Theology needs to grasp its own role in this context.

Some of us are slowly beginning to understand that the pain at the margins affects us all. Consequently, theology in touch with the underside of history can no longer be labeled (in sync with that all-pervasive consumer mentality that has long taken over our theological schools and even the academy) as "special interest theology." The development of common perspectives that include at their heart those who hurt the most is no longer optional.[8] The encounter with those in pain imposes new urgency on the collaboration of theologians across the dividing lines of denominations, countries, and continents, as well as race, gender, and class.

---

5. Gustavo Gutiérrez, "The Historical Power of the Poor," in Gustavo Gutiérrez, *The Power of the Poor in History*, trans. Robert R. Barr (Maryknoll, N.Y.: Orbis, 1983), 107 n. 5.

6. Frederick Herzog, "Liberation and Process Theologies in the Church," *Prism* 5:2 (Fall 1990), 62; also included in *Theology from the Belly of the Whale: A Frederick Herzog Reader*, ed. Joerg Rieger, forthcoming from Trinity Press International.

7. See, for instance, the United Nations' *Human Development Report 1996* (New York: Oxford University Press, 1996).

8. See Joerg Rieger, "Developing a Common Interest Theology from the Underside," in *Liberating the Future: God, Mammon, and Theology*, ed. Joerg Rieger (Minneapolis: Fortress Press, 1998).

New Theologians and New Theology

Fredric Jameson's comment that one of the great challenges of "third world" literature has to do with the function and place of the intellectual also applies to theology.[9] In the encounter with people on the underside of history anywhere, the function of the theologian is reconstructed. The task of the theologian can no longer be relegated to the autonomous self, the center around which the modern history of ideas turns, and whose gravity field keeps interfering even with postmodern pluralism. Neither can her task be confined to rehearsing the various doctrinal canons of selected orthodoxies.

The theologian in touch with the underside gradually becomes an organic intellectual, to use a term introduced by Antonio Gramsci. The difference between what Gramsci calls "organic" and "traditional" intellectuals is not that the reflections of one group are contextual while the reflections of others are not. The difference is that one group is not aware of its own context while the other group is trying to gain greater clarity about the relationship of its reflections to its context. The so-called traditional intellectuals, according to Gramsci, "put themselves forward as autonomous and independent."[10] Because they do not realize that they are in fact shaped by their context, their work easily becomes a function of the status quo and ends up preserving it. It is interesting that Gramsci found many of those intellectuals in the Christendom church of his native Italy. Organic intellectuals, on the other hand, include their context in their reflections. In this way they are led to take into account their own biases. This is not only an analytic move but a constructive one as well: Organic intellectuals can learn how to put their intellectual capabilities to work for themselves and for others.

Yet here we hit on a paradox that is often overlooked in the tug-of-war between liberal "contextual" theologies, and all kinds of theologies that see themselves as orthodox and traditional. What today is called contextual theology is often closer to the position of Gramsci's traditional intellectuals, who see little need to do much analysis of the context of theology. The only difference is that this context is now presupposed explicitly rather than implicitly. "First world" contextual theology often ends up as a celebration of its own context, the context of the modern self. There is not much room for God's concern for the

<hr/>

9. See Fredric Jameson, "Third-World Literature in the Era of Multinational Capitalism," *Social Text* 15 (Fall 1986), 74ff.

10. Antonio Gramsci, *Selection from the Prison Notebooks,* ed. and trans. Quintin Hoare and Geoffrey Nowell Smith (New York: International Publishers, 1971), 7.

underside of history or the context of the other. Both the self and the text have trouble stepping outside their frame of reference.

Organic intellectuals, by contrast, seek to reduce the constant temptation to render their own context absolute. In relating to a different context, the context of those at the margins, an ongoing *self*-critical reflection in the most literal sense becomes possible without rendering any context absolute. In this process, the primary task for organic theologians is to learn again how to listen and to find out to whom to listen. Any transformation of context and praxis is based here. Herzog describes the task of theology thus: "Liberation theology begins as the poor begin to listen to each other before God. Liberation theology continues as we listen to the poor before God."[11]

All would be misunderstood, however, were we to view this, including my reflections on Lacanian thought, merely as a general hermeneutical insight that can be easily universalized by those in charge, and thus added to the rosters of hermeneutical studies in theology as one among others. Herzog cautions, to the point of almost contradicting some of his other remarks on the issue, not to romanticize the poor in this way: "Even the idea of a hermeneutical privilege of the poor has to be examined carefully."[12] For the theologian, the central issue is God's own involvement with the poor, rather than any privileges the poor would own. The task of theology is not primarily to shore up the field of hermeneutics, which has come under attack in a postmodern world, but to reexamine the Christian understanding of God's character and the encounter with Christ in light of the encounter with the underside of history, and to join in God's work. In other words, encounters with the underside, while opening new theological vistas, providing new perspectives, and creating new space, do not allow for reconstructing the security and control of the grand systems of modern

---

11. Frederick Herzog, *God-Walk: Liberation Shaping Dogmatics* (Maryknoll, N.Y.: Orbis, 1988), xxii (abbreviated: GW). This is the difference between "eloquence" and "active participation" in Gramsci's description of the organic intellectual: "The mode of being of the new intellectual can no longer consist in eloquence, which is an exterior and momentary mover of feelings and passions, but in active participation in practical life, as constructor, organiser, 'permanent persuader' and not just a simple orator." Gramsci, ibid., 10.

12. Frederick Herzog, "Kirchengemeinschaft im Schmelztiegel — Anfang einer neuen Ökumene?" in *Kirchengemeinschaft im Schmelztiegel,* ed. Frederick Herzog and Reinhard Groscurth (Neukirchen-Vluyn: Neukirchener Verlag, 1989), 40 n. 20. He prefers to talk about a protection privilege instead: "God assists the poor and the rejected, the widows and the orphans." But that comes close to falling back into the other trap, the trap of charity and doing things *for* the poor rather than *with* them.

theology. Encounters with the underside remind us that things need to be kept open and that theology is never quite finished.

Herzog has experienced the truth of his own comment of the seventies that "we ought to admit the almost insurmountable difficulty for traditional theology to begin anew *in identification with the struggle of the oppressed.*"[13] This task has not gotten any easier, and in the late eighties he still sees this as a pressing issue, for "there is little understanding thus far that exactly in regard to scholarship the poor of the world are calling Western Christianity to account." The fundamental challenge is still the same: "It is part of scholarship not to close one's eyes to reality."[14] We do not need to add much to formulate the major challenge for the twenty-first century.

The theologian as organic intellectual has thus learned one of the main lessons of Gutiérrez's book on Las Casas: "There is no innocent theology!"[15] At stake, ultimately, is the issue of truth, tied to an analytic process that helps theology cut through various layers of untruth. As Lacan has taught us, the encounter with the real, in the form of the "symptom" — the product of the repressions of selves and texts — leads to the unmasking of untruth and an uncovering of unconscious truth, the truth masked up by the powers that be. At this point we are back at the critique of authority and power. The main challenge of theology from the underside is not that it would preach the categorical imperative of social activism in an even louder voice, but rather its examination of the social practices and political identities of all of theology in terms of power and authority.

One aspect of this has to do with Pablo Richard's observation that the strength of a theology from the underside lies in the truth, "that is, simply the truth regarding the economic, political and social reality, especially of the poor majority."[16] This point is echoed even more strongly in another (nontheological) work that grew out of encounters with the underside of history in other parts of the world, Frantz

---

13. Frederick Herzog, "Introduction: On Liberating Liberation Theology," introduction to Hugo Assmann, *Theology for a Nomad Church* (Maryknoll, N.Y.: Orbis, 1976), 17, also included in *Theology from the Belly of the Whale: A Frederick Herzog Reader*, ed. Rieger. Emphasis in original.

14. Frederick Herzog, "New Christology: Core of New Ecclesiology?" Review of several books by Latin American liberation theologians in *Religious Studies Review* 14 (July 1988), 216.

15. Gustavo Gutiérrez, *Las Casas: In Search of the Poor of Jesus Christ*, trans. Robert R. Barr (Maryknoll, N.Y.: Orbis, 1993), 193.

16. Pablo Richard, "The Church of the Poor in the Decade of the '90s," *LADOC* 21 (November/December 1990), 15.

Fanon's *The Wretched of the Earth*. Fanon puts it this way: "Now, the *fellah*, the unemployed man, the starving native do not lay a claim to the truth; they do not *say* that they represent the truth, for they *are* the truth."[17] No wonder this book has had such a strong impact on liberation movements all over the globe. Obviously, such claims can easily be misunderstood in the ego's era and continue to create strong reactions one way or another in the reader. But the decisive difference compared to other human claims to be the truth, grounded in the model of the modern Cartesian self or in the immediate access to an inerrant text, should be clear now: We are dealing with a notion of truth that is no longer a priori and foundationalist but relational. Truth in this sense is not so much a universal category, but points to that which has been repressed and covered up in a specific situation. It cannot be determined once and for all but must be discovered time and again along the way.

Theology in touch with the underside, although it challenges the securities of the modern foundationalisms of the self and the realisms of the text, does therefore not need to buy into the relativism of the postmodern world. It keeps searching for truth. But we cannot find it without solidarity with the ("real") other. This implies two things. First of all, the primary challenge for theology is now to examine self-critically precisely what (or who) fills out the position of the "real" for us. At this point we are not just dealing with an abstract epistemological question on the level of theory anymore. In getting in touch with the repressed real, that which lies at the basis of our inmost desires, our unconscious hopes and fears, a change of both thinking and acting becomes possible. The process of discerning truth is, as Lacan has realized, less cognitive than performative. At the same time, there is no need to identify the empty place of the Lacanian real (or Fanon's definition of truth) with God in a theological or philosophical equation. The main point is that any claim to truth is now no longer related to the "be all," the human being in the place of God controlling the world, but to the "not all," the suffering human being keeping open the place of ultimate authority, thus avoiding the idolatrous trappings of most foundationalist approaches.

A second step is related to the first, for this encounter with the real other opens up to an encounter with God, who can never be fully grasped. Here ends the usefulness of our Lacanian framework; there is

---

17. Frantz Fanon, *The Wretched of the Earth*, preface by Jean-Paul Sartre, trans. Constance Farrington (New York: Grove Press, 1968), 49.

no need to claim any identity between God and the real. Theological truth is uncovered in the double encounter with the marginalized and with Christ. Decentering the authority claims of mainline theology, tied to either the self or the text, does not do away with the task of theology (a constant fear of contemporary mainline theology of various camps) but opens new ways for encounters with its subject matter: God in Christ and the Holy Spirit. This process of decentering is part of a long tradition to which the Reformation and the Second Vatican Council also belong in their own ways, both instances of a "decentering" of the church, clearing the way for an encounter with its real center, which can never be had as a possession. The encounter with Christ on the underside of history, a Christ who (like the people on the underside) cannot ultimately be controlled by the powers and authorities that be — not even by putting him to death on a cross — introduces a much needed next step in this ongoing process. Nothing less than a new reformation is at stake.

Paradoxically, at first sight, in this process the Scriptures and the traditions of the church can be taken more seriously than before since they no longer need to serve as warrants for ultimate authority, which can only be in the hands of God. In this context, the textual realities of Bible and tradition contribute once again to the search for truth and can be read in more constructive ways. Most important, however, this approach leaves room for the Spirit, who appears to be under constant tutelage in other theological approaches, for theology now begins exactly at the point where we become aware of our own *self*-limitations in the encounter with the other.

Only if these moments come together — our observation of how God's work manifests itself in unexpected places, on the underside of history, and our awareness that the real can never be reached or contained — can we hope to develop a spirituality that does not give up concrete historical questions in locating God's presence but is at the same time aware of the continuing need for questioning and self-critique. As I have argued throughout, without encounters with the repressed human other who is different, encounters with the divine Other are unlikely, an insight that, as we have seen, can be traced all the way back to the biblical texts.

For the project of a theology from the underside this may well mean that there are "occasional leaps of thought," as Herzog acknowledges. Theology, developed in places where power structures have become most pressing, is at times subject to violent interruptions. The recent brutal murder of the Guatemalan bishop Juan Gerardi on April 26,

1998, has once more painfully reminded us of this.[18] But there is another reason: "Our leaps of thought are also brought on by our rejection
of any hegemonic solution. Everything we do is *in via*, on the road.
There is no one answer to our search, except the (continually changing) walk itself."[19] Where the hegemonic paradigms of the self and of
the text of much of mainline theology finally meet their limits, another
approach to theology develops. At the end of this book, the last of nine
statements on theological education and liberation theology, formulated
by a group of theologians, has programmatic value: *"We believe that no
final theological formulation of the liberation struggle is possible.* New struggles against oppression continually emerge in ways that demand new
kinds of action and new modes of reflection."[20]

Theology from the underside of history is, therefore, not more pre-
tentious but more humble in the increasing awareness of our own limits.
For good reason the one picture on the walls of Herzog's office at
Duke Divinity School was not of his great theological teachers but of
William Edwards, the disabled African American firefighter who introduced him, Bible in hand, to the underside of history in new ways. This
might well hold the major lesson for theology at the beginning of a new
millennium.

---

18. Bishop Gerardi was beaten to death after his presentation of a report on the
massacres of the civil war in Guatemala; his murder was followed by a wave of death
threats to many other church people.

19. Herzog, GW, xxii.

20. Frederick Herzog et al., "Theological Education and Liberation Theology: An
Invitation to Respond," *Theological Education* 16:1 (Autumn 1979), 11. Emphasis in
original.

Index